PUPPETRY

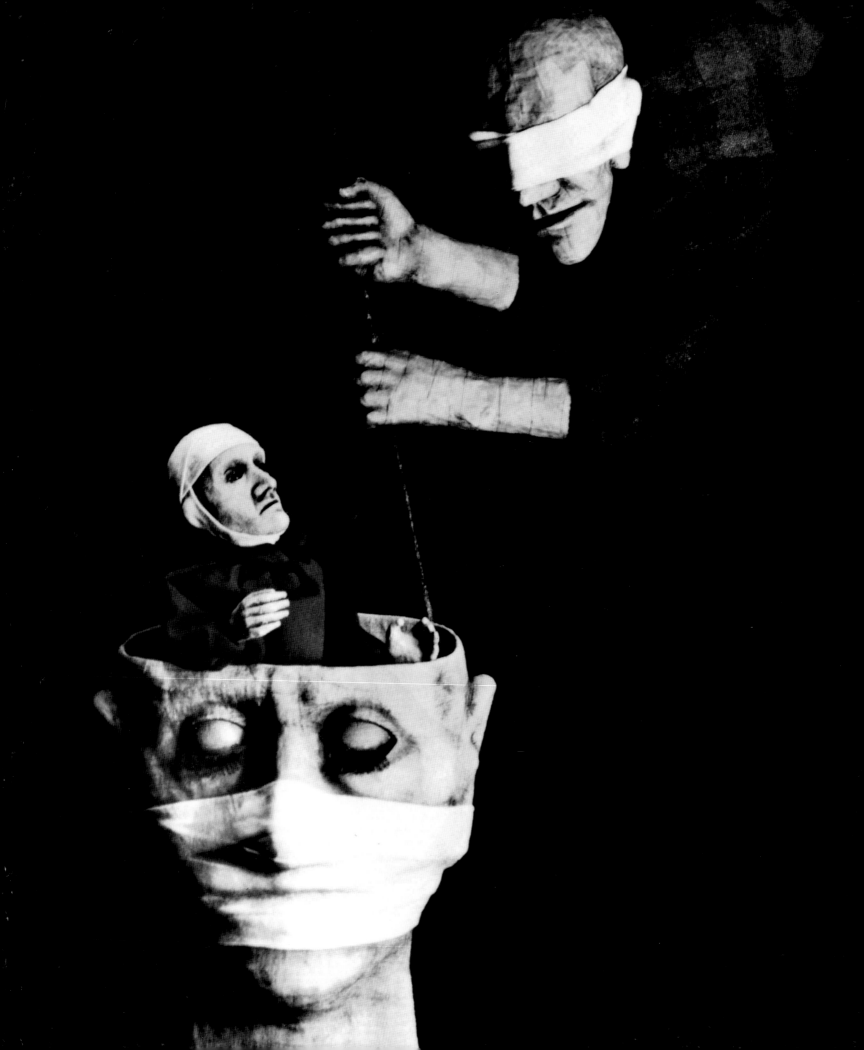

PUPPETRY

A WORLD HISTORY

Eileen Blumenthal

HARRY N. ABRAMS, INC., PUBLISHERS

CONTENTS

Preface

It is not my fault. The puppets did it. More than a century ago, that excuse got a Czech puppeteer out of hot water after his little actors had challenged the government. I will invoke the same defense to explain the unorthodox structure of this book.

Puppetry: A World History encompasses all kinds of constructed actors and performing objects from all times and all places. Given this gigantic scope, the default methodology would have been to sort the material by genre, time, or place—particularly since no other existing study does that job. But the puppets themselves suggested a different scheme.

Over the ages, similar aesthetics have shaped puppetry in disparate cultures whose other forms of expression shared little ground. And around the world, puppets have used similar mechanisms and performed the same astonishing range of social roles—including slapstick entertainer, political dissident, and emissary to the spirit world. Classifying this body of work according to *where, when,* or *how* would mean repeating the same story again and again. It is *what* puppets are, their basic nature, that makes them so special.

This book, therefore, offers just an overview of history and technique and then switches to a thematic approach. Drawing together material from different continents and periods, it examines the distinctive nature and abilities of constructed performers and surveys the kinds of roles they have played in human societies. This system, I hope, will give readers a multifaceted image of the richness of puppet life. True, it may not provide the clearest possible landscape of puppetry in individual regions or centuries. But that trade-off seems worthwhile, particularly since excellent studies do exist of various geographical areas. Henryk Jurkowski's two-volume *History of European Puppetry* and

Olenka Darkowska-Nidzgorski and Denis Nidzgorski's *Marionnettes et masques au coeur du théâtre africain* are treasures of puppet scholarship that have recently been published—although they are, alas, not always easily available. Jayadeva Tilakasiri's *Puppet Theatre of Asia,* nearly forty years old, remains a fine survey. My bibliography lists many, many other excellent studies of puppet art that focus on particular regions and genres.

While looking at the art through a thematic prism, I have tried to draw examples from as many important puppeteers as possible. Readers should get a good sense of the field and a glimpse, at least, of many of its major players.

Puppeteers and puppet lovers are an exceptionally open-hearted group, and I have enjoyed a staggering amount of assistance on this project. Nancy Loehman Staub's donation of her time adds one more chapter to her decades of support to the art of puppetry. Using her extensive knowledge, library, and contacts, she fielded dozens of queries, and her meticulous reading of the text made it clearer and more accurate. Leslee Asch, long a part of the Jim Henson Company and the Jim Henson Foundation, facilitated my access to the thousands of images and hundreds of videotapes in the Henson collection, and provided cartons of rare publications from her personal library. Plus she read the manuscript and offered valuable suggestions. Others at the Henson Foundation, including Heidi Wilenius, Meg Daniel, and, of course, Cheryl Henson, provided all manner of both concrete and moral support. The Institut International de la Marionnette, in northwestern France, provided hospitality and guidance during my research there: The puppet artists Margareta Niculescu, who helped to found the Institut, and Roman Paska, who was then its director, welcomed me and facilitated

ENDPAPERS: A shadow-theater version of a Chinese dragon puppet. In traditional Chinese New Year celebrations, several live actors animate a huge paper dragon from underneath, dancing it through the streets. This late nineteenth-century dragon from Peking is manipulated in the customary way—by several puppeteers beneath it. But in this case, those puppeteers are themselves puppets.

PAGE 1: Mr. Punch, from England. This gleeful rogue was part of a late nineteenth-century traveling company.

PAGE 2: *Metamorphoses* by the Dutch Figurentheater Triangel of Henk and Ans Boerwinkel. See page 98.

PAGES 4–5: *Story of Goblins and Other Realities* by Palo Lluvia of Mexico. See page 62.

OPPOSITE: A butterfly-woman just emerged from her cocoon in *Chrysalis*, by Bruce D. Schwartz, in a 1985 performance.

ABOVE: The author interviewing a performer as Japanese bunraku puppet master Yoshida Tamamatsu looks on.

my stay; and Sophie Bon, then its librarian, guided me through the Institut's collection. In Amsterdam, Dragan Klaić, then director of the Netherlands Theatre Institute, offered me hospitality in his home and the use of the Institute's extensive holdings.

Vince Anthony, executive director of the Center for Puppetry Arts in Atlanta, Georgia, Frank Ballard, who founded the Puppetry Program at the University of Connecticut at Storrs, and Alan G. Cook, who has collected a museum's worth of American puppets, all went to some trouble to provide material from their archives. Alan Louis and Susan Kinney at the CPA also were generous with their time and were of real help. Phillip Dennis Cate, then director of the Zimmerli Museum at Rutgers University, personally shepherded me through its Special Collections. Barbara Mathe at the American Museum of Natural History in New York and the Phototèque staff at the Musée de l'Homme in Paris helped me to navigate their extensive libraries of images. Elisabeth den Otter at the Tropenmuseum in Amsterdam and André P. Larson, director of the Shrine to Music Museum in South Dakota, also were kind enough to provide me with materials. Ray DaSilva, who provides invaluable service to puppetry through his mart for new and out-of-print books, also helped me resolve queries.

Friends and colleagues read the text at various stages and offered suggestions. Julius Novick, one of the smartest contemporary theater critics, read the entire manuscript, and it is clearer and cleaner thanks to his astute notes. The composer Ezra Sims, a walking encyclopedia of the arts, read chunks of the text and pointed me toward arcane examples that landed in the book. Steve Abrams, a trove of knowledge about puppetry, provided wonderful insights and information. The puppeteers Massimo Schuster, Hanne Tierney, and Basil Twist read several chapters at different times and made valuable suggestions, in some cases informing me about interesting puppet work I had not previously known. Other puppeteers and

puppeteer-scholars, including Joan Baixas, Vit Horejš, Larry Reed, John Bell, and Richard Bradshaw provided information and answered queries about other artists' work as well as their own. Kate Dorrell and Paula Lawrence read sections of the manuscript and offered helpful notes.

Many puppeteers have allowed me backstage and into their workshops. The shadow puppet artist I Wayan Wija took me to a dozen of his shows all over Bali. Julie Taymor welcomed me into her studio many times over two decades. Lee Breuer and the bunraku master Tamamatsu Yoshida made me privy to their workshops. Basil Twist and Larry Reed showed me the complex techniques behind some of their shows. Michael Curry devoted more than an hour to showing me the millennium celebrations just hours before they were to perform. Besides these artists, many many others—including the late Peter Baird (Bil Baird's son and successor), Janie Geiser, and Theodora Skipitares—have taken the time and trouble to show me the inner workings of their art.

To supplement the countless puppet shows and videos I have seen, this study relies heavily on the work of other scholars and journalists. Several whose published work I cite in my bibliography, plus a number of others, also offered direct help. Olenka Darkowska-Nidzgorski and Denis Nidzgorski allowed me to draw on research of theirs which has not yet been published in English. Dominque Bénazeth, chief curator of the Coptic Egyptian collection at the Louvre, helped me track the tantalizing (and probably fake) ancient Egyptian marionette theater from Antinoë. Japanese theater scholar Samuel Leiter answered specific queries, and bunraku specialist Michiko Ueno-Herr generously offered her expertise as well as contacts. The late Barbara Adachi was kind and game enough to accompany me several years ago to see old-style puppetry on Japan's remote Sado Island. Terry Miller led me to material on Thai puppets, and let me tag along to his research area in northeastern Thailand. Ron Jenkins, whose field work on Lithuanian puppets graces my Chapter 8, also helped me with material and contacts for Dario Fo. Christopher Cairns let me read his not-yet-published manuscript on Dario Fo's puppets. Beth Cleary and Peter Rachleff sent me their in-process research on the Buffalo Historical Marionettes. John Emigh and Kathy Foley answered queries on Southeast Asian and South Asian masks and puppets, and Laurel Kendall provided fascinating material as well as contacts for Korean and Vietnamese puppet theater. Greg Mann forwarded my questions to list-serves of Africa scholars. Roger Copeland pointed me toward some quirky contemporary work at the edges of puppetry. And many other scholars, including John McCormick and Michael Malkin, were kind enough to answer specific questions.

THE THREE HUNDRED AND FIFTY images in *Puppetry: A World History* owe their presence here to the talents, yeoman labor, and generosity of a number of people. Fay Torres-Yap of Carousel Research, who handled most of the photo gathering, was nothing short of amazing. For my hundreds of specific requests, many re-quiring detective work, she tapped museums, galleries, private collectors, individual photogra-phers, and the estates of photographers and puppeteers on six continents. Plus, she brought hundreds of other images to my attention. I am also grateful to the dozens of photographers whose work appears in the book. Two of these, who have specialized in puppet photography, de-serve special thanks. Brigitte Pougeoise gave me free access to and helped me to search through tens of thousands of photos she has taken over several decades—and even hosted me for sev-eral days at her farmhouse outside Paris to facil-itate the research. In New York, Richard Termine helped me to pore through volumes of contact sheets, slide pages, and prints of his puppet photos. In addition, colleagues and friends of individual puppet artists—including Hans Jörg Tobler for Mummenschanz, Barbara

Busackino for Basil Twist, and Bette Stoler for Robert Anton—gave me access and permission to use pictures, in some cases from their per-sonal archives. Larry Engler also supplied pic-tures from his own collection.

Felipe Gamba, my unflappable, indefatiga-ble research assistant, not only checked hun-dreds of facts but helped to keep the book's gargantuan mass of material from collapsing into chaos. Lauren Acampora provided smart and gracious research assistance at the earliest stages of the project.

A part of my work on *Puppetry: A World History* took place during a residency at the Camargo Foundation in Cassis, France. Rutgers University also has assisted me on this project through a sabbatical leave and other research grants. The Asian Cultural Council provided support for a research trip to Asia. The contacts that ACC director Ralph Samuelson provided me for that trip were invaluable.

At Abrams, it was the enthusiasm of the late Paul Gottlieb, then editor-in-chief, that launched this project. As the book's assigning editor, Diana Murphy nurtured and champi-oned it for two years before leaving Abrams to work independently. Andrea Danese picked up the editing of this very complex book mid-stream to see it to completion. Ellen Nygaard designed a layout and was dedicated enough to the project to complete initial page proofs be-fore leaving Abrams. Shawn Dahl saw the book's design through production, sensitively implementing the many revisions.

I regret that the work of many wonderful artists is not shown or mentioned in this book due to space limitations, the exigencies of the structure, or my ignorance. Any other deficien-cies that remain in this work despite the ex-traordinary help I have enjoyed are, of course, my own.

I dedicate this book to my sister and ally Judith and to the memory of my parents, Diane Blumenthal (October 20, 1911–September 11, 2001) and Philip Blumenthal (January 5, 1915–September 15, 2001).

CHAPTER 1

The Origin of Species

THEY CAN BE GODS, IDIOTS, OR WORMS. They are able to nurture children or terrify adults. They survive indefinitely without normal biological aging but also can die and come back to life again and again.

Whenever someone endows an inanimate object with life force and casts it in a scenario, a puppet is born. And something very like this has been going on, it seems, since the days of Cro-Magnon. Evolving from prehistoric and early-historic figures in stone, bone, leather or wood, puppets have thrived across eons and continents, interbreeding with each other and related species, such as masks, idols, automatons, and, surprisingly, illustrations. Puppets and their mixed-breed cousins have facilitated contact that is otherwise hard to achieve, such as with ancestors and gods, but also have served up slapstick and raunchy entertainment. They have been powerful conservators of social values, but also political subversives. They have given visible form to the vastness of the cosmos but also have shown the intimate interior of a human psyche.

WE CAN REASONABLY begin the story of puppets sometime between 30,000 and 21,000 B.C.E., as glaciers were pushing up the mountain ranges and Homo sapiens were revving up their brain power. Besides hunting and roasting mammoths, Cro-Magnon men or women

carved tiny, voluptuous figurines out of soft stone or the bones or tusks of animals. Although we may never know the purpose of these miniatures, their plump breasts and bellies suggest they had something to do with fertility. In any case, before people had conceived of agriculture or animal husbandry, the earliest humans had taken the phenomenal conceptual leap to create miniature replicas of people.

As history starts to come into focus during the second and first millennia B.C.E., so does the development of puppets. Early societies included some role for crafted beings, objects imaginatively endowed with life. As broad population groups encountered one another and exchanged goods, their constructed actors also exchanged traits, and several interbred traditions spread across vast swathes of territory. One group of puppets reached from Northern Europe through the Middle East, another from the Indian peninsula to East Asia. A venerable family of puppets also spanned sub-Saharan Africa, and constructed actors came to thrive throughout the Pacific islands and in the Americas.

THE ANCIENT CIVILIZATIONS of the Middle East were crafting statues and figurines with movable parts four to five thousand years ago. Excavations in the Indus Valley in modern Pakistan have turned up toy-size terra-cotta

Venus of Willendorf, one of many zaftig little Paleolithic women found over a wide area of Europe. This 25,000-year-old lady, just four inches tall, was carved from limestone and covered with a pigment of red earth.

OPPOSITE: A Teotihuacan terra-cotta figure with movable limbs from 400–650 C.E. Found at burial sites in central Mexico, usually in pairs, figures like this six-inch-tall pigmented doll apparently tended the dead.

Ancient terra-cotta dolls with movable limbs. The six-inch-tall figure above comes from the Greek colony of Cyrene, in North Africa, circa 470–450 B.C.E.; the pigmented pair at right, from a fourth-century C.E. burial complex in Knidos, in modern Turkey. Similar figures have turned up throughout the Greek and Roman empires. Some have a metal rod extending from the top of their head or a metal hook for attaching a rod. Other ancient Greek puppets had cords strung *inside* their bodies, perhaps like Thai puppets (see page 48).

cattle from about 2400 B.C.E. with articulated heads, legs, and tails. The earliest record of a puppet actually performing comes from the Nile basin about six hundred years before Tutankhamen. A twentieth-century B.C.E. hieroglyphic text describes a performance in which a walking statue represented a god. Tombs from the same period contain articulated figurines, sculptures with movable limbs.

As we move into more documented times, the fifth-century B.C.E. Greek historian Herodotus wrote about Egyptian processions in which women carried puppets to honor the god Osiris, a dying-and-rising god associated with fertility. By this time, the fecundity images were male and sported prodigious dying-and-rising penises. Herodotus also described phallic

gies in fertility rites in Greece. There, rather than distracting from the main focus with irrelevant body parts, the celebrants paraded holding colossal replicas of erect penises.

According to Greek writers of the first and second centuries C.E., the legendary inventor Daedalus made wooden dolls with movable parts for the pleasure of King Minos and his family—which means that this sort of articulated doll was known by the time of those writers, at least, and probably much earlier. In fact, articulated statuettes excavated in Greece and Italy plus some ancient texts show that puppets performed for entertainment as well as for ceremonies in Hellenic times, the fifth century B.C.E., and dolls with movable limbs were ubiquitous. Puppets played for common folk at public gathering spots and for the wealthy at banquets. During the third century B.C.E., they even performed in the venerable Theater of Dionysus on the Acropolis, the site of the great Hellenic tragedy contests.

Besides hand-manipulated figures, the Greeks crafted elaborate automatons, mannequins that moved via cogs and levers, sometimes activated by the flow of water. Hero of Alexandria, who lived around the first century B.C.E., described an elaborate miniature Trojan War performance with tiny Greeks hammering and sawing to build ships then setting sail. Some scholars believe the Greeks also had shadow theater, in which audiences watched the silhouettes puppets cast on a screen. (This theory is based in part on Plato's simile that humans understand the world no better than people watching shadows of unseen actions.) Performance by constructed actors apparently emigrated to Greek colonies in Italy and on into the Roman Empire, blending at each step with indigenous traditions.

To the Christian religious authorities whose civil power grew after the fall of Rome, puppetry was anathema. It smacked of idolatry and fun, two well-known devices of the devil. Plus, female puppets raised the specter of carnal

desire, attracting special vitriol from, for example, St. Thomas Aquinas.

Despite this hostile climate, folk puppetry weathered the Middle Ages. Even within the generally despised ranks of entertainers, though, puppeteers were by legal statute "the most vile class," on a level with people who exhibited trained monkeys and dogs. Puppeteers

The earliest known picture of puppetry in medieval Europe: a miniature joust with children controlling their knights' movements via ropes. Their play was used in a twelfth-century manuscript to illustrate ungodly pastimes.

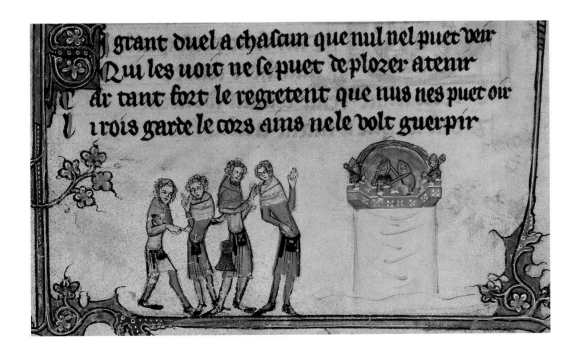

A puppet show painted by Jehan de Grise for a fourteenth-century manuscript of *The Romance of Good King Alexander*. This scene of hand puppets clashing swords and onlookers wielding maces and truncheons suggests the spirited behavior of medieval puppetry.

A weather-beaten puppeteer resting and repairing his actors on a hill outside town in *The Puppet Master*, a 1926 etching by Robert Sargent Austin.

A traditional Polish szopka stage. Miniature cathedrals evolved into these unique stages for nativity plays, probably in the sixteenth century. A single operator manipulated the entire eight-inch-tall cast from underneath the stage, moving rods attached to the puppets along grooves cut through the floor. Like other Christian pageants, szopka shows came to use the bible stories as a framework for local lore and politics.

players often came from outcast groups such as Gypsies and Jews. Indeed, the wandering puppeteer whom Don Quixote encountered in Cervantes's early seventeenth-century novel was a lowlife whose most recent address was prison.

Ironically, medieval puppets found a niche within religion. Crucifixes were rigged so that Jesus could move or bleed, and statues of the Blessed Virgin were made to weep. The church's switch from banning to advocating religious images (in the 1310 Synod of Tiers) encouraged illustrated narrations and enactments of the bible. This boosted the live-actor religious pageants, where puppets played special-effects characters such as the Holy Ghost and the beast-shaped "souls" that sprang from dying villains. As these Mystery and Passion plays became ever more lurid, life-size dummies also stood in for live actors during some of the more colorful tortures visited on Christian martyrs. By the sixteenth century, with this mainly live-actor tradition in decline, versions played entirely by puppets had developed. Audiences now could marvel not only at little angels and devils flying around flapping tiny wings, but at the spectacle of a lifelike, jointed Jesus Christ effigy miraculously resurrecting skyward.

Secular skits and farces continued in the face of (or behind the back of) the disapproving

Church, and puppets, with their knack for low comedy and satire, remained part of this scene. Medieval entertainers also presented automaton dolls and mechanical mini-spectacles.

Meanwhile, at the eastern end of the Mediterranean, puppetry thrived despite Islam's ban on human and animal images. Hand-puppet farceurs entertained the masses as well as rulers throughout the Near East, including Turkey, Iran, and Armenia. Mechanical dolls, much prized by royalty, probably performed for commoners as well. In addition, Egypt's Mameluke culture, from the thirteenth to sixteenth centuries, developed an art of shadow theater inspired by Indian or Chinese models. This type of performance eventually spread from Egypt into much of the Middle East, North Africa, and the Near East, including Turkey and Greece.

By THE DAWN of the Renaissance, streets and aristocratic courts around Europe were hosting all kinds of miniature spectacles. Where live-actor religious plays were banned (in England in 1559 and France in 1548) due to their luridness and to Catholic-Protestant tensions, the audiences for biblical puppet shows only increased. Farces by puppets also remained popular, offering such edifying matter as the theft of a pork roast or the romance of Mrs. Rump, and invariably featuring knock-down, drag-out beatings. Street entertainers narrated and depicted naval battles between pint-sized Christians and Turks or showed entire little towns being sacked. The use of an outside storyteller, still common in Western puppetry, dates back at least to this period and probably to the Greeks. The advent of perspective stage scenery in the live-actor stage also created a new role for puppets: they could substitute for live actors in the upstage areas scaled too small for humans. Sebastiano Serlio's 1545 handbook on stage design suggests crafting pasteboard characters and moving them along grooves on the floor.

For the next several hundred years in Europe, until the verge of the twentieth century, puppetry and live-actor theater ran along parallel tracks, trading influences. As commedia dell'arte and opera developed in Italy and spread through much of continental Europe, so did puppet versions of both. Like their live-actor counterparts, some hand- and string-puppet

A fourteenth-century Egyptian shadow puppet of a camel and driver. Shadow theater flourished in Egypt from the 1300s through the late 1900s. Early puppets such as this had two layers: opaque camel hide carved with lacy designs, and a backing of thin translucent skin dyed to tint the light coming through. After the eighteenth century, puppets were made entirely of translucent hides.

The Crèche, a sketch by Gustav Girrane of a marionette Nativity play in Lyons, France, at the turn of the twentieth century.

The elegant world of puppet opera. The Salzburg Marionette Theatre, founded in 1913, revived this seventeenth- and eighteenth-century tradition.

OPPOSITE: Guards struck with astonishment as Christ resurrects in a scene from the Sicilian marionette theater, recreated by the Museo Internazionale delle Marionette Antonio Pasqualino in Palermo. This style of Sicilian puppetry, used mainly for *Orlando Furioso* and other chivalric epics, took shape in the early nineteenth century, though simpler puppets probably had been enacting those stories for centuries.

A puppet stage for children in the Tuileries gardens of the Louvre. In turn-of-the-century Paris, mothers and nannies brought children in starched frocks and short pants to watch miniature miscreants clobber each other in the Tuileries and other Paris parks. Puppets still play in Paris parks and gardens.

Backstage at Chat Noir cabaret in Paris. During the 1880s and 1890s, the Chat Noir's artists, mainly Henri Rivière and Caran d'Ache, expanded their techniques from jointed cardboard and zinc figures moved in a single plane to multi-layered images that included color.

commedia characters kept their original Italian names, costumes, and personalities, while others developed local identities. Some puppet operas were crude parodies of the live-actor stagings, but others featured finely crafted actors of wood and wax, some of them nearly life-size, with sophisticated controls. Late seventeenth- and eighteenth-century maestros such as Alessandro Scarlatti, father of the composer Dominico Scarlatti, wrote puppet music-dramas that played in Italian palaces, including the Pope's. Farther north, the Hungarian Esterhazy Prince Nicholas commissioned Franz Josef Haydn to compose operas specifically for the wooden performers.

A counterforce to the Italian Renaissance came, as on the live-actor stage, from the rough-and-tumble theater culture of England. Starting in Elizabethan times, English puppet companies as well as live-actor troupes traveled in Northern Europe and Germany helping to shape the traditions there. Able to get away with cruder and more irreverent work than their human counterparts, many miniature actors came to specialize in slapstick and outrageous satire. Puppetry in Spain and Portugal, like live-actor theater there, largely served religion, presenting saints' plays and other Christian stories. Eastern Europe, meanwhile, produced puppet Nativity pageants on elaborate portable altars or, in Poland, on stages shaped like miniature cathedrals.

In the eighteenth century, shadow puppets, spun off from the Eastern Mediterranean models, became popular with bourgeois and upper-class audiences in Western Europe, particularly in France. En route to the Holy Land, or in their free moments between killing Moors and Jews, European crusaders likely had seen these exotic performances and brought the idea, if not actual puppets, home with them. France's "Chinese Shadows" (so named to cash in on the cachet of things Oriental) presented safe, conservative work. After the 1789 Revolution, the main practitioner of shadow theater in France, the Séraphin Theater, survived thanks

A character starts to flip head over heels in a 1988 performance by Greek puppet master Michopoulos Panayiotis. During the nineteenth century, shadow theaters became popular around much of the Mediterranean. They were named for their main character: Karagiozis in Greece, Karagöz in Turkey, Karakos in Syria, and others.

to a hasty shift of repertory and its particular gift for depicting a guillotine in action. A few other respectable and stable puppet theaters also developed, mainly showcasing string puppets, which required more elaborate setups than portable street booths normally allowed.

Aristocratic puppet operas and respectable shadow and marionette theaters notwithstanding, Europe's constructed-actor theater remained mainly a plebian province, and the status of the artists remained sub-basement. Many were ragged itinerant showmen carting their little castelet stage, puppets, and sometimes dogs, cats, monkeys, and porcupines from place to place. Others performed in local

markets as a draw for their main occupation of tooth pulling. In some cases, they were officially classed with Gypsies and bandits.

IN THE NINETEENTH CENTURY, puppetry got a special bailiwick. With the romantic movement's exaltation of pre-civilized innocence, children were increasingly seen not as half-baked grown-ups but as a special group with unique imagination and needs. Puppets took a prominent place in the new field of theater geared specifically to kids.

Then, toward the end of that century, the advent of realism changed the rules for all theater in a way that had a particular impact on constructed-actor work. Before that time, few people had suggested that theater or *any* art should present reality exactly as it was observed. Rather, artists had used real life as raw material to be crafted into something more keenly expressive. Neither live-actor nor puppet theater in Euripides' Athens, Shakespeare's London, or even Victor Hugo's Paris had aimed to present mere copies of people in society any more than those cultures' musicians had confined their compositions to the noise patterns they encountered in life.

But the nineteenth century's romance with science seduced European artists in many genres to try to present "objective data." Given society's new understanding of living creatures as products of heredity and environment, it seemed important to portray characters and their surroundings with as little distortion—as little "art"—as possible. Theater was as susceptible as any field to the pandemic realism that hit Europe and America especially hard.

Some puppeteers bought into the new aesthetic and tried to make their work as lifelike as possible. This was not a propitious undertaking. Realism is one theatrical ground where puppets cannot compete on equal footing with live actors. But the alternative seemed to be accepting society's verdict that a non-realistic form such as puppetry was fit only for children. Since children had usually been a part of the target audience anyway, many puppet artists settled into this truncated role.

To make matters worse, puppetry faced increasing competition from other popular entertainments. Toward the turn of the twentieth century, vaudeville variety shows, spectator sports, and then film grabbed up much of the audience that had once gone to puppet plays. For a time, constructed actors found a niche in vaudeville, working as miniature stand-up comics, jugglers, blackface minstrels, and ventriloquists' dummies. But that venue also dried up a few decades into the new century.

These hard times created a watershed for puppetry. Ill-suited for the style that most theater had embraced, some puppet artists focused more on what they *could* do that live-actor theaters could not. That turned out to be rich territory.

A MAJOR SOURCE of nourishment for twentieth-century Western puppeteers came from halfway across the world: the puppet theaters of Asia. Those interbred traditions date back three millennia in several different regions, each with scholars championing it as the birthplace. As Europe's colonial expansion sparked new interest in exotica, international expositions and returning travelers introduced the West to a new array of constructed-actor theater.

In China, puppets figure in several early legends. Around 1000 B.C.E., a performer condemned to death for flirting with a royal concubine was spared when shown to be a puppet, *already* not alive. Eight centuries later, an artificial danseuse atop the walls of a beleaguered city hoodwinked the enemy general, a woman warrior, into lifting the siege lest this local beauty land in her husband's harem. Not long afterward, a bereaved emperor named Wu took comfort from shadow images depicting his dead wife. However apocryphal these stories may be, they indicate that puppets were known in China during these periods.

Sometime during the first millennium B.C.E., the Chinese also began to use jointed,

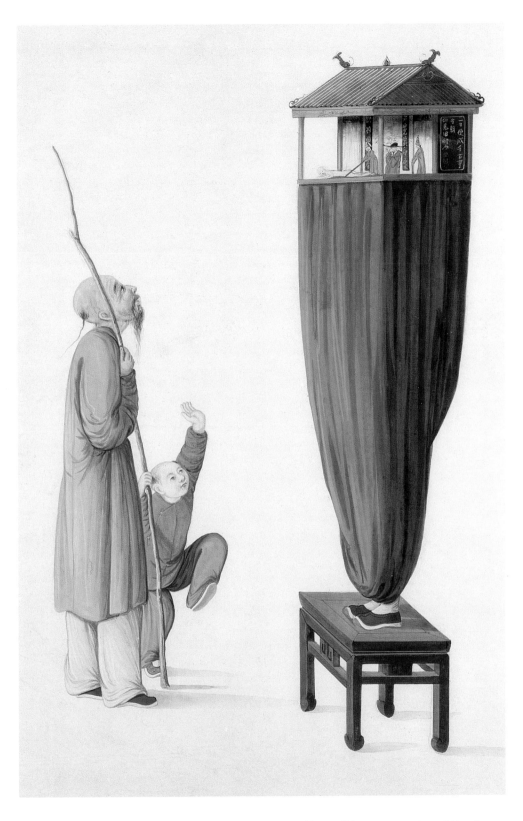

An itinerant Chinese puppeteer in an eighteenth-century painting. Versions of such "walking" theaters have existed all over Europe, Russia, Central Asia, and East Asia.

The temptress Somu in a puppet version of Korea's *Namsadang* folk dance–drama. Somu entices monks with her graceful arm movements trailing long sleeves. This twenty-inch-tall seductress dances without benefit of actual hands or feet: her painted papier-mâché head attaches to a body-stick; her arms, hidden beneath wide sleeves, are dowels loosely bolted to a horizontal "shoulder" bar and operated from below.

A *haniwa* koto player. This two-foot-high clay figure, about 1,500 years old, wears a funerary necklace as well as wrist and finger protectors so that he can play music for the deceased. *Haniwa* often wear paraphernalia associated with shamans, who effect communications between the realms of the dead and the living.

movable effigies to attend the deceased in the afterlife—a humanitarian upgrade that supplemented and eventually supplanted the sacrifice of live retainers. Manipulated by shamans, these puppets developed into funeral entertainers, then into performers for other ceremonies. By the second century C.E., they were performing at parties.

China's Song-dynasty (960–1279) puppets played for all social classes—in designated entertainment districts and along roadsides as well as in wealthy homes and even at court. The tremendous range of three-dimensional and shadow puppets often paralleled and exchanged influence with live-actor entertainments. In addition, sophisticated mechanical dolls performed solos and group scenes. Secret manipulation techniques were passed down through families.

As in Europe, the sometimes high status of the audiences rarely rubbed off onto performers, who were considered lowlifes. Overseers of morality condemned puppetry as fostering bad behavior. But the popular arts prevailed. An attempt by the twelfth-century Confucian philosopher Zhu Xi to ban puppet theater merely made him a favorite target of its satire. Some puppetry was so topical that government agents reportedly attended shows incognito as an early warning system against popular uprisings.

As CHINESE INFLUENCE spread through much of East Asia, including the present Vietnam and Korea, so did China's constructed actors. By 1000 C.E., Korea also had performances by itinerant puppeteers from Central Asia, possibly Gypsies. These imports may have crossbred with indigenous puppets. In any case, Korean showmen developed a distinctive folk puppetry in tandem with their colorful masked dance-drama. As in Europe and China, puppeteers were social outcasts.

Constructed actors, or their near relations, had played roles in Japan since prehistoric times. As early as 5000 B.C.E., clay servants looked after the dead, some having first been "killed" (deliberately broken). By the early centuries C.E., these retainers had developed into the haunting, hollow clay *haniwa*. According to an old chronicle (perhaps slightly fanciful, since it also includes a visit by the sun goddess), these silent attendants had replaced live servants who, when buried to their necks near the deceased, had wailed just awfully as they died.

Some puppetry that still survives in Japan's Shinto temple rites may be ancient and indigenous. Japan also acquired puppet arts directly from China as well as from Central Asia and China via Korea, whose arts the Japanese periodically plundered during occupations. By the eleventh century, "foreign" puppeteers, likely from Korea, also performed at Japanese shrines. The shows were popular: at one, the audience reportedly "split their sides with laughter" watching an old codger pant his way through sex with his young wife. But that imported puppet tradition soon dropped from sight. Some marionettes and mechanical dolls transplanted from China during the fourteenth and fifteenth centuries did take root—among them, the automatons and fake automatons still used in parade floats.

By the mid-fifteenth century, puppets were enacting the recently developed *noh* dramas and *kyogen* comedies. Japan's renowned bunraku puppetry sprang from a late sixteenth-century inspiration to accompany a popular style of storytelling with Shinto puppetry and the music of a three-stringed *samisen*. The constructed actors for these performances began as simple figures controlled by one puppeteer apiece. By the 1730s, the puppets had become so complex that each one required three handlers (who were, uncharacteristically, considered artists). Portraying ordinary people, the domestic tribulations of the great, and swashbuckling melodramas, these puppets became Japan's most popular entertainment.

WITH A LANDMASS and population mix as great as Western Europe's, the Indian subcontinent

A Japanese festival float with its *karakuri ningyo*, or (purportedly) mechanical doll, front, high, and center. Notwithstanding the giant chicken that crowns the float, the *ningyo* beneath the canopy would be the chief attraction, greeting onlookers or performing simple acrobatics. Most of these supposed "automatons" have help from a hidden puppeteer. With long shadows and no spectators in sight, the *dashi* car in this photograph seems to be heading for the festivities just after dawn.

BELOW: A 1765 performance showing the *ningyo joruri* manipulation system, using three handlers per puppet. Doll theater became so popular in eighteenth-century Japan that its tearjerkers about star-crossed lovers were blamed for inspiring a rash of copycat double suicides. After a lull in popularity, this puppet form was revivified in the late eighteenth century by the puppet-theater manager Uemura Bunrakuken IV, for whom the tradition is now called "bunraku." It attracted increased interest again in the 1940s as a fortuitous byproduct of enflamed nationalism and then, in recent decades, with the help of government subsidies.

spawned a prodigious range of puppetry that influenced the arts far beyond its home territory. Shadow puppets in India may descend from 2,500-year-old leather cutouts from Central Asia that, perhaps, migrated south with populations into the subcontinent and possibly eastward into China and westward to Egypt. In India itself, the earliest reference to what may be shadow puppetry is in the Hindu epic *The Mahabharata,* written between the second century B.C.E. and the second century C.E. By the thirteenth century C.E., India clearly had performances that used shadows to enact a story. Modern India's tremendous range of shadow puppets includes some that are intricately carved and others that are unpatterned, some opaque and others translucent, some with joints and others unarticulated, some less than one foot tall and others more than six feet tall. Some figures represent a single character, others a complete scene. Some styles use only one light source, others many lamps in a row.

A clue to the early history of three-dimensional puppets in India occurs in a second-century B.C.E. treatise on drama, which refers to a director of *live* theater as the "string holder." Since controlling even recalcitrant live actors does not normally involve ropes, the term appears to be borrowed from marionettes. India's string puppets may, then, be older than its earliest known live-actor theater—that is, older than the fourth century B.C.E.

India's three-dimensional puppets include not only figures operated by strings, but some

worked from above with rods, some moved from underneath with rods, and some that have the operator's hand inside. The repertory ranges from sacred, heroic, and elegant to satiric, raunchy, and slapstick. At one extreme, in a popular Rajasthani form, the story is just a frame for variety acts such as juggling or transformations. At the other, puppets native to one village in Kerala, in southwestern India, play nothing but replicas of live-performer *kathakali* dance-drama enacting the two major Hindu epics, *The Mahabharata* and *The Ramayana*. Some puppeteers have enjoyed royal patronage. Others have lived more like the vagabond outcasts of Europe or East Asia.

THE HINDU EPICS imported from India to Southeast Asia became the core of puppet traditions there. The hub of Southeast Asian shadow puppetry is the island of Java, where the art has thrived for at least 1000 years. Originally solid leather cutouts, the puppets over time became gorgeously unrealistic, elon-gated and carved into lacy semi-corporeality, possibly because of Java's conversion to Islam (culminating by about 1550), which forbade human images. The repertory, however, remained centered on the Hindu *Mahabharata,* with Islamic philosophy and remnants of older religions folded in. Javanese still view shadow puppeteers as a composite of artist, priest, teacher, social critic, and comedian. The puppets perform at most public and private religious ceremonies and star in media from television satires to cartoons and fabric design.

Java's shadows spread across the region, both on the mainland, likely including Malaysia, Thailand, and Cambodia, and to nearby islands, such as Bali. They arrived in these new homes over several centuries and at different stages of development. Cambodia's shadow theater may descend from late eighth-century puppets that the Khmer ruler Jayavarman II brought from Java, where he was raised before starting the Angkor Empire. Bali's shadow puppets, less stylized than the

Villagers gathered by a riverbank in Mali to see a traditional showboat during the French Colonial period. This type of performance is documented in the area for over a hundred years but may well be centuries older. It remains popular today.

Javanese, likely reflect those of fourteenth- and fifteenth-century Java, when Java's Majapahit rulers, fleeing Islamic invaders, occupied that smaller island.

Many three-dimensional puppets in Southeast Asia are essentially plumped-out versions of the leather characters, operated much the same way but seen directly, not as shadows. Other non-shadow puppets in the area—including highly developed traditions in Burma, Thailand, and northern Vietnam—are mainly imports from India or China, revamped to a greater or lesser degree.

ALONG THE ARCHIPELAGOS from Southeast to East Asia and out to the Pacific Islands, some old traditions have survived. Puppets' chief task in this region has been hosting disembodied spirits—often family members from previous generations who no longer have usable earthly bodies. Further east, in the Hawaiian islands, old stories describe puppets that either were favorite toys or, in some cases, miraculously came to life.

And although Christian missionaries virtually wiped out such "vanities of the heathen" and performing "idols," shards of evidence reveal that, besides any ritual function they served, puppets were entertainers, performing hula dances and satirical skits for the pleasure of audiences.

HALFWAY ACROSS THE WORLD in sub-Saharan Africa, legends recount how certain objects came to life when they were honored or disturbed. In some tales, craftsmen carved organic materials, such as wood or butter, into children or fiancées or tomb guardians, and the sculptures became animated. But these seemingly alive people invariably became inert again due to mistreatment or to the normal course of events, such as the sun melting a person made of butter.

Sub-Saharan Africa may have inherited some of the puppetry of ancient Egypt. Much of Africa still has species of puppets whose most prominent feature is an awe-inspiring phallus—much as Herodotus reported of ancient

A 1992 performance by Hausa puppet artist Alassane Saidou in Niger. Concealed under a little tent held up by his body and a few sticks (far right), the puppeteer pushes wooden characters into view between draped cloths or skins. Offstage, male puppets standing in the sand lean backwards to counterbalance the weight of their prodigious penises.

Snake puppets at a Hopi planting-season ceremony in 1899 in Walpi, Arizona. In a firelit *kiva*, a below-ground sacred chamber, handlers animated serpents through holes in the decorated screens. For other rituals, the puppeteer remained in view and wore a fake arm to replace the one inside the snake.

Egypt. Like those earliest Egyptian puppets, many contemporary African puppets have a religious or social function. Puppets carried on boats, still seen in Mali, *may* have ancestors as far back as the second century C.E. (though the chief evidence for this, a miniature marionette theater in a tomb at Antinoé, is likely a fake).

A few early writings document puppets in Africa as much as 700 years ago. A fourteenth-century Arab visitor to Mali saw an artificial bird dance to a poetry recitation. A seventeenth-century Italian friar in Congo witnessed a priestess animating wooden dolls by banging them together as part of an invocation. By the nineteenth century, more plentiful foreign accounts describe what are clearly direct ancestors of living traditions, including the colorful animated antelopes of Mali, which sport smaller moving puppets on their backs and horns.

THE ADVANCED EARLY cultures of the Americas left tantalizing clues to roles that constructed performers played in their worlds. The Teotihuacan civilization of central Mexico, which thrived around 600 C.E., buried its

dead with terra-cotta attendants, whose movable arms and legs presumably made them fit to carry out their duties. These ancient people also molded mysterious hollow statues with tiny figurines nestled inside their chests, abdomen, and limbs. Further south in what is now Guatemala, a pre-Columbian bas-relief shows a man with a glove puppet. And in South America, among Incas and in other ancient Andean societies, ritual vessels bear small terra-cotta replicas of people engaged in important activities (such as sex), suggesting that perhaps the little figures were acting out the activity to which the ritual offering pertained.

More recently, people native to the Americas—from Alaska to the Andes and from ocean to ocean—have used puppets in their ceremonies. During the sixteenth and early seventeenth centuries, European colonials in Mexico, the southwestern U.S., and eastern Canada described jointed puppets including tiny figures that danced on a magician's hand. Powerful Hopi "corn maiden" puppets that performed at planting times have been documented as recently as 1979 and may still be active. In the Pacific Northwest, such potent spirits as Raven and Killer Whale still alight in the exquisite bodies carved and painted for their use.

European puppets settled in the Americas with the earliest Spaniards. Hernando Cortés's entourage on a gold-hunting expedition in 1524 included musicians, an acrobat, and a puppeteer. While much of the European interaction with indigenous American societies took the form of annihilation, some vigorous hybrid cultures did develop, particularly in Mexico, Haiti, and parts of South America. As styles, beliefs, symbols, and people interbred among Native American, Spanish, Portuguese, French, and African communities, puppets with complex, intercultural heritages emerged to perform rituals, social functions, and entertainment.

FAR-FLUNG PEOPLES have exchanged ideas and arts as far back as records exist. But starting in the nineteenth century, improved travel and communication increased contact among very disparate traditions. The Japanese began to perform Ibsen, and the Balinese to paint for a Western tourist market. European and American artists discovered the stylized and planar aesthetics of East Asian landscape painting and found new timbres and musical structures in Indian raga and Indonesian gamelan. The visual polyphony and stylization of African decoration and sculpture transformed Western plastic arts. All this interplay nourished a burgeoning Western avant-garde already searching for ways to escape realism, to express the realm of the subconscious, the world of the imagination, and even the nature of art itself.

Among puppeteers, the foreign influence sometimes was cause-and-effect direct. The Czech-born Viennese puppeteer Richard Teschner saw Javanese rod puppets in Dutch museums in 1911 and proceeded to develop his own gemlike universes peopled with similar figures. Paul Brann, who opened the Munich Artists' Marionette Theater in 1905, drew inspiration from Asian masks and puppets (as well

as the work of Munich's master marionettist, "Papa" Schmid, and the contemporary live-actor avant-garde). He used pared-down forms and undisguised theatricality to evoke sharp, distilled worlds.

Beyond specific borrowings, Europe's expanded artistic horizons sparked a general boom of experimental puppetry. The Hungarian-born painter Geza Blattner, influenced in part by Teschner and Brann, began his *Arc-en-ciel* (Rainbow) theater in Paris during the late 1920s. His performers included folded-cardboard geometric figures, animated musical instruments, and an emcee with a radio-antenna head and bicycle-wheel feet. Just after World War II, Fred Schneckenburger created a cabaret in Zurich with satirical grotesques whose odd assortment of limbs and facial features made them resemble modern paintings more than people. Yves Joly in France often worked with found objects, casting some of his most famous plays with umbrellas or gloved hands.

Sergei Obraztsov, working under Josef Stalin's official mandate for realism, delivered some "correct" realistic work, but also explored *kukolnost*, "puppetness"—qualities that made constructed actors *different* from life. He exaggerated some characters into comic impossibilities and pared down others to the simplest possible forms and gestures, even making actors from unadorned little spheres on his fingertips (see page 132).

All over Europe, constructed actors garnered interest and praise outside puppetry circles. The German playwright Heinrich von Kleist's long-ignored 1810 essay "On the Marionette Theater" now inspired artists with its claim that true grace could exist only with total lack of self-consciousness—that is, "in the marionette and in the god." Several major contemporary critics championed constructed actors, including French Nobel-laureate novelist Anatole France, who extolled little wooden actors as more "artistic" than live ones.

Puppets were featured in the work of theorist-practitioners as diverse as the Italian

A pre-Columbian hand puppet in a bas-relief discovered in the Bilbao region of Guatemala.

"The Latest Thing at the Museum" by Fred Schneckenburger. This 1951 museum docent from Schneckenburger's Zurich cabaret appears to be explicating the finer aesthetic points of—well, nothing. Notwithstanding her unusual assortment of features, this lady boasts one of the less disturbing physiognomies and anatomies among Schneckenburger characters, which are generally two to three feet tall.

RIGHT: Sergei Obraztsov's ice skaters in a 1950 performance. These realistic skaters could glide, wobble, sprint, and stop. Obraztsov more typically caricatured gestures into gravity- or anatomy-defying movements that only puppets could execute.

OPPOSITE TOP: *The Good Soldier Schweik* with cartoon puppets by Georg Grosz. In this landmark 1928 production in Berlin, director Erwin Piscator incorporated two-dimensional puppet characters that moved along a treadmill.

OPPOSITE BOTTOM: Punch and Judy at Coney Island, New York, in an 1880 painting by S.S. Carr. During the eighteenth and nineteenth centuries, puppet shows frequented beach resorts in Europe and America.

Futurists, zealous to trash traditions, Edward Gordon Craig, with his lofty ideas about art, and Erwin Piscator, committed to political theater. Prominent playwrights such as Maurice Maeterlinck, Paul Claudel, George Bernard Shaw, Michel de Ghelderode, and, later, Federico García Lorca wrote works specifically for puppets. Eric Satie and Manuel de Falla composed music to accompany constructed performers, and the Colette/Maurice Ravel opera *The Child and the Enchantments* (1925), choreographed by George Balanchine, included singing furniture and toys.

Some plastic artists working in the theater, imbued with the adventurous contemporary aesthetics of painting and sculpture, used puppets to break from the realism inherent in human performers. Maurice Dénis created actors as well as sets and costumes for the avant-garde Théâtre d'art in Paris. Fernand Léger's designs for the ballet *The Creation of the World* by Rolf de Maré included puppets, and Léger created characters for the company of French puppet master Jacques Chesnais. Pablo Picasso, working with Ballets Russes impressario Serge Diaghilev and, later, with Mikhail Larionov, incorporated two-dimensional and sculpted characters in mainly live-performer dances. Salvador Dali's designs for the Strauss opera *Salome* at Covent Garden in London also included puppets.

Across the Atlantic as well, constructed-actor theater was coming of age. America's eighteenth- and nineteenth-century puppetry

Giant puppets in a sketch by Robert Edmond Jones for Igor Stravinsky's 1926–27 oratorio, *Oedipus Rex.* Stravinsky had called for masked singers. Instead, this 1931 performance by the Philadelphia Orchestra used ten-foot-high effigies moved partly from above with strings (suspended from a forty-foot-high platform) and partly from below with long sticks. The puppets were designed by the American puppeteer Remo Bufano, whose extensive career included children's shows and stagings of Shakespeare, Molière, and Lorca.

Ventriloquist Edgar Bergen and Charlie McCarthy. Bergen designed Charlie in 1919, launching a lifelong collaboration. After success in vaudeville, Edgar and Charlie became radio stars—quite the feat for a ventriloquist. Charlie sparred on the air with the likes of W. C. Fields, and performed an "Adam and Eve" skit with Mae West so racy that the actress was subsequently barred from radio for fifteen years. Bergen and his wooden partner also played in films and on television.

had largely paralleled Europe's lower-class shows, with hand-puppet farces and trick puppets dominating an increasingly marginal field. Then in the early twentieth century, Tony Sarg brought puppet art into the mainstream, performing at major venues such as the 1933 World's Fair and nurturing the next generation of artists, including Sue Hastings, Bil Baird, and Rufus and Margo Rose. These Sarg disciples created permanent puppet theaters and also appeared at World's Fairs, on Broadway, and in films. As in Europe, innovative artists in live-actor theater—including Robert Edmond Jones and Norman Bel Geddes, two of America's most prominent set designers—occasionally incorporated constructed actors in their stagings.

BY THE SECOND HALF of the twentieth century, puppet life was flourishing. In the West, masters such as Obraztsov, Joly, and Baird helped to inspire the next generation—including

Albrecht Roser from Germany; Josef Krofta from Czechoslovakia Republic; Michael Meschke, a Polish-born Swede; Joan Baixas from Catalonia, Spain; Henk Boerwinkel from the Netherlands; Philippe Genty from France; Richard Bradshaw from Australia; Ana Maria Amaral from Brazil; Massimo Schuster, an Italian-born Frenchman; Peter Schumann, a German-born American; and the Americans Jim Henson, Roman Paska, and Julie Taymor. At the same time, constructed-actor traditions in Asia and Africa bred and cross-bred new kinds of puppets to express the new, often cross-bred realities of their societies.

Contemporary live-actor directors have continued to use a casting pool beyond performers as they occur in nature. Lee Breuer has included puppets in most of his theater works. Julie Taymor has mingled live and constructed cast members in most of her plays and films. Other artists who sometimes use such

Peter Brook's production of *Conference of the Birds* (1974), one of his rare uses of constructed actors. This stage version of a poem by the twelfth- to thirteenth-century Persian mystic poet Farid Uddi Attar was by Brook and Jean-Claude Carrière.

Jim Henson and Kermit the Frog on the set of
The Muppet Show, circa 1980.

mixed casts include the Americans Richard
Foreman, Robert Wilson, the Wooster Group,
Peter Sellars, and George C. Wolfe, the British
Théâtre de Complicité, and the Canadian artist
Robert Lepage.

Finally television brought constructed-
actor theater to a vast audience. In 1946 in
Britain, Ann Hogarth, Jan Bussell, and
Annette Mills launched the long career of
Muffin the Mule, possibly the first celebrity
(live-actor or puppet) created entirely by television. American puppets entered childrens' TV
the following year, and soon included such
stars as Snarky Parker, Howdy Doody, Lamb
Chop, and Kukla and Ollie. As television became widespread in Europe and Asia, so did
TV puppet shows aimed at children. In addition, television's variety shows for adults included vaudeville-like puppet entertainment to
adult audiences—including traditional acts,
such as Edgar Bergen with his dummy Charlie
McCarthy, and quirkier work, such as Wayland
Flowers with his foul-mouthed Madame. Most
important, Jim Henson and his Muppets, a
growing presence beginning in 1954, endowed
generations worldwide with vivid theatrical
imagination.

Puppetry also developed an organizational
support structure. By 1929, an international
puppet union, UNIMA, was holding international festivals for traditional and experimental
work. In 1966, puppeteer Frank Ballard created
a degree-granting program in puppetry at the
University of Connecticut, the first in America.
In 1981, Jacques Félix established an international school and institute for puppetry,
l'Institut International de la Marionnette, in
Charleville-Mézières, in northwestern France.
It trains performers, holds festivals, and pro-
duces puppet-related books and journals. In
1998, Julie Taymor's version of *The Lion King*,
teeming with puppets, garnered Broadway's
Tony Award for Best Musical. The puppet production *Avenue Q* received the Best Musical
Tony in 2004. And mainstream presses are
now publishing books like this one.

Julie Taymor designing lead actors for *The Lion King*. She is sculpting a clay model for the treacherous Scar. The young hero Simba and his father Mufasa are in the foreground.

Two live actors flanking a life-size puppet in *Spunk* (1990), based on writings by Zora Neale Hurston, adapted and directed by George C. Wolfe. Wolfe, who for many years headed New York's Joseph Papp Public Theater, often mixes live and constructed actors in his casts. His *Tempest* included islanders ranging from half to twice human size. *Bring In Da Noise, Bring In Da Funk* featured a tap duet between a puppet Shirley Temple and a live-actor Bill "Bo Jangles" Robinson. American puppeteer Barbara Pollitt often designs and sometimes manipulates the constructed actors for Wolfe.

CHAPTER 2

Show Breeds

Puppets have one critical drawback as performers. Their operating systems, unlike those of live actors, are not self-contained. Once an inanimate object is cast in a scenario, it usually has to *do* something, and puppets cannot perform even the simplest tasks on their own. For certain borderline breeds, the issue is moot, since the puppets' activities are invisible to human audiences anyway. They may take place in the realm of the dead, or they may be entirely spiritual. But most puppets need to execute some kind of perceivable action. Artists have devised all kinds of techniques to make their actors act.

Westerners usually categorize puppets into six main types: hand or "glove" puppets, moved by a puppeteer's fingers inside the character's head and arms; marionettes, manipulated from above by strings or, sometimes, sticks; rod puppets, controlled from below via a center post plus additional slender wands; body puppets, which totally envelop the handler; bunraku-style dolls, worked by a visible, onstage handler or handlers; and shadow puppets, which appear to audiences only as the shadows they cast on a screen. In fact, though, constructed actors require a broader taxonomy.

Hand puppets belong to a larger class that solve the inertia problem by physically attaching to a source of life, a puppeteer. The host wears the parasite character, which gets the animation

it needs from the puppeteer's anima. Puppets in this group have most often favored the hand, that most agile of human parts, for their infrastructure and host. Little characters moved by fingers inside their head and arms have been some of the world's most popular actors—including slapstick rapscallions in Europe, virtuoso acrobats in China, and superhuman heroes in India. Puppet characters also can live on a single finger. These include contemporary crocheted or squishy creatures for children, bawdy comedians of seventeenth-century Russia, and subtle characters made from just a mask or head on a fingertip. Some of the most admired works of Sergei Obraztsov and the American puppet artist Robert Anton used one-finger actors. Two-finger puppets, common in some Inuit traditions, have a very different body architecture and range of movement.

A variation of hand puppets is the mitten-head: A manipulator's thumb animates the character's lower jaw while the other four fingers make a malleable face. Most of Jim Henson's mouthy Muppets use this basic system. Mitten-heads can employ additional devices to move their arms and legs, should they require movable arms and legs, and can appropriate the manipulator's forearm (becoming evening-glove puppets). Traditional Hopi snakes, for example, are animated by the manipulator's hand and arm inside them.

An Inuit puppet head that lives on two fingers. Worn by women dancers during ceremonies, these beings are considered incapable of embodying spirits and so are theatrical rather than sacred.

OPPOSITE: An arrogant hunter taking a direct hit of chimp urine on a miniature puppet stage atop a *gelede* body puppet (whose head sits on top of the puppeteer's). Yoruba Gelede puppets in southwest Nigeria and Benin often satirize social faults. Strings, including one that releases the water, are accessed from inside the costume.

Sergei Obraztsov's evening-glove-puppet swans. Inserting his thumb and four fingers into a simple "beak" at the end of a sleeve, Obraztsov turned his hand and arm into a swan. This pair is engaged in a discussion about swimming.

BELOW: Robert Anton painting one of his tiny, fingertip puppets. Anton cast his finely detailed characters in troubling little scenarios, performing for fewer than twenty spectators at a time.

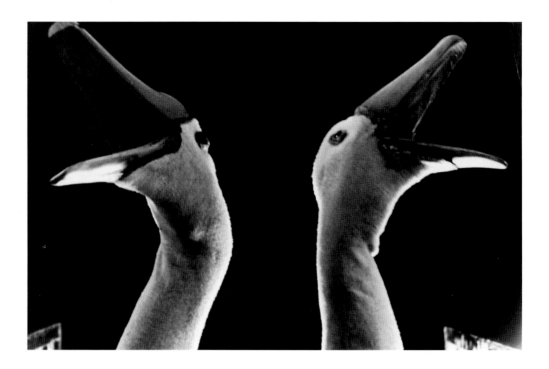

A Yup'ik ritual face puppet made of painted driftwood and feathers. When the doors in its chest are closed, the puppet's body is plain white. Dancers wore mask-puppets like this in ceremonies concerned with the hunt for meat or driftwood, a precious commodity on the treeless Alaskan tundra. Sometimes pairs or trios of these characters appeared in sequence to illustrate a chant. The puppets were nearly wiped out of Yup'ik life by missionaries in the early twentieth century.

The puppeteer's head, despite its unimpressive range of motion, is a popular site for parasite puppets. Proximity to the center of consciousness seems to give the puppet a leg up on coming alive: "I'm attached to the brain, which thinks; therefore I am." Some puppets are complete characters worn over the face, like masks. Inuit duck puppets have eye-holes for the host-puppeteer around their wing tips as they swim straight up toward the sky. Other head-puppets sit on their hosts like hats. Painted wooden turtles perch right atop the heads of Nigerian Yoruba performers, anchoring cloths that conceal the handlers.

Puppets have lived on nearly every part of the human body. Sergei Obraztsov used his elbow for a baby's head. Puppeteers in Korean *baltal* plays and in one Japanese tradition perform lying on the ground with their legs in the air, wearing the characters' heads on their feet. The contemporary German puppeteer Peter Waschinsky also has animated creatures with his feet and lower legs. Julie Taymor filled the ranks of a ragtag American revolutionary army in *Liberty's Taken* (1985) with Sad Sack trios consisting of one live actor and a mannequin attached to each arm. Mel Brooks did the same for his Nazi storm troopers in *The Producers* (2001).

A PARASITE CHARACTER ALSO can completely envelop its handler. What distinguishes these puppets from masks and costumes—and those borders are murky—is that a separate being with its own anatomy is created. (In many areas, including West Africa, words for "mask" or "masquerade" refer interchangeably to any performance disguise.) Having very different proportions from the manipulator or having its own body parts usually makes a figure more

A German hand-puppet theater, as depicted in the *Illustrierte Chronik der Zeit* in 1886. Actors not currently on stage hang by their costumes on a rope in front of the puppeteers. The performers' instruments for drumming up audience lie on the chair and the floor behind them.

puppet than masked actor. The towering *barong landung* of Bali has a handler under its sarong, barely reaching its waist. Bread and Puppet Theater angels often have a papier-mâché head held above that of a puppeteer draped in sheeting. Full-body puppets may have additional characters attached to them. Some Yoruba body-puppet ladies, for example, carry puppet babies.

Total-body puppets need not be anthropomorphic. The Bamana of Mali create animals and supernaturals by hiding performers inside movable haystacks with a few conventional features: A straw tuft atop the hillock, for example, makes a porcupine. In Benin, in western Africa, the supernatural *Zangbeto* night patrols

look like ambulatory fourteen-foot-high gourds made of bush grass. The handler breathes, sees, and speaks through a small face-height window of plaited slats.

Finally, instead of living *on* the handler, a puppet can purloin uncostumed parts of the handler's body. Pieces of the puppeteer, chosen for size, shape, and movement capabilities, become body parts for the puppet. A handler's arm might play the character's leg, or a finger poking through a face might become the growing nose of Pinocchio. The contemporary Peruvian/Bosnian duo Hugo and Ines have created such prodigies as a toothy grin made of fingers and a face made from a bare belly, with the navel as its puckered mouth. The

A flock of hat puppets at a Bulgarian winter festival. At a mid-winter festival on St. Basil's Day, January 13th, celebrants call for spring's renewal of the earth by animating a sky full of birds (made from dead birds plus sheepskin).

A hat puppet of a dog (left), from East Sepik Province, Papua New Guinea. The 1927 photo (above) shows its forbears in action. More than four feet long including the tail, the dancing dogs have painted, carved wood heads and bodies sewn from bark. Each animal perches on a grass "hill," which conceals its (nonexistent) legs, and hides the head and body of the animator.

John, the puppet hero of Lee Breuer's 1980 *A Prelude to Death In Venice*, joined at the waist with his manipulator and cohort, Bill Raymond. John uses Raymond's hands to hold the telephone, as well as to dial phone numbers and play a Bach fugue on the touch-tone buttons.

A Buenos Aires street performer, joined at the feet with his dance partner.

Carnival puppets in Lobbes, Belgium. This trick gear makes the puppeteer seem to be toted in a basket by an elderly woman—actually a puppet he controls. Versions of this masquerade character have carried on for centuries in parts of Western Europe and Turkey.

RIGHT: A body puppet of a mother with a conjoined puppet baby—in a performance by the Yoruba Gelede Society in Benin. A secret society of specially trained actors, the *gelede* performers serve to defend community values against social and supernatural threats. Here the dance courts the favor of the occult female powers by presenting an affirmation of motherhood.

OPPOSITE: The beautiful and virtuous Yayoroba, a combination of shoulder puppet and body puppet, performing in Nyamina, Mali. Her sculpted upper body fits over the handler's head and rests on his shoulders, while her colorful robes conceal him from the audience. He controls her arms with rods from inside the puppet. More than ten feet tall, Yayoroba bows on one knee to the honored guests and female chorus, then dances within the circle of spectators. This popular Bamana character also appears in much smaller rod-puppet versions and has a similar-looking cousin, Yoke (a mother), among the Baga people of Guinea.

Australians Simon Morley and David Friend have devised a revue of characters, including a fruit bat and a wind surfer, by contorting their penises and scrotums.

THE SECOND MAJOR class of puppets comprises ones operated from outside rather than worn by the puppeteer. The most basic technique for moving puppets this way is by hand. Manipulation can be as simple as holding an unarticulated figure at its base and moving it through the action. Carved wooden puppets in Niger and other parts of sub-Saharan Africa often work this way (see page 27). Direct-animation by hand can also be subtle. In American artist Winston Tong's *Bound Feet* (1977), for example, a small strategic adjustment to the neck of a cloth puppet makes her whole body shiver with a frisson of sexual ecstasy (see page 137).

More typically, puppeteers who move their actors from the outside use equipment. One of the oldest and most common devices is string. Early puppet systems in Egypt, Greece, India, East Asia, the Americas, and (probably) Africa all used systems of cords.

Puppet strings sometimes run through the interior of the body, lengthening or shortening like anatomical muscles to effect movement. Such systems, like biological ones, are invisible from the outside, apart from whatever exterior mechanism controls the strings. Pantins, the simplest of these puppets, have a single pull-cord at the bottom that makes the character's arms and legs fly up (see page 187). Internal stringing also can facilitate far more sophisticated movement. The ancient Greeks ran cords through hollow channels to emerge through a tube, probably at the top, so that they could be moved individually. Some early nineteenth-century Italian marionettes operated the same way. Elaborate puppet crèches in southern France, during the eighteenth and nineteenth centuries, used internal stringing with the cords all coming out at the bottom, to be operated from beneath the stage. Traditional Thai puppets evolved a similar technique, apparently from a Chinese model.

Henri Signoret and, later, Geza Blattner created variants on the system for their late nineteenth- and early twentieth-century Paris theaters, attaching the string-ends to small levers, like piano keys. And at a miniature opera house in Chicago in the 1950s, one-foot-tall divas moved via internal cords that extended through grooves in the floor to substage handlers, who scooted about on wheeled stools. The traditional antelope and buffalo stages of Mali have adapted internal stringing to a mobile stage. (See page 64.)

Puppets' strings, unlike human muscles, also can run *outside* their bodies. "Jigging" puppets, or marionettes *à la planchette,* have a single cord threaded front to back through the chest of one or more dolls. One end is fixed to a plank or post, and the other tied to the puppeteer's leg. These figures, country-fair fare in Europe through the nineteenth century, played at least as far east as Turkey. In an African version of this technique, the string ends are tied to the big toes of the puppeteer, who sits on the ground. Some Balinese rituals use other variants of the arrangement.

Marionettes, the most familiar string puppets, hang suspended and controlled by thin cords fixed to strategic points on their bodies. This system allows the puppet more dynamic movement and also, usually, increases the physical distance between the handler and the character. For some puppeteers, this factor—the degree of intimacy or distance from the puppet—is the most important one in de-

termining the basic nature of any puppetry technique.

Marionettes can be as simple as those traditionally used in some Rajasthani and Sri Lankan examples, which have only one or two strings. Such a basic system relies on the balance and jointing of the puppet plus the artistry of the puppeteer to create expressive gestures. At the other extreme, Burmese marionettes can have nearly two dozen strings that control everything from haunches and shoulders to knuckles and jaws. These puppets' virtuoso turns include acrobatics, such as somersaults that they somehow execute without strangling themselves. Some contemporary puppeteers have designed marionettes almost twice as complex as the Burmese.

The demon princess Pirakuan, an internally strung puppet from the Thai royal tradition of *Hun Luang*. To reproduce the fluid movements of live dancers in the court dance-drama, the three-foot-tall puppets have complex mechanisms (including arms jointed in four places) controlled with strings that emerge from the base. Costumes and jewelry are replicas of those worn by live court dancers. Contemporary artists are attempting to reconstruct this lost puppet art, which thrived from the seventeenth through the early twentieth century.

Henri Signoret's system of internal strings linked to piano-type "keys" for his Paris theater, 1888-1892.

BELOW: A performer with *planchette* or "jigging" puppets. In this early nineteenth-century French engraving, a ragged showman makes his puppets dance by moving the string attached to his leg—while he also plays the drum and flute. According to witnesses, jigging puppets on the leg of a virtuoso could cut a mean caper. Teater Taptoe of Gent, Belgium, is reviving this technique.

French puppet artists Jacques Chesnais and Madeleine Chesnais with their Comédiens de Bois (wood actors). The puppeteers lean on a railing that helps them support the weight of the puppets and also holds rolled-up backdrop cloths to be unfurled as needed. Offstage cast members hang from a pole at the back of the bridge. The company's name probably puns on Comédiens du Roi (The King's Actors), France's first important theater, founded in the 1550s.

Marionettes, like internally strung puppets, employ various devices for operating the strings. Rajasthani traditional puppeteers just hold them or tie them to fingers. More typically, the string-ends are attached to a control-piece, such as a wooden cross or "I" shape, that allows the puppeteer to move or tilt all the strings together or to raise them one by one. For complex marionettes, the puppeteer may use two controls, one regulating the general body stance and the other moving individual limbs or one

controlling the upper body while the other moves the legs. Puppetmakers often invent new stringing systems to meet the specific needs of a character.

Another twist on string technique involves rigging all the cords for all the figures over some high structure and then to a central manipulation area. Some Hopi ceremonies feature beings whose strings extend up, across a high beam, and finally out of the underground *kiva*, or ceremonial hall. Many Asian and European peep shows—puppet stages inside a box, viewed through holes—operated similarly, with all the cords emerging through the top, back or sides of the carton.

The other main type of external manipulation uses rods. In Asia, rod puppets have usually been worked from below with the puppeteer hidden from view. Javanese *wayang golek* have a center stick that supports the puppet and turns its head, and a thin wand fixed to each wrist to move the arms. Puppets in parts of Thailand, Korea, and India use a similar system, but the wands are attached further up the arms and concealed under the costume. Large, heavy rod puppets in China's Sichuan province

and in West Bengal, India, rest their center stick against the handler's waist to support the weight, like a parade flag. Some smaller puppets, such as the *Tay* puppets of northern Vietnam, use a similar technique.

In Europe, rod puppets have mainly been manipulated from above. These have sometimes been called "marionettes"—the spatial orientation of puppeteer to puppet (that is, above or below) determining the nature of the beast more than whether or not the controls are rigid. The earliest known European rod puppets, those excavated from ancient Greek and Roman sites, seem to have had a single pole either attached at the top or run through the head

Hanne Tierney animating a group of dancers in *Incidental Pieces for Satin and Strings* (1991). Using fishing wire threaded over a ceiling grid, Tierney handles a stageful of characters, usually semi-abstract. Her casts have included metal coils, lengths of fabric, strings of beads, air-conditioner hose, and aluminum triangles.

The violinist Zelig, created and manipulated by Joseph Cashore. This American puppeteer's marionettes use as many as forty-four strings. They perform actions as subtle as writing and playing music or as tricky as trapeze stunts and climbing onto the puppeteer's shoulders. Zelig, twenty-six inches high and made from papier mâché, uses a mere eighteen strings.

A royal character of Sri Lanka's traditional string-puppet theater. Dignified characters such as royalty are controlled only at the head and wrists. Dancing girls and acrobats may have strings attached to their head, elbows, wrists, knees, and ankles. Made from lightweight local *kaduru* wood, the marionettes are three to four feet tall.

Portugal's *Boñecos de Santo Aleixo*. These eight-inch high angels dance in perfect unison, a sign perhaps of their divinity, while vertical strings across the proscenium opening help to camouflage their control rods. One of Europe's oldest puppet traditions, dating back to the sixteenth century, the *boñecos* died out in the twentieth century but were revived in 1979 and continue to perform.

Knights of the Sicilian "marionette" theater. The main rod, extending through the puppet's head to the neck, controls head movements and gait: By inclining the puppet slightly from side to side, the handler frees each leg in turn to swing out and take a step. These soldiers from Palermo are the smallest of the breed, about three feet tall and less than twenty pounds. Their cousins from Catania, up to four feet tall, can weigh in, fully loaded, at forty pounds. Those alpha males of European rod puppets clomp around the stage on rigid legs, whacking and impaling each other.

OPPOSITE: Backstage at a Javanese *wayang golek* performance. These three-dimensional rod puppets use a manipulation technique and stage setup similar to those of Javanese shadow puppets, from which they apparently developed. A system very much like *wayang golek* once was popular in Japan, but has disappeared.

and hooked onto the neck. One tradition in Belgium still works that way. The handler controls these puppets' limbs, which swing freely from jointed shoulders and hips, by shifts of weight and angle.

Most European rod puppets have additional poles attached to hands and, sometimes, to knees or to props. Sicily's *pupi*, active for about 200 years, use right-arm rods (in Catania and Palermo) and strings to help handle limbs, weapons, armor, and special effects. Many traditional Czech and Slovak puppets also hang from a center rod and have strings to control their limbs.

UNLIKE LIVE ACTORS, puppets need not be three-dimensional. If they are manipulated from outside, they can be flat. Two-dimensional constructed actors can use most of the movement techniques that full-bodied characters do—including strings, rods, and hands-on manipulation.

At their simplest, flat puppets can be unarticulated figures made from cardboard, wood, or sheet metal. The contemporary American puppet artist Janie Geiser has sometimes used one-foot-high plywood puppets with no movable parts at all, held from above on a rod. During the eighteenth and nineteenth cen-

turies, when live-actor stage sets were mainly painted wings and backdrops, several publishers printed miniature "toy theater" versions of popular shows. Amateurs could assemble the stage, scenery, and cast by pasting the printed paper images onto cardboard, and put on their own home versions of hit plays (see page 207). Some contemporary puppeteers, including the New York-based companies Great Small Works and Ninth Street Theatre, create original works for this format.

Twentieth-century artists have played with many variants of flat actors. The Théâtre Sur le Fil, founded in France in 1970 by Claude and Colette Monestier, cut its sets and actors from paper or corrugated wrap. David Hockney's 1981 designs for Stravinsky's *The Nightingale* presented the citizenry as stylized faces painted on flat circles atop long poles; when public opinion changed, the chorus just flipped the circle-faces from the sad to the happy side. In James Lapine's *Sunday In the Park With George* (1984), the leading character, painter Georges Seurat, left life-size cardboard copies of himself to keep chatting up rich patrons at a gallery opening while he continued to work the room.

Two-dimensional puppets have most often been used to cast shadows. Shadow puppets can be opaque, creating a black image (as in Java), or translucent, projecting color onto the screen (as in much of China). They can be solid (as in eighteenth- and nineteenth-century France) or intricately carved (as in medieval Egypt). They may have no movable joints (as in Cambodia's "large format" tradition) or several hinges (as in Turkey). They can be held flat against the screen to create a sharp picture (as, usually, in Greece), or at varying angles, to create a shimmer of form (as in Bali). The main manipulation rods may extend below the puppet (as in all of Southeast Asia) or poke out behind (as in the Near East and parts of China). There can be a single light source, making the brightness modulate across the screen (as in India's Orissa province), or many lights, creating a more uniform field (as in Kerala, in southwest India, where lamps six to nine inches apart run the length of the twelve-foot screen).

Three-dimensional objects, including humans, also can be used to cast shadow figures on a screen. Performers using their hands to create shadows of animals have been documented in Central Asia and the Near East for more than three centuries. This form of puppetry may be as old as sunlight and hands.

SYSTEMS FOR ANIMATING puppets have mutated and cross-bred all over the map. Haida puppets worn on the head often have some movable parts controlled by strings: A head-puppet killer-whale can arch its fearsome body; a bird perched atop a mask can flap its wooden wings. The *bommalattam* marionettes of southern India use an unusual combination of rods and strings, with the puppet suspended from the manipulator's head. Richard Teschner's puppet technique resembled that of the Javanese rod puppets that had inspired him, but he added internal strings to control the head and waist. The American puppet artist Bruce D. Schwartz often held a puppet behind its neck and used slender rods to operate its hands. Japanese bunraku, with three puppeteers per character, combines hands-on (for the feet), complex control-rods (for the arms), and internal stringing (for the head). Jim Henson's basic Muppet technique mixed mitten-mouth glove puppetry for the heads and Asian-style rods-from-below for arms.

Finally, all manner of eccentric puppet techniques have been passed down in long traditions or invented for a single show. In parts of the Balkans and Near East, generations of solo puppeteers have animated three puppets at once while lying on the floor: a glove puppet on each hand and a third puppet between them on a knee. In rural New England and Appalachia, loose-limbed little wooden characters bounce against a board to dance as the handler taps a rhythm. Japanese *kuruma ningyo* performers scoot around seated on small wheeled boxes,

connected ankle-to-ankle and usually head to head with four-foot-tall actors. Humanettes, used by contemporary European and American performers, are hybrids combining live actors and puppets, with a fake body under a live actor's head (see page 74).

Puppeteers have harnessed nearly all the basic elements—air, water, fire—to animate their actors. Tony Sarg pumped helium into jumbo characters made of rubberized silk for Macy's Thanksgiving Day parade. (Sarg's colleague Bil Baird called these airborne puppets "upside-down marionettes," since the handlers worked them from underneath with strings.) In *Red Beads* (2002), Lee Breuer and Basil Twist used the wind from electric fans to move featherweight performers.

Some ancient Greek and Turkish automatons were set in motion by flowing liquid. In rural north Vietnam, centuries of lightweight wooden actors have performed floating on ponds. And several contemporary puppet shows, including Basil Twist's 1998 *Symphonie Fantastique,* have played inside tanks filled with water, which alters how figures move and look to an audience.

Blowups of eighteenth-century William Hogarth engravings in Theodora Skipitares's staging of *A Harlot's Progress* (1998). Puppeteers half-hidden behind the figures move them around the stage. Skipitares invents new species of actors for each show—from these flat unarticulated characters, to marionettes, to life-size realistic mannequins, to human-headed cat-size buffalo, to fanciful meldings of inanimate objects and humans.

"Murder at the Cabaret," a part of *Charta*, four plays that Massimo Schuster performed in war-torn Sarajevo in January 1994 using easily transportable paper puppets. The French painter Hervé Di Rosa designed the characters for this Humphrey Bogart take-off, one of *Charta*'s three comedies. Schuster developed the fourth play, "Sarajevo," on site, using puppet designs by Peter Schumann of the Bread and Puppet Theater and the Italian artist Enrico Baj. Based in Marseilles, France, Schuster has run his Théâtre de l'Arc-en-Terre since 1975.

OPPOSITE: Backstage at a *wayang kulit* shadow puppet performance in Bali in 1983. The *dalang*, puppeteer I Wayan Wija, holds the carved-leather characters so that only their tips touch the screen, making the shadows soft-edged and ephemeral. He manipulates and speaks for all the characters in the four-hour performance. Clowns translate the ancient language that higher-ups speak, improvise jokes, and perform slapstick routines. These particular oafs serve the usurper Kurawa clan in *The Mahabharata*.

OVERLEAF: Silouettes that suggest cave art in *The Song of the Bear,* performed in Paris in 1994 by the French troupe Amoros et Augustin with members of the Lapp National Theater. Luc Amoros and Michèle Augustin, who founded their company in 1976, use a wide range of shadow forms. Here, hand-held lights helped to create a mysterious air for a story set in the liminal world of Lapp shamanism. Their *Señor Z* (1991) was a wind-blown cartoon melodrama. *Sunjata* (1989) created with the Ki-Yi Mbock theater of Ivory Coast, included multi-character images inside shields (see page 239). *360° In Shade* (2000) featured artists slapping small paint bladders onto a screen.

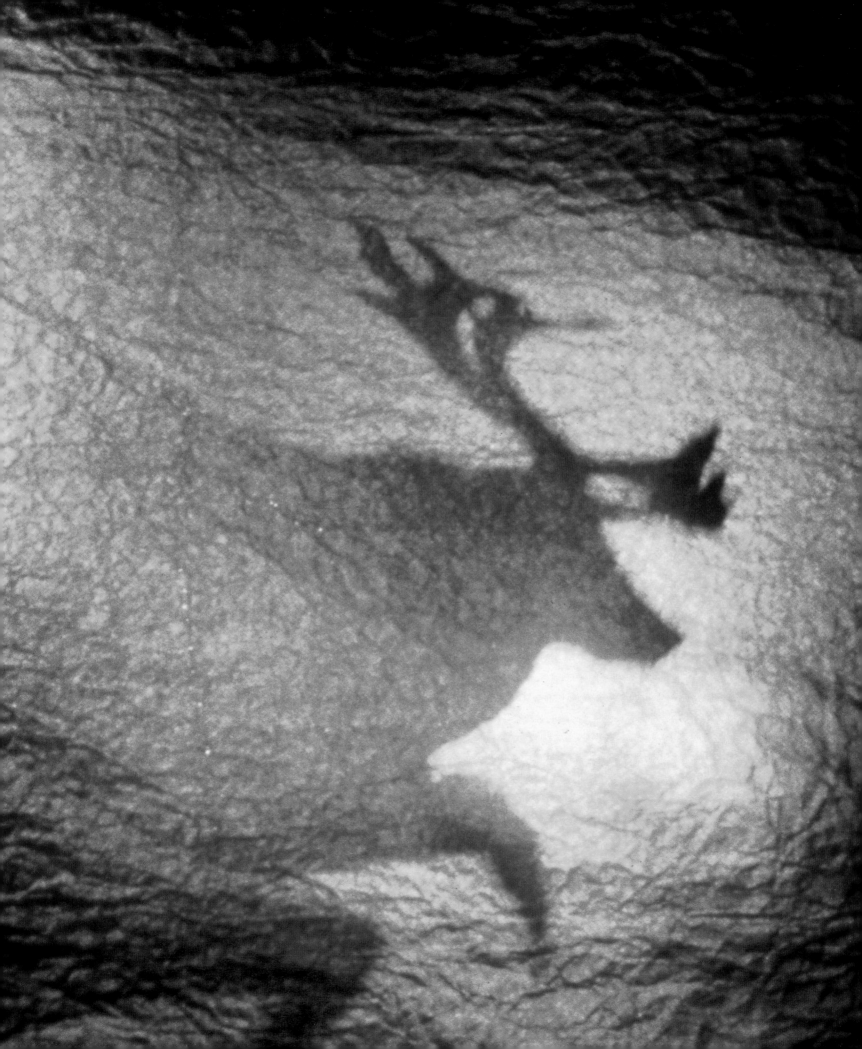

An itinerant exterminator advertising his business in Paris's nineteenth-century theater of "Chinese Shadows."

The Mexican Palo Lluvia company's 1989 shadow performance of *Story of Goblins and Other Realities*. Opaque and translucent characters move through landscapes of dark crags and pastel washes, water made of patterned light, and a cataclysm created with mylar.

Artists even have animated puppets, in a way, by setting them on fire. Ilia Epelbaum, director of Moscow's experimental Shadow Theater, transformed a woman into a swan in his *Swan Lake* (2000) by burning away the initial character made of paper to reveal the foil-covered shape underneath. The contemporary Polish artist Grzegorz Kwiecinski fashions actors and environments from paper—some of them toy-theater size, others human scale—then torches them. Their act consists of disappearing with this single blaze of energy. At the opposite extreme, the Théâtre du Fust, based in Montélimar, France, has used puppets made from ice, which melts during the play. In *Un Cid,* the company's 1996 version of Corneille's classic, the characters start out with detailed features and opulent, glistening period costumes, then progressively drip away until, by the end, they are bare sticks. At this point, the characters have transcended physical presence to exist in the realm of pure imagination.

Artists have also made evanescent, incorporeal performers out of reflected light. These images have ranged from abstract to figurative. In the early 1920s, Bauhaus artists Ludwig Hirschfeld-Mack and Kurt Schwerdtfeger created a show using reflectors and stencils to control various colors, shapes, and intensities of light. Designing Andrei Serban's 1984 production of *The King Stag,* Julie Taymor helped to create the fairytale world of Carlo Gozzi's play with magical deer made of light reflected off mirror Plexiglas—ephemeral figures gamboling in and out of existence along the theater walls. The contemporary American puppeteer Jane Catherine Shaw has used mirrors to shape and bounce figures made of light and to show audiences the reflected images of flat puppets they could not see in person.

Characters can also be made of direct, unreflected light. Tinkerbell in *Peter Pan* has usually appeared on stage as a twinkle in midair or, starting in the late twentieth century, a dancing laser beam. In Ping Chong's *Kwaidan,* a bluish shimmer of luminescence plays a

The shadow theater of Prasanna Rao. This puppeteer from Calcutta, India, brings his imaginary world to life with just a light and his two hands.

A drawing of the mechanism of a Bamana animal puppet-stage.

RIGHT: A buffalo body-puppet that is also a mobile stage for internally strung little actors, in a 1980 performance in Mali. Other Bamana animated stages are shaped like antelopes (the most popular), giraffes, and birds.

ghost that wafts into a room and steals a corpse. Holograms have made possible three-dimensional actors with no physical substance. Julie Archer's design for Mabou Mines's *Hajj* (1983), and Linda Hartinian's for the company's Imagination *Death Imagine* (1984) both feature holograms, giving these journeys of self-discovery a mystical air.

Still another eccentric clan of puppets comes to life by producing sound rather than by moving. Some pre-Columbian ceramic figures of animals and humans whistled when someone blew into them. In the southern Congo well into the twentieth century, human-shaped trumpets expressed their anima by singing. The French *marotte*, a mock-septre with the head of a jester, both spoke the words of the "fool" who held it and used its own voice of bells.

BESIDES ALL THIS DIVERSITY of techniques, puppets vary tremendously in style. Naturally, they reflect the aesthetics of their homelands. A cloth antelope puppet from Mali looks more like its sculpture and textile neighbors than like its distant bunraku or *wayang kulit* puppet cousins.

Another fundamental variation among constructed actors lies in how they deal with their odd lot in life—namely that they don't actually *have* life. For their performance to succeed, constructed actors must induce the audience to overlook that they are fakes. This is no small matter. The distinction between living and inert matter is basic to how humans sort out the world. The range of puppets' approaches to this conundrum cuts across manipulation techniques, centuries, and geography.

At one end of the spectrum, puppeteers devise to camouflage their actors' fraudulence at least to some degree. Making puppets move or, for that matter, do *anything* works to belie that they are inert. Besides this, the obvious way to mask puppets' scam is to make them resemble live humans. Delicately carved rod puppets of ancient Rome had the detail and even individu-

A drawing of a system of interior stringing for the face of a ventriloquist's dummy. This puppet was designed by Frank Marshall, who made the original Charlie McCarthy.

A demonstration of a *bommalattam* puppet from Tamil Nadu, India. The puppeteer, hidden during an actual performance, connects head-to-head with the puppet, bearing its weight (up to twenty pounds). He controls its jointed arms with rods. Although most Indian puppets have no legs under their long skirts, *bommalattam* dancers, who may be four and a half feet tall, have complex legs, with joints at their hips, knees, and ankles. Assistants sometimes help the main puppeteer move the limbs.

Water puppets of northern Vietnam. In the Red River delta, puppets have performed on ponds and lakes since at least the twelfth century. The actors, up to three feet tall, are carved from the lightweight wood of fig trees, then painted with waterproof pigments. Manipulators, thigh deep in water and hidden by a bamboo screen, operate them with long poles that include contraptions for moving individual parts. The dancers in this picture wave their little arms and execute precise choreography. Other popular characters breaststroke, fish using poles or baskets, and climb trees. Sea serpents, whose segmented bodies are connected with bicycle chain, swim, slither, dive, and spew water or fire.

BELOW: A drawing of a water-puppet theater setup, seen from backstage.

aity of the period's portrait sculpture. Japanese bunraku puppets' gestures often include not just moving limbs but the rise-and-fall chest motions of breathing. Among contemporary Western puppets, Theodora Skipitares's early performers included life-size, realistic mannequins of Thomas Edison and Marie Curie, and sculpted portrait heads of New York planner Robert Moses. The principal characters in *Tinka's New Dress* (1994) by Canadian puppeteer Ronnie Burkett looked more or less like people.

Puppeteers' common practice of hiding their mechanisms is obviously geared to help camouflage the actors' fakeness. Puppet designers have run strings inside the puppets' bodies and concealed manipulation rods under costumes. Artificial actors in Hopi ceremonies and in contemporary western theater have had their workings obscured with dim or sharply focused lighting. Portugal's centuries-old *Boñecos of Santo Aleixo* and their eighteenth-century marionette offspring in Brazil had a

ABOVE: A Tsimshian sound-maker puppet. The hollow wooden head of this nineteenth-century Northwest Coast puppet is a rattle, allowing him to "speak." He moves his arms via a string threaded through the neck. Made of buckskin and birdskin as well as carved, painted wood, this sixteen-inch-tall character probably was used in ceremonies to dramatize a "spirit name."

LEFT: A family of wooden trumpets from the Bembe region of Congo. In 1966, local musicians breathed life into these already long-dormant figures. In their prime, such wooden singers participated in funeral services and ceremonies for ancestors. In the group pictured here, the largest, the "father," is fifty-two inches high. Certain African drums carved with human images are also considered to contain spirits.

An ostrich ballet by French puppet artist Philippe Genty using black theater technique. These maladroit danseuses, part of a 1981 revue *Breath*, lose their underwear, their legs, and their cool. Black-clad puppeteers remain invisible in darkness behind the puppets' narrow strip of light. Genty uses evening-glove-puppet technique for the ostriches' necks and heads, plus hands-on and rod techniques for the legs and tutus and (don't ask) the eggs and hatchlings.

OPPOSITE: Mixed-method manipulation of a puppet ballerina in the German Figuren Theater Tübingen's 1998 *Flamingo Bar*. In this solo performance, puppeteer Frank Soehnle controls the puppet's stance with a short protrusion behind her neck. He also uses rods attached to the wrists, strings to adjust the tilt of the head, and direct hands-on manipulation.

pattern of thin vertical strings across the front of the stage to help mask the puppets' strings and rods.

Since the presence of a manipulator is a dead giveaway, puppeteers often conceal themselves. Many have played from behind a screen, wall, or curtain above, beneath, or beside the stage opening. Handlers in "black theater" remain invisible by wearing black and keeping clear of the corridor of light where the puppets play. "Black light" technique another variant, makes the constructed actors visible, because they are painted to reflect that light, but lets their manipulators remain unseen. Puppeteers who do stay visible during a show sometimes justify their presence by having a role in the puppets' world, interacting with the characters. Shari Lewis chatted with Lamb Chop. Edgar Bergen endured Charlie McCarthy's sass.

Finally, of course, all these tactics fool no one. Apart from the occasional trompe l'oeil work or certain religious ceremonies where belief ratifies the illusion, nobody watching a puppet show thinks for one moment that the constructed actors actually are alive. And yet puppetry has thrived through the eons. It works, despite its utter lack of believability.

Or because of it. Intriguingly, puppeteers in virtually all times and all places have deliberately, grossly undermined their own illusion. Even when they fashion relatively realistic-looking actors, they throw in something that gives away the game. Those finely sculpted Roman puppets had uncamouflaged rods protuding from their heads. Bunraku characters are dwarfed by visible onstage handlers. Skipitares's life-size Edison and Curie shared their stage with a herd of miniature human-faced buffalo, and the Moses heads were riding, sans body, on a Ferris wheel. Burkett's Tinka and her fellow characters lived on a carousel turntable.

Puppets are savvy creatures. The bogusness that logically should prove the fatal flaw of the species actually is a key to its success. This paradox bears closer examination.

CHAPTER 3

High-Wire Acts

THE SHEER DARING OF IT TAKES YOUR BREATH away. Tightrope walker Trixie LaBrique teeters just a bit but keeps her balance, perched on the head of The Great Brikini. Stage lights glint off Trixie's sequined tutu adding to the drama as Brikini The Clown, riding a unicycle, carries her across the high wire.

Actually, the performers are perfectly secure. Their tightrope is only a few feet off the ground. And they are eight-inch-high figures held in place by puppeteers. In fact, as anyone can plainly see, Trixie and Brikini are ordinary construction bricks, one sporting a skirt of pink tulle, the other a clown nose, and their unicycle is a furniture caster. The bravado in this nervy act is not the circus performers' but the Puppetmongers': Their show will fall flat if they cannot launch the audience into an imaginative leap of lunatic scale.

ALL THEATER ENGAGES its viewers in a double reality. While film can lock onto the imagination and virtually transport the audience, spectators at live theater never quite forget where they are, however much they buy into the fabricated world on stage. This double vision—seeing both, say, Kevin Kline a few yards away right now and Hamlet at Elsinore centuries ago—is part of the pleasure of live theater.

In puppet theater, this so-called "willing suspension of disbelief" becomes a high-wire

act as the gap between normal reality and stage truth becomes a chasm. Making audiences see two L-shaped blocks of foam rubber as lovers nuzzling—which the Swiss mimes Mummenschanz did in their debut show—is like tying the spectators' imagination to bungee cords. Never mind that Mummenschanz's chunks of foam lack such acting skills as "emotion memory" and vocal articulation or that the Puppetmongers' tightrope dancer has neither flexibility nor grace. They make up for it by spurring their audiences to canyon-spanning feats of disbelief suspension, which are like amusement-park rides for the imagination.

Since lack of believablity amplifies the theatrical kick, and believability is rarely an option

A high-wire act in the Puppetmongers' "Brick Bros. Circus." Created in 1978 by the Canadian sister-brother team Ann and David Powell, the brick circus tours widely, tapping local talent (bricks) for each show.

OPPOSITE: Massimo Schuster with his cast in a 1998 performance of *Dieu! God Mother Radio*, a zany, troubling adaptation of Christopher Marlowe's *Massacre at Paris*. In this case, the puppeteer does have a role in the play that justifies his presence on the stage: Schuster plays a combination radio announcer and God. But the illusion is nonetheless daredevil, since the role he plays is far-fetched, putting it mildly. Schuster created this show with the American puppet artist Roman Paska.

A 1994 performance of *The Teachings for Women*, by the great bunraku playwright Chikamatsu Monzaemon, at the National Bunraku Theatre in Osaka, Japan. This scene shows the houses of doomed lovers separated by the Yoshino River. Innocent victims caught in a complicated intrigue of high-level corruption and murder, both lovers will commit suicide rather than serve a perfidious usurper. Bunraku master Yoshida Tamamatsu is the principal puppeteer for the young man, Koganosuke, at far right. Across the river, (right to left) puppeteers Kiritake Itcho, Yoshida Tamae, and Yoshida Minojiro are the head puppeteers for the visiting princess Tachibana and two maids. All twelve manipulators remain visible to the audience; the four principal puppeteers are not wearing hoods.

anyway, puppet artists generally have not even tried to create real-looking beings living in a plausible world. In fact, they have gone out of their way to tease and shake up the suspension of disbelief.

Even as puppeteers make their actors gain credibility by moving, they may deliberately undermine the effect by having them move in blithely incredible ways. Hand puppets, which could enter from the side at stage-floor level, as people would, pop up from below, where everybody knows the manipulator is. Instead of walking from place to place, marionettes often bound across the landscape or up staircases in a single hop.

Puppeteers also challenge the illusion by remaining visible when they have no business in the characters' world. The artists who developed Japanese bunraku deliberately altered their stage setup so that the audience could see the puppeteers. During the early eighteenth century the manipulators progressed from being totally hidden in a substage area, to being semi-visible through sheer cloth, to being on the stage, covered head to toe in black. Starting a century later, the lead puppeteers often played without hoods, letting audiences see their faces.

European planchette players and African toe-puppeteers have never concealed that their leg movements, agitating the string threaded through the puppets, provided the actors' life. In the glove-puppetry that survives in India— *kundhei-nacha* in Orissa and *kathakali* puppets in Kerala—the handlers sit on mats in full view (see page 202).

Modern Western marionettists are similarly brazen about being visible in a world where they supposedly do not exist. By the 1920s and 1930s, puppeteers—including Karl Schichtl in Germany and the Yale Puppeteers in the U.S.— were using either a waist-high masking curtain or none at all. Other prominent puppeteers adopted the practice, including Frank Paris in America and Albrecht Roser in Germany. The American marionettist Alice May Hall started playing unconcealed in her 80s, at first just in living rooms so that fellow artists could watch her technique. Everyone liked the effect so much that, like bunraku artists nearly three centuries earlier, she never hid again. By now, this innovation is common practice.

Contemporary non-string puppeteers also stay visible to the audience. New York's Crowtations hold their Muppet-like do-wop crows overhead as if the handlers were either

within a traditional castelet puppet booth or outside the frame of a TV camera—except there is no castelet or camera. The *Avenue Q* puppeteers similarly remain in full view as they operate Muppet-type figures that exist only from the waist up. For *The Lion King's* many full-body puppets, Julie Taymor keeps the live actor's face visible, wherever it happens to be in the puppet character's body.

These trespassing performers not only increase the theatrical bravado but often allow the audience to watch their technique. At the same time, seeing the puppeteers' concentration on the characters can intensify the audience's focus.

Puppet artists sometimes up the ante by letting audiences see characters being assembled. In "Adventures of a Hole," the Théâtre Sur le Fil cut characters out of paper and arranged them with clothespins on a line, all within the audience's view. Heightening the game another notch, the French Théâtre Bululu (directed by Horacio Peralta, an Argentinian) arranged four sticks and a giant bean as limbs and a head, with no body at all in the middle. In *Lost Soles,* the contemporary American tap-dancer and puppeteer Thaddeus Phillips went even further: He conjured a person just by moving tap-shoes with his hands, leaving it to the audience's imagination to fill in the body from the ankles up.

PUPPETEERS' MAIN TRICK for challenging the illusion, though, is to make the actors outrageously unrealistic. The heroes in Southeast Asian shadow plays cast lacy silhouettes even though everyone knows that the bodies even of defeated warriors are not riddled with holes. The antelope puppet/puppet-stage figures in West Africa have complexions of bright patterned fabrics, a far cry from the fur of any living antelope.

A popular formula for flaunting puppets' fakeness is leaving raw materials undisguised. For the Siberian-born American puppeteer Basil Milovsoroff, tree branches or roots created the basic shape and character of a puppet. Milovsoroff then defined its features with marbles, metal springs, and other found materials. The contemporary American artist Ralph Lee has created such prodigies as a mammoth dung beetle with undisguised toilet brushes for its hairy legs and red rubber gloves for its cockscomb and waffle.

The more outrageous the better. In *Highway to Tomorrow* (2000), the American experimen-

OPPOSITE: Even a *live* actor becomes an implausible being in Teatro Tinglado's *The Repugnant Story of Clotario Demoniax*, in a 1996 performance. Playing Señora Lola LaGorda as a humanette, Ramón Barragán, at lower left, supplies the head and animates the feet (with his hands), while another actor provides the arms. The señora appears later in the play as a hand puppet—with a miniature of Barragán's bearded head atop a buxom body. This deleriously demented Pulcinella play layers Scheherazade-like stories within stories, making the audience lose its bearings on reality. Founded in 1980 by Mireya and Pablo Cueto, Tinglado continues a three-generation Cueto family tradition of puppetry in Mexico.

LEFT: In the Sandglass Theater's "That is No Country for Old Men" (1998), actors arrange ordinary logs to create a horse. From that moment on, the beast, although still obviously held together by actors, is as alive as anyone else. The Vermont-based theater, founded by Eric Bass and Ines Zeller Bass, adapted this and another short play from stories by Castle Freeman Jr., calling the double-bill *Never Been Anywhere*.

A Paper Tragedy (circa 1955) by French innovator Yves Joly. The tribulations visited on these characters included attacks by real scissors and fire—underscoring that the characters were actually made of paper. In another Joly show, a nuclear family of undisguised umbrellas and parasols was invaded by walking-cane intruders. He also used his bare hands as puppets, making them play everything from lovers to octopi.

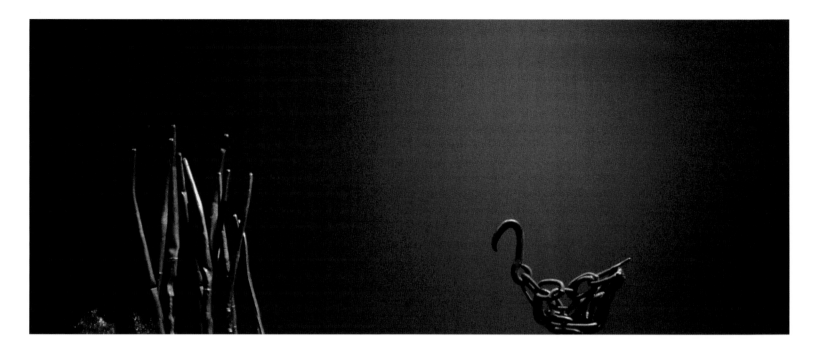

A chainlink duck in *Obstacles* (1992) by the Dutch theater Tam Tam. The chain for this odd duck came from director Gérard Schiphorst's grandfather's farm, and the pond reeds were old organ pipes. The inappropriateness of the materials—rusty metal and a meat hook are a far cry from eider down—only gooses the illusion. Tam Tam, founded in 1979 by Schiphorst and Marije van der Sande, also has cast long-handled blacksmith's pliers as leggy ballerinas (able to pirouette and leap) and cleaning products as a human throng with twist-off or spray-top heads.

tal Elevator Repair Company's loonily updated version of Euripides' *The Bacchae*, two adhesive-backed eyes slapped onto one of the theater's architectural pillars created an elder statesman. To avert the man's gaze from his murdered son, a performer peeled the right eye off the pole and moved it to the other side of the left eye. The Vermont-based Bread and Puppet Theater, led by Peter Schumann, even shows the audience the no-tech raw materials of its props and stage effects: four tin cans tied to a broomstick make a "lawnmower," an onstage performer slowly turning an egg-beater creates the patter of rain.

One time-honored class of raw material is raw produce (and other food) appealing precisely because it is so deliciously inappropriate. A tantalizing example is the 1902 Munich production of "A great potato-, radish-, beet-, and apple-tragedy, staged and performed with his own fruit and vegetables by Paul Larsen." The French *Théâtre de Cuisine* took its name from its first show, in 1979, which starred vegetables and leftovers. Andrew and Bonnie Periale's New Hampshire-based Perry Alley Theatre cooked up a *Snow White* (1993) from groceries, featuring Prince Rigatoni. But Swedish performer Lasse Akerlund takes the cake, staging

Macbeth with a sausage take-out dinner. A tomato brandishing a weiner (dagger-wielding Macbeth) savages the innards of a ketchup bottle (King Duncan) that has removed its cap (crown) for the night. A bottled beer (Cawdor) undergoes summary decapitation (with a bottle opener), spewing out its inner fluids, and generating, amazingly, a touch of horror as well as humor.

Verbal and visual puns and jokes also can tease the illusion. Among the miscellany of performing trash in American puppeteer Paul Zaloom's political monologues, a sports trophy played President Ronald Reagan and a model-railroad bush was George Bush père. In *Highway To Tomorrow*, The Elevator Repair Company cast an uncostumed *thermos* bottle as the god Dionysus, making a malapropian pun on *thyrsos*, the leaf-topped staff associated with that god. American puppeteer Jonathan Edward Cross begins one Cosmic Bicycle Theatre sketch with hand-puppet lightbulbs switching on and off in conversation. Enter the grim reaper, played by a shrouded hammer. One whack on the bulb's head and—blackout.

Suspension of disbelief can notch up to the second mathematical power when puppets perform the role of actors who are playing other characters. The Lyonnais puppet-star Guignol not only had a variety of biographies (tailor, cobbler, political candidate) but played the hero in such classics as *Guignol and Juliet, Guignol Tell, Faust,* and *Cyrano.* Jim Henson's Kermit, Miss Piggy, and their cohorts have starred not only in such obvious vehicles as *The Frog Prince* and *Three Little Pigs,* but also in *The Musicians of Bremen, Treasure Island,* and Charles Dickens's *A Christmas Carol.* Puppet thespians even adopt live-actors' techniques and limitations. The Thai marionette version of *Kaew Na Ma,* about a woman born as a horse, does not initially show the heroine as a horse puppet but rather as a human puppet wearing an equine mask.

Another way puppets launch suspension of disbelief to the second power is by turning puppeteer. In miniature versions of the popular Asian lion and dragon dances, tiny manipulators peek out from under lion or dragon puppets. Eighteenth- and nineteenth-century commedia dell'arte marionettes sometimes animated miniature selves or other characters. The twentieth-century French puppeteer Louis Valdes took it even further, inventing a marionette that held string controls for a smaller marionette, which manipulated a

TAYMOR

Julie Taymor's design for three gazelles—and their puppeteer—leaping through the velt in *The Lion King.* Taymor's uncamouflaged handlers prance and bound about the stage, seeming to be members of the herd—but at the same time they are understood as "not there."

Hands totally out of hand in a 1998 performance of *Ginocchio* by Hugo and Ines, Peruvian mime Hugo Suarez and Bosnian artist Ines Pasic.

Señor Wences and his mischievous sidekick Johnny. The Spanish-born ex-bullfighter Wenceslao Moreño constructed Johnny in front of the audience at each performance, folding his hand into a fist, adding the wig and eyes, then drawing the lips and nose. Their act also included Pedro, a disembodied head in a box, whom Wences periodically checked up on ("You all right?" "S'al'right"). A long-time New Yorker, Wences performed into his 90s, moving from vaudeville to television.

Kukla and Ollie costumed for an urban drama. Burr Tillstrom's Kuklapolitans often staged plays-within-the-puppet-show, tackling not only species-appropriate roles (St. George and the dragon, for example) but also such artistic stretches as "three little maids from school" in Gilbert and Sullivan's *Mikado*. Tillstrom created Kukla in 1936 and gradually expanded the troupe. Their live interlocutor, Fran Allison, joined in 1947 when they moved to live television. Always ad-libbing, the Kuklapolitans covered such topics as pushy houseguests, income tax filing, and political campaigns (Ollie ran for office), and had adult as well as child fans.

BELOW: The Little Players puppet repertory company, created by Francis Peschka and W. Gordon (Bill) Murdock. One of New York's longest-running repertory theaters, its actors were the Standwell family and their German maid, all hand puppets. From the 1950s into the 1970s, this troupe of miniature thespians performed works by Shakespeare, Molière, Oscar Wilde, Noel Coward, and the like. They even raised the suspension of disbelief to the third power when the Standwell's maid, played by a puppet, played Marlene Dietrich playing a film character.

A puppet mischief-maker in "The Red Scarf" by contemporary Dutch puppet artist Feike Boschma. No sooner has the puppeteer sewn this little character into existence, then it starts to wreak havoc with all the tools until, finally, the scissor decapitates it. Repaired, it promises to behave but, of course, does not.

Charles Ludlam and his deranged dummy Walter Ego. In the berserk spirit of the Ludlam's Ridiculous Theatrical Company, his puppet alter ego was committing adultery with Charles's wife and plotting with her to murder Charles. Ludlam was known mainly for outrageous, extravagantly theatrical live-actor shows, including performances in drag. He brought the same lunacy that infused his live-actor shows to this ventriloquism act and the Punch and Judy show he performed as "Professor Bedlam," which won an Obie (off-Broadway theater) award in 1975.

third, which performed a juggling routine—all while a fourth puppet, peeking over the largest marionette's shoulder, tried to get into the act.

PUPPETEERS SOMETIMES go beyond challenging their illusion to flat-out breaking it with in-your-face reminders that the actors are fakes. One game involves teasing the audience into guessing and second-guessing which actors are really alive. The expatriate Hungarian Squat Theater's *Dreamland Burns* (1986) began with over-sized trompe l'oeil puppets that, since everything on stage was at their scale, seemed to be live actors. Then, actual humans entered the scene, to unnerving effect. In Philippe Genty's *Stowaways* (2000), spectators could not tell that a live actor, silhouetted by back-lighting, had been replaced with a two-dimensional copy. Not, that is, until his head flew off.

Or puppeteers may deliberately blow their illusion by ambushing spectators into looking for action from puppets that obviously have no manipulator. In Dutch puppet artist Neville Tranter's *Macbeth* (1990), the drama mounts as Macbeth waits for Macduff to return his greeting. In the American Figures of Speech Theatre's *Nightingale* (1996), tension rises as a character refuses to greet the emperor properly. But both of these silent characters are very obviously sans puppeteer at the moment. Despite such potshots at the theatrical illusion, the action continues on track.

Another plucky deed of daredevil theatricality is puppet mutiny. The ornery ventriloquist's dummy will *not* say hello to the nice lady or stop mimicking everything the puppeteer says. In Togo, Danaye Kanlanféi's dummy is none other than the Goddess of Fortune: Although he is visibly controlling Madame Fortune, she

Complex puppets in *The Trees of Life* (1983) by the Figurentheater Triangel of Ans and Henk Boerwinkel in Meppel, the Netherlands. Here, a twenty-eight-inch-tall bunraku-type puppet carries not only a mask but another character, creating layers of illusion. And then there is that tree that might also be a woman. These glued-paper and cloth figures are part of a four-section play evoking the seasons of the year—and the cycle of life, death, and perhaps rebirth. Since 1963, the Boerwinkels have performed haunting vignettes often on the edge of both humor and nightmare. They combine overhead string marionettes (worked by Henk), glove-puppets (manipulated by Ans), bunraku-type puppets, body-puppets, and masks, often using multiple techniques within one sketch.

BELOW: The title character working with a junior colleague in the Harlequin Marionette Theater, founded by English puppeteer Eric Bramall in 1958.

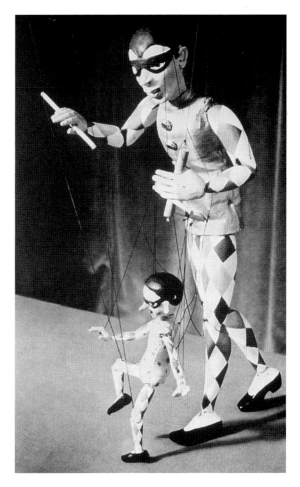

Salomé, animated by Neville Tranter, growing furious at the stony silence of John the Baptist in a 1997 performance at Charleville-Mézières. The dramatic tension builds, even though the John the Baptist mannequin has no manipulator and so could not possibly answer Salomé. Tranter's Stuffed Puppet solo theater, begun in 1976, uses a variety of puppet media, testing the outer boundaries of theatrical illusion and, sometimes, taste.

A life-leeching puppet in *The Gertrude Story* by Yael and Revital puppet company, as performed in Charleville-Mézières, France, in 1977. Here an elderly-woman puppet purloins her creator's sexy legs. This is part of the character's scheme to take all the most desirable parts of the puppeteer for herself—a metaphor, perhaps, for art's plunder of the artist. Yael Inbar and Revital Ariely's company is based in Jerusalem.

Belgian dancer and puppet artist Nicole Mossoux being attacked by her own creation in a 1996 performance of *Twin Houses*. Various life-size alter-egos in the show struggle to dominate and even obliterate their creator. Inspired in part by a psychoanalyst's description of a multiple personality disorder, Mossoux uses puppet mutiny to express the terrible power of art to savage the artist. She and Patrick Bonté, who directed *Twin Houses*, are co-founders of Compagnie Mossoux-Bonté and have worked together since 1985.

keeps tripping him up. Many puppeteers—including the Argentine artist Ariel Bufano, Albrecht Roser, Henk Boerwinkel, Philippe Genty, and Joe Cashore—have performed skits in which a marionette, often the character Pierrot or Pulcinella, tries to escape from its handler. In Hanne Tierney's *Drama for Strings* (1997), the upstart is a scarf of strung beads grousing about Tierney's animation, until she retorts, "then do it yourself," and drops the controls.

Puppet insurrectionists even assault their handler. In an old Turkish routine, a man rests his turban and cloak on a stick—and the figure promptly comes alive and attacks him (having usurped one of his arms as its own). The beating stops only when the character is dismantled. One of Philippe Genty's insubordinate marionettes dismembers him and packs him into a valise. In *Manipulator and Underdog* (1985), Neville Tranter's creation tries to strangle him. Puppets killing their creator also feature in several twentieth-century plays, including *Caroline's Household* (1935), by Michel de Ghelderode, and *Mr. Pygmalion* (1921), by Jacinto Grau, which was staged in Paris in 1923 by the prominent live-actor director Charles Dullin.

"The Frog Prince" from Preston Foerder's *Tales of the Brothers Grimy* in a 1999 performance in New York's Washington Square Park. Here the frog (a sponge) chats with the golden-haired princess (a feather duster sporting sunglasses). Stringmops and old bluejeans serve as castle battlements, and day-glo dusters become spring flowers visited by a squeegie-mop butterfly. Wearing an overturned bucket as a crown, Foerder plays the king. Taking young audiences on a theatrical trapeze ride, the show underscores how imagination can transcend unpromising material circumstances.

At its best, puppetry's audacious teasing of the illusion serves the theme of a show. In the British Théâtre de la Complicité's *Mnemonic* (2001), partly about the quest to know one's past, performers dismantle a wooden chair by unfolding it, stick by stick, so that its form makes less and less sense. Then suddenly, at the climax of the play, one last fold makes it into a stick figure of a man—a living figure, evoking the 5,000-year-old "ice man" discovered in the Alps. In Belgian artist Nicole Mossoux's *Twin Houses* (1994), exploring, in part, the process of making art, one life-size puppet she manipulates tries to rape her; another snatches her pen to usurp creative control, then tries to stab her.

Mabou Mines *Peter and Wendy* (1996), a version of *Peter Pan*, knots and yanks at strands suspending disbelief. Handlers shrouded in white lawn fabric manipulate the puppets, while a single reciter, Karen Kandel, narrates. But Kandel also plays Wendy, and speaks the dialogue for all the puppets. So, at times, she simultaneously recounts an incident, physically plays a role in it, and speaks the words of the other characters, even arguing with herself. Moreover, the family dog, a floppy brown rag of a puppet, disguises itself to play the crocodile in Neverland. What better way than with such brazen, slippery puppets to express the magic and the perils of fantasy— and the fabulously, dangerously porous border between imagination and reality.

Peter Pan and Captain Hook face off with rapiers in the Mabou Mines *Peter Pan*, adapted by Liza Lorwin, and directed by Lee Breuer. Julie Archer created the puppets, which were operated by seven handlers, including master puppeteers Basil Twist and Jane Catherine Shaw. Karen Kandel, in the background, narrates the action and speaks for all of the characters.

CHAPTER 4

Casting Characters

In the early decades of the twentieth century, Edward Gordon Craig proposed replacing live actors with "übermarionettes," super-puppets. Only made-to-order actors could be perfect, with no irrelevant or inappropriate traits. Only they could express spiritual states without ego worming its way in and distorting the artist's vision. While Stanislavski-based training taught actors to attach their own emotional history to characters, for Craig this was tantamount to letting performers hijack art into narcissism.

Flesh-and-blood actors have other drawbacks. Physically, they are extremely limited. Even using stage make-up, even with cross-gender casting, live performers can play only characters that are reasonably similar to themselves physically. Sir Laurence Olivier would have been hard put to play Juliet, no matter how well he could empathize with the character and deliver her lines. Finding actors to play anatomically unusual characters, such as the amputee war-wounded in *The Veterans*, by New Zealand's Strings Attached Puppet Theater, can be exceptionally difficult. The live-actor casting pool is more like a puddle.

"Found actors," that is, actors as they occur in nature, come in a narrow range of dimensions and materials. Even outliers on the spectrum of human size fall within a shallow band. Puppets, on the other hand, can be crafted to whatever measurements a play requires. Constructed giants have performed all over the world almost as far back as records exist—including the oversized Egyptian gods from 2000 B.C.E., huge turbaned dancers in eighteenth-century Turkish royal entertainments, and Bali's twelve-foot-tall barong landung. Peter Schumann's Bread and Puppet Theater includes characters so large they need more than a dozen puppeteers with long poles to manipulate them. The creatures Michael Curry invented for New York City's millenium celebration included a Saharan-desert horse nearly a city block long.

Puppets can play colossal characters even indoors despite walls, ceilings, and floors. They harness the audience's imagination to extend through these physical barriers. An early eighteenth-century play, *The Sneeze of Hercules*, called for a character so gargantuan the audience saw only his enormous nose or hand. The rest of Hercules continued offstage in space imaginatively purloined from the rest of the building, the street, and right through the earth's crust. In the child's-perspective world of the Colette/Ravel opera *The Child and the Enchantments*, the mother is scaled too large to fit on stage. She appears as a singing skirt. Bread and Puppet Theater indoor shows have included bigshots so big that only a single foot or hand fit on stage.

A *bunshichi* head being sculpted during a workshop-demonstration at the International Institute of the Marionette in Charleville-Mézières.

OPPOSITE: A *bunshichi* head, used for noble characters harboring a secret grief. This puppet, now in the Osaka City Museum, no longer performs, but its complexion—aging lacquer on a carved wooden head—shows how the puppet's materials can contribute to characterization.

Itinerant *kugutsu*, or puppeteers, in a 1787 Japanese painting. Showmen like these, carrying their stage and actors in a box hung around their neck, played in Japan as early as the eleventh century.

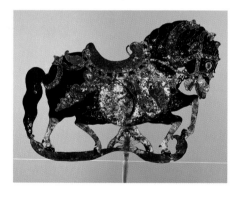

A Javanese shadow-puppet horse from the nineteenth century or earlier, made from painted and gilded water-buffalo hide.

OPPOSITE: The title character in Royal de Luxe company's *A Giant Dropped from the Sky* in Nîmes, France, in 1994. This thirty-foot-tall puppet promenaded through streets and sailed down rivers in several European towns, stopping traffic with his awe-inspiring and road-blocking presence. The Nantes-based troupe, founded in 1980 by Jean-Luc Courcoult, performs for free in public places.

Crafted actors also can be smaller than live ones. This helps itinerant showpeople to transport entire productions. And it allows artists to present characters that are tiny within the scale of their own world. The Appalachian puppeteer Hobey Ford has crafted rod-puppet elves small enough to swim laps across a teacup. In Fernand Léger's 1923 designs for the ballet *The Creation of the World,* twenty-five-foot-tall puppets playing gods shared the stage with twelve-foot-high demi-gods, normal-size humans (the live performers) and little puppet animals.

From Rajasthani court drama to *Beatlemania*, plays have often included historical characters. Live-actor theater must make do with the best available compromise between physical resemblance and talent. Puppets, on the other hand, can be made to order. In recent decades, portrait puppets have played virtually every head of state—including Cleopatra, Queen Elizabeth I, Queen Elizabeth II, Louis XIV, Woodrow Wilson, FDR, Adolf Hitler, Charles de Gaulle, Marien Ngouabi, Mikhail Gorbachev, Jacques Chirac, Margaret Thatcher, George Bush, and Bill Clinton—as well as all manner of other politicians, dissidents, scientists, writers, warriors, bureaucrats, saints, entertainers, and bandits. Beyond the cheeky suspension of disbelief that any puppet creates, portrait puppets spark that peculiar pleasure of recognition that impersonators and impressionists evoke.

Using puppets for animal characters circumvents problems of reliability, decorum, and hygiene. Plus, they can talk. Puppet actors also can embody the many anomalous species common in plays but absent from the live-actor pool—characters such as the human/goat mixes of Greek satyr plays, the elephant-headed Ganesha of *The Mahabharata*, multi-limbed Hindu deities, and cloven-hoofed, humanoid Christian devils.

Live actors, with their limited agility and endurance, are ill suited for such classic stage business as, say, flying and hemorrhaging. Puppets, on the other hand, can be designed to possess exceptional skills or withstand extreme physical insults. Chinese glove-puppet martial artists often exit the stage with a backward flying somersault to defenestrate through a second-storey window. Certain bunraku puppets and Sicilian marionettes get their skulls cracked in half, and some combatants in Indonesian shadow theater literally get their heads knocked off. Characters in Alfred Jarry's *Ubu* plays, originally written for puppets, get impaled on spikes, sliced in half, flushed down toilets, and expelled from a pig's anus—all actions few human performers would attempt.

Then there is gravity. Since puppeteers can counteract the natural pull downward, as Heinrich von Kleist pointed out, constructed actors can achieve kinds of gracefulness impossible for a live actor. And for certain characters, exemption from gravity is fundamental. From fairy tales to religious dramas, theatrical roles call for flying or at least rising off the ground. To accomplish this, live actors need harnesses and wires, equipment that usually is out of place in their stage world. But flying puppet actors need no gear that their earthbound costars do not also have, nothing that is not already a convention in the play. Wooden Sicilian marionette angels, clunky though they might be, get hauled through the air by the same sort of metal rods that *all* beings in their world have.

Trick puppets have been great favorites in Asia and the West. Popular characters in the Rajasthani Kathputli theater undergo a (reversable) sex-change by turning around 180 degrees or flipping upside down. Some nineteenth-century European puppets had similar sexual bipolarity. Other favorite stunt puppets in Europe and America included skeletons that fell apart and reassembled themselves, and characters that could expand or shrink. Flat puppets have their own brands of tricks, often changing their shape by flipping or folding. Nineteenth-century German audiences watched a painted-cardboard Salome whose hoop skirt turned into a hot-air balloon that flew away.

Fred Astaire and Ginger Rogers, twenty-four-inch-high plastic-wood string puppets created circa 1935 by The Rufus Rose Marionettes. Margo and Rufus Rose often invented new control mechanisms for their complex marionettes. Besides touring widely, the Roses were pioneers in puppet industrial films. Rufus Rose may be best known, though, as the manipulator from 1952–1958 of television's cowboy-marionette star Howdy Doody.

A unique display of relativity. Albert Einstein reportedly pronounced the Yale Puppeteers' 1931 marionette of him "good, but too thin," and stuffed a wad of paper under its smock. Founded in 1920 by college roommates Harry Burnett and Forman Brown, the company had its own off-Hollywood Turnabout Theater from 1941–1956 featuring a puppet stage at one end, a human-scale revue stage at the other, and eleven rows of recycled railcar seats with backs that could flip to reverse the orientation. Yale Puppeteers also brought master live-actor stage designer Norman Bel Geddes to create the sets and actors for their *Bluebeard* and *Hansel and Gretel* productions in 1928.

ABOVE AND RIGHT: A hand-puppet theater outside a temple in Taipei, circa 1980. The backstage view reveals how characters execute their flamboyant exits through second-storey windows. In a virtuoso turn, the puppeteer flings the puppet off his hand, making it somersault backward over the first cloth "wall," through one of three second-floor windows in the backdrop behind him, and onto a cloth rigged to catch it.

Besides sight-gags, puppets can handle the tricky transformations that certain roles require. The Faust story, with Mephistophiles' infernal stunts, was a German puppet play before Christopher Marlowe or Goethe wrote a live-actor version. An eighteenth-century staging of *The Prodigal Son* (1736) by Voltaire featured a hanged man who fell from the gallows in pieces, reassembled himself, and ran off. In northern China's shadow theater, a wily legendary fox masqueraded as a beautiful woman by folding his snout back behind his body, giving him an alluring human profile.

In all types of theater, directors sometimes want spectators to see aspects of characters or situations that no one within the play knows.

Live-actor drama can clue audiences in by means of various devices, including visual symbols, music, and verbal asides or leitmotifs. Puppet artists use all these tactics, but they have additional means for communicating what is hidden.

Puppet theater can show what kind of stuff characters are made of by, literally, showing what kind of stuff the characters are made of. Construction materials can provide insight into a character's nature. Even small children intuit that a "monster" sewn from blue fake fur can not be all that malevolent, even if it does eat its friends' cookies. It is obvious that brightly colored little actors atop Yoruba Gelede body-puppet "masks" have a different line of

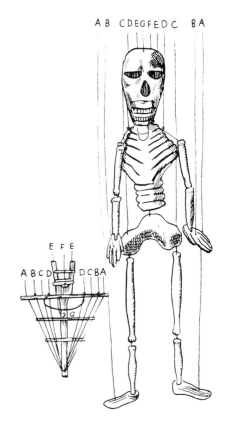

The working diagram of a come-apart skeleton that reassembled when the puppeteer let the strings go slack. This marionette belonged to the Lanos family, three generations of American puppeteers (descended from at least two more in Europe) that toured frontier communities from the early 1800s through the 1930s. Other Lanos trick marionettes included a woman whose skirt turned into a trapeze, a character that split into six people, and various jugglers. Lanos puppeteers, like many others, sometimes enhanced their shows with rope-walkers and trained-bear acts.

A nineteenth-century puppet transsexual from the Netherlands.

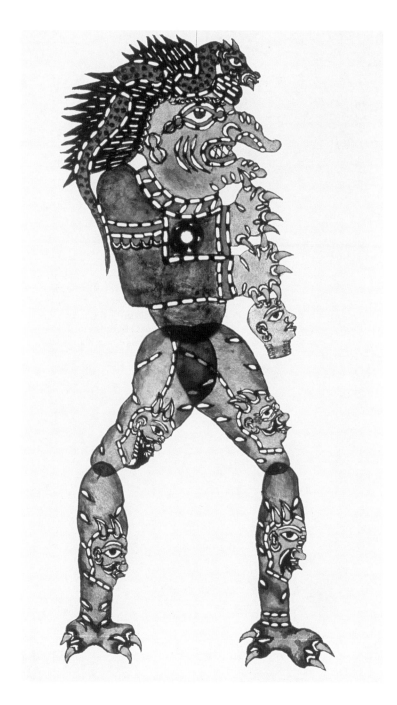

A *djinn*, a supernatural troublemaker in Turkish Karagöz shadow theater. The puppet incorporates the djinn's unusual anatomy, which often includes several spare heads. Many Karagöz plays require composite-character puppets. The bungling title character is forever getting his own head grafted onto the body of some undignified beast, such as a donkey, goat, chicken, or turtle (see page 149). Karagöz's blunders also result in such prodigies as a donkey with its back attached upside down.

RIGHT, TOP AND BOTTOM: A nineteenth-century German transformation puppet from Saxony. This hinged cardboard figure embodies the racist insult *Judensau* (Jew-pig), a phrase recorded as early as 1460. Although singularly vicious, this creation is far from alone in the worldwide ranks of racist puppets.

Superkangaroo flying to the rescue. Here, the marsupial superhero, created in 1972 by Australian puppeteer Richard Bradshaw, is blocking government bulldozers about to flatten an aborigine's hut. (Bradshaw eventually removed the Union Jack from Superkangaroo's cape, to avoid suggesting that the hero supported the government's policies.) Bradshaw has been performing solo shadow-puppet shows in Australia and around the world since the 1960s.

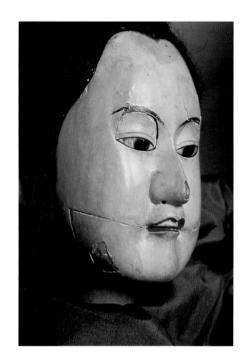

A woman whose sweet face hides a fiendish nature in Japanese *ningyo joruri*. This head typically portrays the lovesick, vengeful Kiyohime (above) in *The Cherry Trees Along the Hidaka River*. Pursuing her recalcitrant beloved, Kiyohime turns into an avenging demon (right) by way of a string attached to mechanisms inside the puppet's head.

Spirits that change form in the Chinese shadow play, *The Chaos Box*. The wily rogues Lizard and Centipede have taken on a human form as part of their plan to capture T'ien-shih. Although they fool other characters in the play, the audience can see their real natures revealed on their headdresses.

Having connived their way into T'ien-shih's presence, the demons have reverted to their proper shapes.

Characters with roughly carved wood "skin" in *Woyzeck on the Highveld* (1992) by the South African Handspring Puppet Company and William Kentridge. The puppets' texture meshed stylistically with the depictions of the characters in the show's animated films. The figures' earthy quality also made them, paradoxically, seem more organic, more alive than the live humans on stage. Founded in 1981, Handspring began doing puppet theater for adults in 1985. This adaptation of Georg Büchner's *Woyzeck* (1837) began their ongoing collaboration with Kentridge, an artist renowned for prints and animated films.

A probe of psychic depths in "idée fixe" by the Dutch Figurentheater Triangel of Henk and Ans Boerwinkel. The vignette begins with a twelve-inch-high bandaged head on stage. A blindfolded rod puppet enters from the side, unwraps the bandages and removes the crown, exposing the inner life. This short piece, with puppets made from fabric glued over paper, was part of *Metamorphoses*, which the Boerwinkles developed and performed for nearly forty years, until 2000.

OPPOSITE: *Nonlemgila*, a puppet of the Nishka people of British Columbia designed to reveal its inner self. Doors in the chest open via strings to show the face of a spirit. Strings also move the arms. This thirty-inch-tall wooden puppet is covered with buckskin and has hair made of animal fur.

work than their fellow Benin puppets made from wild clumps of raffia and bare wood. The little painted characters perform social satire, whereas the raffia figures perform secret nocturnal ceremonies. Using different materials for characters within a play can underline distinctions between them. In a shadow-puppet section of *The Way of Snow,* Julie Taymor's first directing project, rural characters were made from carved leather, and city folks from hard-edged Plexiglas.

Puppeteers even can reveal their characters' inner beings by providing x-ray vision. For a stetl bride in *The Golem,* the contemporary Czech-American puppeteer Vit Horejš cast a puppet (by Prague sculptor Jakub Krejčí) with a baby curled into a grotto beneath her heart—a poetic vision of her life's role of motherhood. To show what is in a character's mind, puppeteers can show the interior of the head. Its contents may be as straightforward as comic-book thought-balloon-style visions of glory, sex, escape, food, whatever. But they also may be more poetic or mysterious. When a puppet pianist in Eric Novak's Bacon/Mingus Triptych (2004) starts to play, his head literally splits

apart into bird- and fishlike creatures that dance to the music, then reassemble to re-form his head when he stops. In Taymor's *Way of Snow,* a psychiatrist fishing inside a patient's head hooked hand tools and fish skeletons. Remnants of evolutionary past? Symbols of personal experiences? Rancid garbage? All at once?

Puppet designers can use all the expressive tools of sculpture. Besides choice of materials, they can harness style, shape, and proportion. They may use artistic license to help express their actors' personality and character. Villains have craggy, off-kilter faces. Slack jaws hang to the waist. Grins go literally from ear to ear. Beside-the-point features (ears, legs, sex organs, whatever, depending on the character) can disappear to keep the focus on traits that matter (ears, legs, sex organs, whatever, depending on the character). Puppet artists also can use symbols, puns, and associations to create multiple levels of meaning.

The twentieth century's innovations in visual arts, such as abstraction and cubism, did not generally seem useful for the construction of humans that could function, and most puppet-

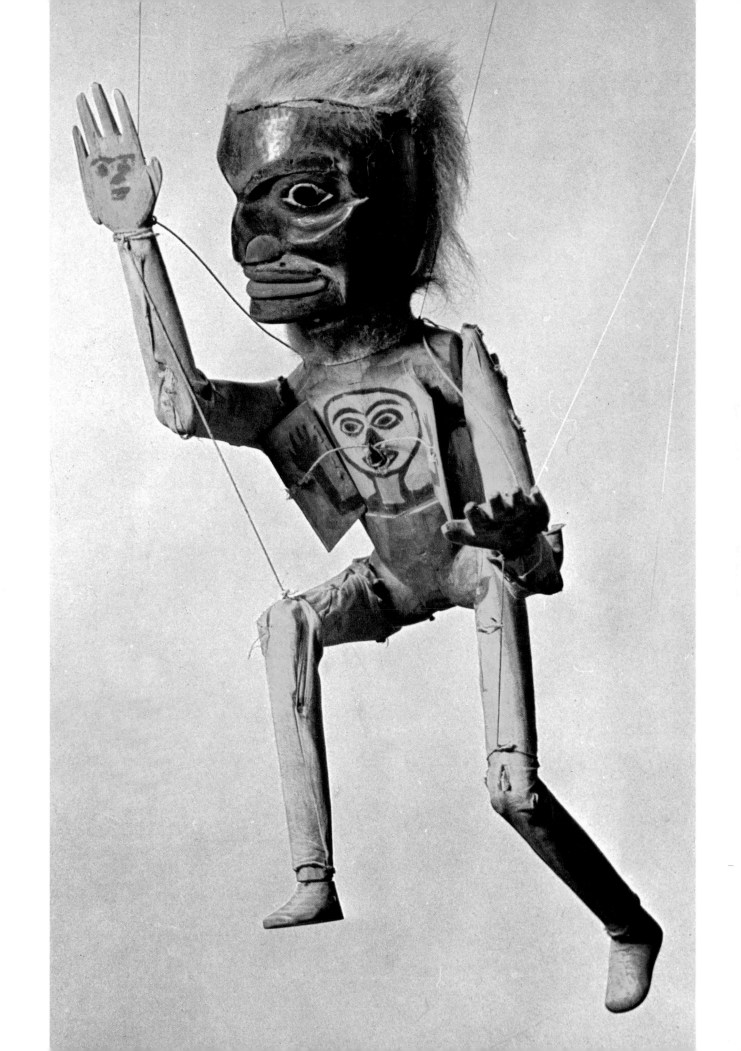

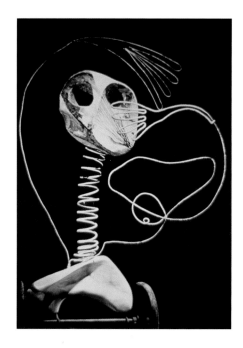

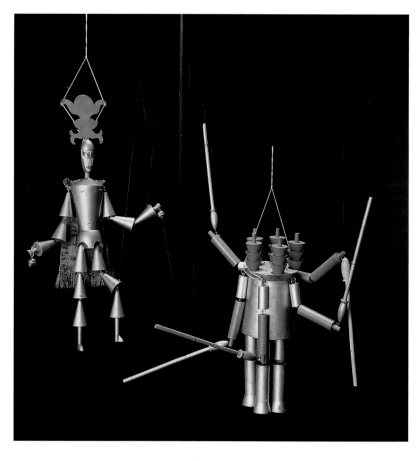

Hellishness on wheels, circa 1954, from Harry Kramer's Mechanical Theater in Berlin. After working with mixed casts of live dancers, articulated dolls, and wheeled humanoids, Kramer pared his troupe down to rolling sculptures moved from above with rods. His creatures often exuded Kafkaesque ghastliness.

TOP RIGHT: Puppets by Sophie Taeuber-Arp for Alfred Altherr's 1918 production of *The King Stag*. Tauber-Arp, who was active in the Dadaist "Cabaret Voltaire" (and was married to the sculptor Hans Arp) created painted-wood puppets for this updated version of Carlo Gozzi's tale. She not only built her actors from geometric rather than organic shapes but even made some of them composites—such as this five-headed palace guard. The show tweaked Gozzi's bizarre and magical love story to mock Freudian analysis of the female psyche.

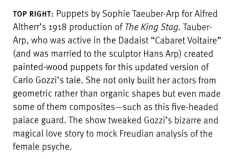

RIGHT: Puppeteer Jane Phillips' "Miss Junk" (1967), featuring a watering-can-spout nose that makes smelling the flowers an exercise in kindergarten humor. Phillips' Caricature Theater in Cardiff, Wales, produced shows for adults and children from 1965 until 1984, collaborating with prominent writers and designers.

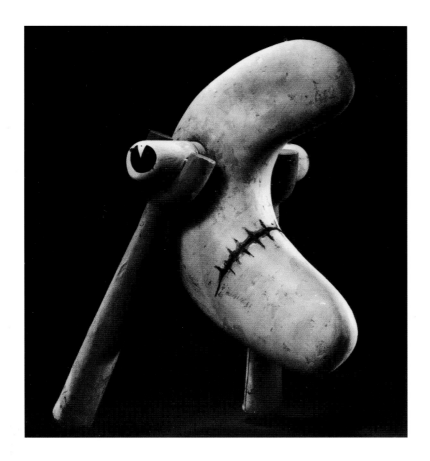

Crutch-face from American puppet master Bil Baird's 1960s *Science Fiction*. Baird heightened the character's pathos by giving him a line of stitching, like an old repair, for his mouth. The twenty-inch-high string marionette, made from Celastic, moved by swinging its blue support legs full circle.

makers, like most surgeons, ignored them. But puppet artists who did explore this new ground discovered broad new possibilities. Why, after all, did puppets need to suggest *any* real-world model? Why not have non-figurative characters such as, say, performing trapezoids and cones? Why not have puppets offer multiple simultaneous perspectives as cubist art did? Why not use these new approaches to help make puppets reflect the century's shaken sense of humanity and to express its war-ravaged psyche?

Geza Blattner made characters for his pre-World War II Paris theater from flat planes folded into 3-D shapes and held from below on rods. The Russian artist Alexandra Exter, also working in Paris, experimented with cubist marionettes in the 1920s. In Zurich, Fred Schneckenburger's sculptures-come-to-life featured tree branches and pipes as scrawny limbs, not always in the customary locations, and eyeball-spheres, not necessarily in pairs, sitting inches off the head on wrinkled wires.

Visual punning and double-entendres, as in Picasso's sedan-headed ape statue, easily jump from sculpture into puppetry. A blabber-mouth in Jonathan Edward Cross's Cosmic Bicycle Theater had dental work made from old typewriter parts. In *Hiroshima Maiden* (2004), American puppet artist Dan Hurlin used broken-eggshell shapes for the heads of young women disfigured by the atomic bomb. This ability to be two things at once allows puppets to create polyphonic performances: while the story unwinds, associations thread in and out.

This, finally, is the real gift of puppets. By freeing actors from the constraints of the human body, they allow theater into the non-literal territories that music, painting, and sculpture inhabit. Puppets are, as Joan Baixas puts it, "the imaginary incarnate, in bodily form, switched on." And they can populate conjured universes of all kinds—including worlds where humans have no place.

The Devil's Violin, a traditional puppet from Gdansk, Poland, embodying a view of secular music as diabolical. As often happens, popular culture had long included a device newly "discovered" by the avant-garde—in this case, visual-pun puppets. The wooden violin-man used its bow for a second leg, the string-tightening screws as eyes, and boar-hair for its coiffure.

A schoolmaster and his hooligan pupils in the original 1988
production of *Juan Darièn*, by Julie Taymor and Elliot Goldenthal.
Taymor underscored the kids' rowdiness by making the schoolhouse
the sort of one-man ambulatory stage used for knock-down
slapstick. The oversized teacher wore four pairs of spectacles and
had hair made from the flapping pages of a book. (Actor Leonard
Petit looked out through a hole in the puppet's chest.)

OPPOSITE: *Gesell Chamber* (1996) by the Argentine company El
Periférico de Objetos. Using old, tattered baby dolls as actors, the
play calls up subliminal vulnerability that wafts through the action.
When a teenage runaway's grown-up friend rapes her, what the
audience sees is a large male baby doll assaulting a smaller female
one. The violation is all the more harrowing because it ruptures a
world that suggests innocence. Founded in 1989 by Daniel Veronese,
Emilio García Wehbi, and Ana Alvarado, El Periférico often mixes live
and constructed actors, and plays at the border-crossings between
the living and the inert, between reality and fantasy.

CHAPTER 5

Puppet Masters

Creating a population is only one step in the genesis of a world. Puppet artists make complete universes, including light, terrain, and accoutrements. These environments *may* imitate familiar chunks of reality, perhaps in altered scale. But they do not have to.

Artists may set their puppets in worlds that resemble no known place, no existing model. Fanciful fauna and flora are just the beginning. The creator can reinvent rules of physics as liberally as those of biology. Isaac Newton be damned, why not make a world where two bodies can occupy the same space at the same time? It is possible, especially if at least one is made of light. Or, for that matter, a single body can be in two places at once. The artist simply constructs a copy for each location.

Or how about a realm with cockeyed gravity? Tony Sarg's helium-filled upside-down marionettes naturally rise rather than fall. The basic pull in Hanne Tierney's puppet worlds is sideways or diagonal or up, thanks to her use of an overhead grid and counterweights. In Basil Twist and Lee Breuer's *Red Beads,* wind currents from fans govern the movement of featherweight objects and characters.

Since puppets do not need to breathe air, artists have fashioned puppet environments in liquids. Sometimes the characters are meant to be underwater. Other times, pup-

A universe of floating memories in *NetherWorld, A Morality Vaudeville*, by Jonathan Edward Cross's Cosmic Bicycle Theater in New York.

peteers just utilize the different movement and visual properties of objects submerged in water.

Puppet universes can give concrete form to such normally invisible forces as metaphysical energy, emotional power, magnetic fields, and supernatural auras. In the American company Puppetsweat's shadow-theater version of "The Tell-Tale Heart," by Edgar Allan Poe, the narrator's mounting terror appears as a color change from blue to red and jagged scribbles shooting across the screen, defacing and finally effacing

OPPOSITE: A visual composition that includes the puppeteers in Tandarica Marionette and Puppet Theater's 1979 performance of *Tyl Ulenspiegel,* directed by Cátálina Buzoianu. Formed in 1949, Tandarica became Romania's premiere puppet theater under Margareta Niculescu. Niculescu also was key in forming both UNIMA (the international organization of puppeteers) and the International Puppet Institute, in Charleville-Mézières, France. The story of Tyl Ulenspiegel, popular in Central and Eastern Europe, includes an immolation, a werewolf, and instantaneous international travel, theatrical challenges that invite the sort of special effects at which puppetry shines.

The three-tiered stage of Faulty Optic's 1996 *Bubbly Beds,* including a flooded basement staged in a water-filled tank. The top level of the set shows a live video feed of the inches-high puppets on the other tiers, switching between the downstairs briny, where giant fish, drifting skulls, and just-flushed toilet paper menace the husband, and the upstairs living room, where his wife is seducing the plumber. Faulty Optic was founded in London in 1987 by Liz Walker and Gavin Glover, veterans of London's Little Angel Theatre.

everything else. *Limbus,* a "mechanical opera" by Jay Bolotin, gives physical form to the metaphysical forces gathering in the seconds just before a catastrophe: Giant sculptures and their surroundings begin to lumber and menace, incarnating latent destructive power amassing to explode (see page 241).

Inanimate actors need not even be distinct from their environment. Characters can absorb into their surroundings. Scenery can come alive. Part of one large actor may serve as the set or stage for smaller ones. In the Russian company White Goat's *Women's Songs,* performed in New York in 2000, a puppet's diaphanous scarf becomes the Neva River, where her long-gone lover once swore fidelity. Character/environment double identities can also be more protean. When a purple lamé cloth playing Herod in Hanne Tierney's *Salomé* (2000) reaches two "arms" out in lust, the shape also suggests a royal throne. The single, semi-figurative form incorporates both the king's lewd grasp and the symbol of his power.

Freed from the stylistic and biological limitations of human actors, creators of puppet worlds can design characters and their surroundings in tandem, with compatible proportions, textures, fluorescences, and so forth. Just as individual constructed actors can utilize all the expressive tools of the plastic arts— including scale, shape, proportion, texture, color, associations, and even puns—so can entire puppet universes. The result can be totally fanciful realms.

Aesthetic unity in these worlds may come from style. In Michael Meschke's landmark 1964 production of *Ubu Roi,* for example, all the characters, sets, and props were white cartoonish creations sketched or outlined in black lines. But within that mode, characters were variously two-dimensional, three-dimensional, inches-high, larger-than-life, and so forth (see page 159).

THE UNIVERSES that puppet artists have conjured over the centuries range from holy to brutish, elegant to madcap, claustrophobic to extragalactic, figurative to abstract. At one end of the spectrum, puppet shows can be blithely rough affairs. Makeshift characters perform simple, often coarse routines in rudimentary, even jury-rigged theater setups. But puppetry also can be an art of great subtlety. A bunraku performer traditionally works for thirty years to master the necessary precision of gesture and spirit. The eighteenth-century marionettists who performed Mozart and Haydn operas aimed to match the sophistication of the music.

In fact, puppetry often confounds standard categories of rough versus high art. The same performers may offer refined theater and slapstick. American artist Bruce D. Schwartz performed graceful scenarios of love, longing, and loss, using delicate-featured puppets—and also knock-down, crude, lewd hand-puppet farces. High and low, dramatic and comic, mix even within shows (as they do in Shakespeare and much Southeast Asian dance-drama). In

A section of corrugated-paper wall separating out as a character in *Toporland* (1999) by Warsaw's Impossible Theater Company (Unia Teatr Niemozliwy). The metaphysics in this wordless "suite for cardboard and double bass" are especially slippery because the man-shaped hole in the wall sometimes appears to be a character—but also serves as a door. The darkly comic play is based on work by Polish-born writer and cartoonist Roland Topor.

RIGHT: A motel-and-motel-keeper combo with hand-puppet guests in the Budapest State Puppet Theater's 1977 production of *Motel.* In Jean-Claude van Itallie's script, which calls for three oversize puppets, the motel guests tear up first the room and then their hostess. The motel-keeper does proclaim early on, though, that she *is* her motel. Director Kató Szönyi and designer Iván Koós took her at her word.

Balinese shadow theater, pratfalls and fart jokes splat through dramas that have serious philosophical messages. *Faust* puppet plays in nineteenth-century Europe, for all their weighty concerns about hubris and damnation, also featured clowns.

Puppets can go beyond mingling tones and genres to melding them. Cartoon characters can be simultaneously loony and serious. The hero of Georgian director Rezo Gabriadze's *Autumn of My Springtime* is a scraggly, felonious little bird that robs a bank, flies into a movie screen to be with Vivien Leigh, and gets

so drunk at an orgy that he passes out in a champagne glass. But the crux of his story is heartbreaking and angry—about a widow who cannot afford electricity and the perfidious narcissism of human beings wreaking havoc on the earth and its creatures.

MANY OF THE PAST century's innovative puppeteers have come out of the worlds of plastic arts rather than live-actor theater. Geza Blattner had been a painter in his native Hungary. Richard Teschner had been a painter, sculptor, and architect. The affinity of visual artists for

A whoosh of diaphanous silk in Basil Twist's 1998 underwater animation of Hector Berlioz' *Symphonie Fantastique*. Cloths, streamers, feathers, colored tubes, fringe, and abstract cutouts swirl through the water in a 1,000-gallon tank. They morph from pure design elements into quasi-character and quasi-set pieces much as Berlioz's programmatic music flows between abstract and figurative. Puppeteers operate from the sides and back of the tank and from above it, suspended in harnesses.

ABOVE: A population and environment all made of Matisse-like shapes in a work by the Little Angel Theatre of London. Founded in 1961 by John and Lyndie Wright, the company created shows for both children and adults. It originally used only marionettes, but later included other techniques, including rod and shadow puppets.

TOP RIGHT: A multilayered, kaleidoscopic sea world in the Italian Teatro Gioco Vita's *Fishmousecrocodile* (1985). The shadow worlds the company creates vary from monochrome to multicolor, hard-edged to shimmery. Some of their shows use only one screen, others use several. The manipulators are sometimes visible, sometimes hidden. Founded in 1971 by Diego Maj, Gioco Vita has concentrated on shadow theater since 1978.

BOTTOM RIGHT: Electric light-switches become energy-sucking southern California houses in Great Small Works' *BB in LA* (1988). Here a miniature Bertolt Brecht muses on life and art in a 1940s Los Angeles made of outsized cars, sunshine, improbably colored plants, and houses with mercury-switch windows. The New York-based company, founded in 1995, consists of John Bell, Trudi Cohen, Stephen Kaplin, Jenny Romaine, Mark Sussman, and Roberto Rossi. It creates topical plays on breadbox-size stages inspired by toy theater of eighteenth- and nineteenth-century Europe.

puppetry is not surprising. Unlike directors of live actors, they are accustomed to the sort of total control over their work and the aesthetic freedom that puppetry allows. These modern painters and sculptors just extended their previous stylized or abstract art into four dimensions, and to the brink of aliveness.

In addition to the visual artists who set up shop more or less permanently in puppet and object theater, many others made forays into the field. The Russian avant-gardist Alexandra Exter created a cubist commedia dell'arte show. A small hand-puppet theater that Paul Klee designed for his son later became resident at the Bauhaus. Alexander Calder built a tiny circus and performed with it over several decades (see page 231). Many of the painters and sculptors who designed sets and costumes for Serge Diaghilev's Ballets Russes also peopled the ballets in part with constructed actors: Mikhail Larionov put the dancers inside body puppets totally incongruent with their own anatomies; Natalia Goncharova mixed live actors with marionettes on stage. Pablo Picasso and Henri Matisse also designed actors for Diaghilev.

Not surprisingly, visual artists working in puppetry often were among those who blurred or ignored borders between characters and environment. Visual artists typically work holistically, choosing how, how much, or *if* a composition will distinguish figures from surroundings. Titanic god puppets in Fernand Léger's 1923 *Creation of the World*, moving along the back wall on rails, were as much a part of the set as they were characters. Pablo Picasso's scene design for the 1924 Diaghilev ballet *Mercury* included both free-standing and hanging human sculptures made of wood and rattan. They had movable body parts and played roles in the narrative—that is, although part of the set designs, these pieces also were, by any definition, puppets. The hundred mobile characters and the stationary figures in Jean Dubuffet's hour-long animated tableaux *Coucou Bazar* (1973) matched the style of their environment and were all but indistinguishable from it (see page 255).

A clothed wooden bucket serving as a puppet in an 1893 woodblock print by Mizuno Toshikata, part of his series *36 Beauties*.

BELOW: One of Robert Anton's strange, wordless miniature worlds, which he presented for invited audiences of eighteen people. Here, as a Gypsy woman lights incense and candles, the jingling of her minuscule bangles and bells breaks the silence. Then dust sprinkles onto her head, and her ornaments, her hair, even the color in her face abandon her, leaving a haunting, haunted incarnation of bereavement. In another of Anton's shows, the dislodged brain of an aged beauty, attached by a wire, was burned in a candle flame.

Other visual artists played at the edges of puppetry. Several created non-figurative forms to play in time and space. Between 1912 and 1928, Vassily Kandinsky fashioned universes of simple two-dimensional shapes moving in an environment of changing colored light. In 1926, Piet Mondrian, looking to make a theater of "sound, rhythm, word music," designed a miniature world composed of rectangles and stripes. The "play" consisted of one vaguely humanoid rectangle altering its position while the rest of the scene underwent gradual color changes.

The Italian Futurists experimented with constructed-actor theater as well. Fortunato Depero's 1918 *Plastic Ballets* were performed by Rome's most prominent puppet company, the Teatro dei Piccoli, headed by Vittorio Podrecca.

ABOVE: Three hand puppets by Paul Klee: (left to right) a "Portrait of Emmyu-Galka Scheyer" (1922); a "White-haired Eskimo" (1924); and a "Crowned Poet" (1919). Klee began creating these puppets in 1916 for his son Félix's ninth birthday, then added new characters each year.

Richard Teschner's miniature fantasy realm for *The Watersprite* (1936). Teschner staged his own versions of traditional Eastern and Western tales. Like most Javanese *wayang golek* puppeteers, whose work had inspired him in 1911, he crafted and manipulated the sixteen-inch-high rod puppets himself and also narrated. (His characters never spoke.) Teschner also designed music and lighting for his shows, which audiences saw by looking through a round glass window.

The show included a larger-than-life "Great Savage" puppet-cum-set-piece, whose fold-down belly formed a stage for smaller cohorts. Depero also staged a more radical show, in which monochrome geometric figures controlled by strings "spoke" abstract sounds.

The Futurist leader Enrico Prampolini built a stage world populated by geometric shapes, some of them lit from within, and hung human-shaped flat actors like scrolls. He tried eliminating the distinction between things and beings, animating different elements of an elaborate stage construction in turn. Giacomo Balla staged the Igor Stravinsky ballet *The Firebird* in 1917 by animating abstract shapes and lights. The printed program for this show, at Rome's Teatro Constanzi, listed the "performers" as "rhythms of colored lights." Fedele Azari tried to make a theater in which airplanes became characters with personalities—in effect, puppets animated by their pilots. The pilot-handlers would express the planes' spirit through the dance of their flying movement, the music of their engine noise, and such discharges as "colored and perfumed dust, confetti, rockets, parachutes, puppets." (Half a century later, Lee Breuer choreographed a dance-theater piece starring a phalanx of industrial forklifts.)

Bauhaus workshops during the 1920s and 1930s also explored puppet and object theaters far more radical than Klee's fairly traditional Bauhaus puppet theater. Several members, including Laszlo Moholy-Nagy, Farkas Molnár, and Oskar Schlemmer, wrote about stage performances based around shape and rhythm rather than strictly human events. Schlemmer, who headed the stage workshop, advocated replacing human performers with "art figures, personifications of the loftiest concepts and ideas, made of the most exquisite material." These made-to-order actors, he wrote, "would permit a theater of shape, material, and movement, not tethered to the physical and aesthetic limitations of the human being. "They could be made of metal or glass. They could be as geo-

ABOVE: "The Three Graces" in Pablo Picasso's design for the 1924 ballet *Mercury,* choreographed by Léonide Massine to music by Eric Satie. In *Mercury,* essentially Picasso's brainchild, every scenic tableaux included articulated, movable characters, which Picasso called "practicables." A dancer concealed behind each of the figures here extended or shortened the rattan lattice to move the character's head.

LEFT: The American Manager in Serge de Diaghilev's 1917 Ballets Russes production of *Parade.* It was Picasso's idea to create three Managers—oversize body puppets—to present the ballet's pageant of acrobats, harlequins, and other fairground acts. One Manager, a dummy astride a two-actor horse, toppled off its mount during dress rehearsal and was cut from the ballet, leaving the horse to play the role alone.

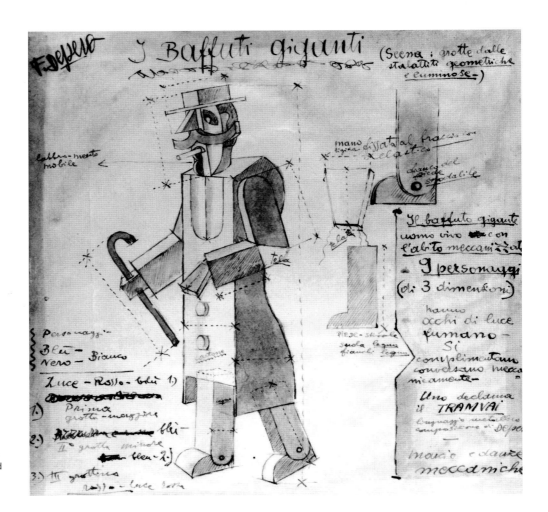

Depero's sketch of "Man with a Moustache" for his 1918 *Plastic Ballets*. As this hefty gentleman lumbered across the stage, smaller replicas of him in various colors and sizes paraded behind. They shared the stage with a geometric ballerina, mechanical mice, and a predatory puppet cat.

A sketch by Oskar Schlemmer for his "Figural Cabinet," using body puppets and other constructed actors to make the performers as geometrical as their environment. Schlemmer's several versions of the "Cabinet," beginning in 1922, included collage exhibitions and performances using both live actors and puppets. In this sketch, the manipulators are indicated by dotted lines. Between 1916 and 1926, Schlemmer also made successive incarnations of his *Triadic Ballet*, danced by constructed actors and live performers whose costumes modified their shape.

metric and abstract as any imaginary universe the artist envisioned." Bauhaus members Heinz Loew, Kurt Schmidt, Alexander Schawinsky, and even Marcel Breuer also designed theater works for mechanical or human-controlled forms.

BESIDES FASHIONING ALL manner of worlds, puppeteers can manipulate how viewers see those worlds, controlling the angle, field and sharpness of vision. Long before the advent of photography and film, puppet artists could produce the effects of wide-angle and telephoto lenses, different camera angles, panning, tracking, zooming, and altering the clarity of focus.

Directors of constructed-actor theater manage audience perspective partly through scale. The contemporary French artists Jean-Pierre Larroche and Serge Dutrieux used such a tiny scale and such a powerful wide "lens" in part of *The System of the World* (1990) that the audience's view encompassed the heavens: half a dozen cherubs carried tiny planets. At the other extreme, puppeteers can produce "close-ups" much as film directors can by filling the whole stage with just a character's face.

Changing scale within a scene can make the action move closer or farther away. The mid-

nineteenth-century puppet theater that Maurice Sand created (with help from his mother, the writer George Sand) included different-sized figures for the same character seen at various distances. Contemporary artists use the same trick. In the Bread and Puppet Theater, a far-off character may appear as a small puppet crossing the stage back and forth, until it gets "close" and is replaced by a larger copy or even a costumed actor. In *The Lion King* (1998) Julie Taymor and Michael Curry turned the modest depth of a Broadway stage into miles for a stampede of wildebeests, starting with tiny figures upstage and increasing to life-size as the animals charged toward the audience.

Puppeteers even use different scales simultaneously, creating a theatrical picture-within-picture effect. The images may show a single scene with certain details enlarged, or else two entirely different scenes. In *The Fish* (1989), by American puppet artist Janie Geiser, the audience watched events unrolling in an entire village presented in miniature on a tray, and also saw a "closeup" of the title character, a magical fish, presented as a life-size wooden puppet. In Shadowlight Theater's 1994 *In Xanadu*, the face of Kubla Khan's wife in gigantic closeup filled one side of the screen, while Khan's exploits (in her

Backstage at a 1994 performance of *Wayang Listrik: Electric Shadows of Bali* (1998) by Shadowlight Theater and Balinese dalang I Wayan Wija. Director Larry Reed creates wide shots, closeups, and special effects by choreographing actors, puppets, and mobile scenery between three 1,000-watt lamps and a screen that covers the entire stage front. The puppeteer at the far left is manipulating Balinese *wayang kulit*. Closer to the screen, appearing smaller, is a popular clown puppet. In the foreground of the photograph, a piece of scenery catches light from the center lamp, creating a muted setting. And a human performer in *wayang*-like ornaments, casts a silhouette. The unseen stage-right lamp creates the remaining shadows visible on the screen.

A scene-shift that works like a tracking shot in film in a 1996 performance of *The Tale of the Lopsided Chimney* by the Forman Brothers (Czech identical twins Petr and Matej). A scrolling backdrop (seen from backstage, above), allows the audience's field of vision to follow two bungling workers as they climb from the ground floor (opposite bottom) onto the roof (opposite top). The eighteenth-century ersatz baroque opera by Karel Loos is the first opera written in Czech.

imagination? in reality?) stretched to the other end in tiny-scale panorama.

To create the effect of panning or tracking, puppeteers slide, rotate, or scroll their set, following the action as it moves from one location to another. They also can pivot the set between scenes to give the audience a different viewing angle. Although live theater can also use these devices to a degree, the exigencies of size, weight, and gravity restrict its possibilities.

The quintessentially filmic devices of blurred focus and distorting lenses have pre-photographic equivalents in shadow puppetry. Two of Bali's best shadow puppeteers— I Wayan Wija from Sukawati village and I Made Sija from Bone village—have developed distinctive ways to show the enormity of the great war that climaxes each play. A ferocious demon or god may begin as a barely perceptible haze, a presence far off in the cosmos, then become a denser cloud and develop a shape as it approaches closer and closer and finally smacks into focus against the screen. Or a battle may arc from one bottom corner of the screen up toward the center then down to the other corner, using a fish-eye lens effect to show carnage spanning the horizon, covering the planet.

GIVEN THEIR long-standing use of these movie-like techniques, puppeteers might have been expected to have a special affinity for film, the new medium that emerged near the turn of the twentieth century. Puppetry even had conventions to deal with early film's most severe limitation: lack of sound. Some puppeteers did incorporate film into their acts, but the great majority ignored it.

In fact, moving pictures, which began in the early 1890s, lagged far behind puppetry in exploiting expressive possibilities: At first, movies just documented single actions with one stationary camera. So film seemed to have little to offer puppeteers. Even when pioneer Georges Méliès began to string film "takes" into a narrative, each scene was a single-take shot by a fixed camera. It took years for moviemakers to start taking advantage of camera angles, different lens lengths, and film's unique potential for cutting and editing within scenes.

Even when innovators such as Edwin Porter and D.W. Griffith did finally develop the shooting and editing vocabulary that turned filmmaking into an art, few puppeteers embraced the medium. After all, they already could create many of the same effects. And filmmaking was time-consuming and expensive.

But film offered one wild new possibility for constructed-actor theater. Making movies normally involves documenting an action with a rapid sequence of individual pictures and then projecting those images at the speed they were

RIGHT: Meredith Monk and Robert Een peopling a miniature tundra with tiny human figures in the preface to Monk's 1990 duet *Facing North.* The human-scale action that followed was understood to be set within that broad landscape.

BELOW: Warfare seen through multiple lenses in *Voice of the Hollow Man* by American puppeteer Warner Blake. Blake's dining-room-table stage contains moving planets, battalions of inch-high Napoleonic soldiers, three-inch busts of Napoleon and his marshals, a TV news talking-head with films of war atrocities inside his mouth, a framed baby picture (a reminder that each soldier is someone's son?), and human actors reading testimonies about war. The texts include excerpts from Napoleon's letters to his wife and Tolstoy's *War and Peace.* Two dozen spectators, some seated at the table, follow the action with the aid of binoculars. *Voice of the Hollow Man* is the middle play in *Soup Talk,* a three-part epic created by Warner Blake between 1985 and 1996.

OPPOSITE: The world of Samuel Beckett's *The Lost Ones* seen as if in an aerial view in a 1974 Mabou Mines production directed by Lee Breuer. Using scores of tiny actors on a small table, David Warrilow created the society of Beckett's prose narrative, a world of miserable people plodding between futile hope and pointless routine.

filmed. (Initially forty frames a second, the rate became standardized at about sixteen per second for silent movies.) Watching the quick series of images, a viewer's brain read continuous movement. A few film mavericks and puppeteers turned this technique inside out: Instead of shooting a rapid sequence of images, they shot one frame at a time, with infinitesimal alterations of the subject between shots. They took a sequence of sixteen pictures for each second of real-time action, and then played it back at sixteen frames a second—and the viewer saw a continuous action that had *not* taken place. Instead of recording action, they fabricated it.

With this stop-action filming technique, virtually any object that could be changed from one stable position to another could seem to move of its own accord. By 1906 experimental filmmakers were using frame-at-a-time shooting to present not only puppet versions of bible stories, *Faust*, and other plays, but also the picaresque adventures of ordinary household goods. One of the most innovative and prolific artists, the naturalist-turned-puppet animator, Ladislas Starevitch began around 1910 by filming models of insects (having learned from experience that live ones behaved unprofessionally). He soon moved on to fiction, including a bedroom farce involving a wanton beetle's infidelities with a dragonfly and a grasshopper. Over the next half century, Starevitch animated miniature actors of many species, including human, first in his native Russia then, after the Bolshevik revolution, in France. The Czech artist Jiri Trnka worked with marionettes and as an illustrator before embarking on animated film. Often considered the greatest puppet-film artist, Trnka directed some fourteen constructed-actor films, including traditional Czech stories, a full-length *Midsummer Night's Dream*, and political allegories.

Stop-action film technique also could animate two-dimensional figures. Lotte Reiniger began in the 1920s to make movies with jointed puppets made from black cardboard

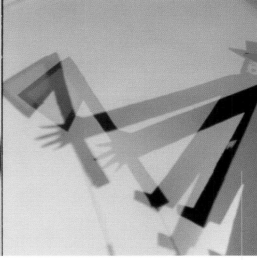

A triptych of views in Puppetsweat Theater's 1992 *Der Signal*, about a railway worker who makes a red flag with his own blood to avert an accident. Here, the left and center screens present different, simultaneous views of the hero signaling with the flag, while the right screen zeroes in on his arm streaming ribbons (literally) of blood. At other points during the show, he runs across a three-screen-wide, continuous landscape. Periodically, the oncoming train lumbers along a two-screen-long length of track, while the hero, viewed from the front on the third screen, races to save it.

OPPOSITE: A radical shift of viewing angle in Ping Chong's production of *Kwaidan (1998)*. First, the three areas show separate scenes in different scales. At left, a priest, a 3-D puppet, keeps vigil over a corpse. At right, larger-scale villagers appear as silhouettes. In the center, a wide shot of the village shows the priest (from the left frame) in a window. Then the set is flipped onto its side and the three panels form one contiguous scene viewed from *above*. A pale blue shimmer of light—an incorporeal demon—wafts in and steals the corpse, whose shape under the shroud (in the center frame) gradually shrinks to nothing. Chong adapted and directed *Kwaidan* (1998), based on Japanese ghost stories by Lafcadio Hearn. The lead puppeteer was Jon Ludwig, who often creates his own edgy, experimental shows for children and adults.

and sheet-lead. Using a camera rigged high above a glass table, she shot one frame at a time, much as the 3-D animators did. Additional parallel glass panels allowed for extra foreground and background action as well as sets, including painted scenery scrolls that Reiniger rolled a tiny bit between frames to create the effect of a journey.

Almost from the start of stop-action filming, artists devised ways to mix their constructed characters with live performers. Those techniques, combined with the sort of size tricks puppet artists had used for centuries, opened new possibilities for special effects. An inches-high puppet striding across a miniature Tokyo could become Godzilla. Enlarged models of insects could be filmed in comparably enlarged environments, creating the effect of extreme close-ups—or they could be placed on miniature sets to look monstrous. Willis O'Brien, one of the special-effects greats, honed his technique in stop-action puppet farces such as *Prehistoric Poultry* before creating the puppet animation for such classics as *King Kong* and *The Lost World*. Computers have augmented the range of these techniques and special-effects.

Since 1964, Trnka's fellow Czech artist Jan Švankmajer has been creating eerie puppet-film collages using extreme editing and camera

placement as well as stop-action, often evoking decay and destruction. The American-born Brothers Quay, now based in England, follow in Švankmajer's path. Other contemporary puppet artists, including Janie Geiser and the South African William Kentridge, animate puppets or drawings using techniques similar to these but to express very different sensibilities.

THE MID-TWENTIETH century's new medium, television, was a natural for puppets. Audiences already were accustomed to seeing puppets on the scale of the television box. And the variety-show format of many early television programs lent itself to the short acts many puppeteers favored.

Early television, mainly produced live, became a medium for presenting traditional puppet performances to wider audiences. Puppeteers such as Edgar Bergen (with Charlie McCarthy), Wayland Flowers (with Madame), and Señor Wences (with Johnny) became regulars on *The Ed Sullivan Show, The Dean Martin Show, The Red Skelton Show* and similar programs.

America's first-generation television puppets for children, like their live-actor counterparts, often were cowboys. The post-World-War-II baby boomers grew up with Howdy Doody, a freckle-faced, singing-cowboy marionette, whose

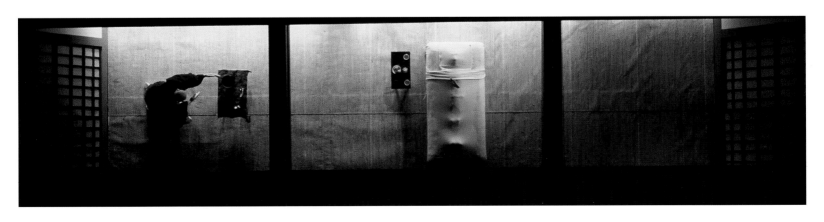

program ran from 1947 until 1960. In 1950, Bil and Cora Baird's first television series, *Life With Snarky Parker* (which actor Yul Brynner directed for a time), also was a western. Puppet television shows ranged from low-budget affairs to a Baird version of *Peter and the Wolf* that used top talent from the live-actor theater, including writers Ogden Nash and Sheldon Harnick, director Burt Shevelove, and actor Art Carney, who narrated. As European television developed, French, German, English, and Italian children got puppet stars of their own.

Puppetry *for* television rather than simply *on* television came into its own with Jim Henson and his Muppets. Henson created a stable of quirky characters—including Kermit the earnest frog, Miss Piggy of ego extraordinaire, and sundry endearing monsters. He also developed puppetry specifically geared to the medium. Besides sharing the technical advantages of film, television allowed puppeteers to watch their work on monitors in real time, seeing it from the audience's perspective. In his feature-length film *Dark Crystal* (1982), Henson invented a universe from scratch, including not only fanciful animals but flora that could wave in greeting or morph into predators. Henson's work survived his death in 1990 and continues to be broadcast throughout the world.

As contemporary artists have mastered so much of puppetry's rich creative possibility, the genre is again being used for serious expression in the West as well as the East. More and more theater with constructed actors is aimed at adults.

Straight Arrow, a radio hero from 1948 through 1951, making his only foray onto television as a puppet-theater premium on a box of Nabisco Shredded Wheat. These finger puppets replicated television's multiple-camera style by using the old puppetry technique of indicating distance through scale. The subject here is Comanche warrior Straight Arrow, a kind of Wild West superman who usually appeared as the mild-mannered cattle rancher, Steve Adams. The hero changed from Adams into Arrow and sprang into action (and into Comanche dress and war paint) whenever forces of evil threatened to strike.

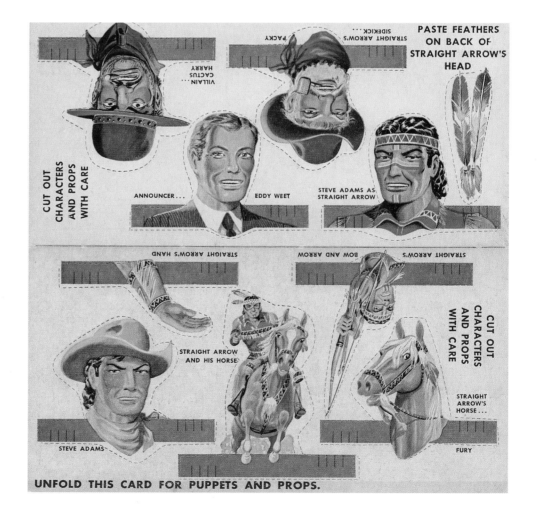

Lotte Reiniger making infinitesimal changes to the position of a horse for a stop-action shadow film. Freed from the need to operate the puppets in real time, Reiniger crafted figures with dozens of joints and movable articles of clothing, creating subtleties of gesture impossible in live shadow theater. Eventually, her films included color.

BELOW: The Gelfling heroes of Jim Henson's film *Dark Crystal* riding off to save the day on their "landstriders."

CHAPTER 6

Sex

SINCE THEY ARE NOT, STRICTLY SPEAKING, CARNAL creatures, puppets might be presumed to be poorly suited for sexual acts. Yet from the earliest times to the present, crafted actors have been sexual players running the gamut from mythic to erotic to raunchy.

Through much of history, puppets and their amulet cousins have performed as agents to invoke fertility. This makes perfect sense, in a way: Given that puppets cross from inertness to a sort of vitality themselves, why not call upon them to help humans generate new life? And while the supernatural dimension of amulets puts them on somewhat different footing than simple entertainers, the two categories are not always distinct. Fertility puppets sometimes shift between ritual and secular performances. And certainly charms share the most basic puppet trait. They are inanimate objects imaginatively endowed with vitality.

Puppets' and amulets' role in fertility may go back to the Paleolithic Venuses with their swelled breasts and bellies. One scholar has even proposed that these statuettes' odd physique resembles a very pregnant woman's top-down, foreshortened view of her own body. Before very long, though, men and male images had assumed top billing in the matter of procreation. In pre-dynastic Egypt, six thousand years ago, it was figures of the male god Min, usually depicted holding his erect penis, that

apparently officiated at fertility rituals. Sixth-century B.C.E. statues of the Egyptian male god Osiris also were associated with fecundity and even had movable penises. Around the world—including Africa, North America, and Europe—into the twentieth century, constructed male actors with oversize phalluses have been involved in fertility ceremonies.

Rawhide cutouts that were suspended from the top of a pole during the annual Sioux Sun Dance ceremony a century ago. Effigies of the sacred buffalo and sometimes of men played a variety of roles in Native American rituals. Ones like this thirteen-inch-tall man and eight-inch-tall buffalo displaying their impressive phalluses were accompanied by chants to invoke fertility.

OPPOSITE: Bil Baird's sexpot stripper Miss Bubbles LaRue.

Toe puppets in Burkina Faso in 1931. Puppets with plug-and-socket genitalia used this technique to perform sex acts during fertility ceremonies in Central Africa. This pair of West African puppets served, instead, as aids to divination. As they moved along the cord, their curved bases allowed them to lean, shimmy, and sway, conveying coded messages from the spirits. Toe puppets, including anatomically explicit figures, also have performed in Africa as street entertainers and children's toys at least since the 1930s.

In many cases, ritual penises of wood or stone have not even been attached to a body (it being widely agreed, apparently, that the organ has a life of its own). Through the ages, these *linga*, some of them tree-trunk size, have been venerated and sometimes animated. Free-standing mobile penises have figured in rites not only in ancient Greece, as Herodotus reported, but also in cultures as widespread as East, Central, and Southeast Asia and sub-Saharan Africa.

Many societies, not surprisingly, have used puppet couples rather than individual figures to summon procreative forces. In Orissa, India, giant "King" and "Queen" effigies that dance at weddings are associated with sex. Fertility rituals among the Yoruba and Fang of western Africa include anatomically explicit figures being joined in coitus. In Congo, male and female puppets with exaggerated genitals are strung like European "jigging puppets" on a single taut cord stretched between the seated

handler's big toes. He slaps a rhythm on his legs, vibrating the cord, and the man and woman approach one another until they consummate their act.

Small amulets, possibly standing in for developing fetuses, have been used to safeguard pregnancies. Some researchers believe that three-thousand-year-old Olmec stone figurines from eastern Mexico depict unborn babies, and may, one can guess, have had protective powers. To this day, pregnant women in parts of sub-Saharan Africa harbor small, potent carved statues to safeguard their fetuses.

Puppets have long modeled fertility for flora as well as fauna. Five thousand years ago, Egyptian effigies of Min, penis in hand, not only imparted sexual prowess to humans but took part in annual festivals to open the harvest season. At rice-planting time in one village in eastern Bali, a ten-foot-tall puppet couple engage in a cycle of temple ceremonies, then copulate in front of villagers and are thrown into a stream.

As BELIEF EDGES toward suspension of disbelief, many fertility figures shed their supernatural trappings and evolve into secular puppets. But the border between the two can be murky. Certainly some ancient Egyptians knew that women carrying fertility statues controlled the figures' awe-inspiring erections by pulling their strings. But those people might still have believed that the puppet handlers were possessed by gods, or that the women's actions drew divine spirits into the figures, or that the rites triggered sympathetic magic. Well-endowed twentieth-century male puppets in Africa and Europe (including Spain, Portugal, and Hungary) also supposedly had supernatural collaboration in moving their parts. Again, the audiences must have regarded these figures with a mixture of faith and suspension of disbelief. Ritual and theater probably meet, too, in a New Guinea fertility ritual Joseph Campbell described: Men held prosthetic genitals made from bark and cones at their crotch and put them through their paces, miming masturbation and spraying imaginary semen all over the village and nearby fields.

Some Indian, Southeast Asian, East Asian, and North African jesters may actually be defrocked fertility demons that have moved so far along the ritual/theater spectrum that now they are mainly entertainers. The oafish clowns in shadow-puppet theater frequently are gods of an older generation, slumming incognito as buffoons to keep an eye on human affairs. And until very recently, many of them displayed private parts that were anatomical marvels. Some Javanese *wayang* wielded enormous penises comprised of nearly a dozen sections, with the end piece shaped and carved like the head of a bull. The genitals of one Syrian jester reached nearly to his feet, and one southeast Indian clown sports testicles that almost sweep the ground. Fertility is irrelevant to the clowns' present occupation, and sex is not even the main feature of their humor. While some scholars have proposed that the prominent genitalia are devices to dis-

tract or repel evil spirits, it seems likelier that they are vestiges of a previous portfolio that included fertility. In a few cases, remnants of the old purpose remain. In northern Japan, *noroma* puppet farces end with the main character pulling out his penis and urinating (water) on the audience—anointing any women his shower hits with the blessing of children.

While many puppet clowns have excised the sex from their act, other ritual-sex puppets have

A fertility spirit embodied in a puppet from Congo. Although his head, trunk, and legs are one solid piece of wood, his penis is moveable (as are his arms). He has dyed plant stems for hair, a costume of animal skin, and body paint of white clay.

A well-endowed jester from Andhra Pradesh, India.

kept the sex when they dropped their ritual dimension. When ceremonies that once were their raison d'être fade away, these popular puppets retool for secular theater so that audiences can continue to enjoy their acts and the release from social restraint that the old rituals allowed. The oversize prosthetic penises that comic actors wore in ancient Greece must have descended from the giant phallus amulets actors used in the *komoi* rites from which comedy developed. In Eastern Turkey, some secular folk plays contain sections virtually identical in form to phallic rituals. The technique for Congo's jigging fertility dolls became adapted for totally non-ritual puppets and toys, both sexual and non-sexual.

For some cultures, though, sorting out rites from entertainment is not only impossible but wrong-headed. In their world views, the physical and supernatural planes of being interweave into a single, complex reality. Constructed beings can easily straddle ritual and entertainment, or move between them. Addressing supernatural versus human spectators just amounts to shifting the demographics of the target audience.

MOST PUPPET SEX, of course, is no more ritual than most human sex. And puppets have been involved with sex acts for pleasure at least since ancient Greece. The legendary inventor Daedalus supposedly constructed a cow body-puppet with a strategically placed orifice to help King Minos's wife fulfill her lust for a bull (thereby conceiving the part man/part bull minatour). Puppets probably were performing sex acts for spectators' entertainment in fifth-century B.C.E. Greece. They have kept it up ever since in both popular and elite theater. Asian constructed actors also have been carrying on sexually for centuries—from Ur-bunraku puppet farces on Japan's Sado Island to traditional *nang talung* shadow puppets in southern Thailand, which sometimes copulated on screen. In Sub-Saharan Africa, the repertory of many puppets includes graphically sexual comedy.

Constructed actors have performed sex acts, first of all, because they have been allowed to. Some risqué entertainments (by live or constructed actors) that descended from rituals were grandfathered in. In general, though, puppets' patent fakeness has given them a broader license for licentiousness than their human counter-

OPPOSITE: A Javanese clown displaying his ample girth—and the family jewels. At first, he seems modestly endowed compared with some fellow clowns, but his bulbous belly presumably obscures great lengths.

A young woman undressed clear down to her mechanism in Roman Paska's *Uccelli, or The Drugs of Love* (1988).

parts. And authorities have not worried that the actors would moonlight as prostitutes—a concern voiced about live actors from ancient Rome to seventeenth-century Japan and America.

In Africa, the contrast between acceptable behavior for live actors and for puppets is especially striking. In most traditional sub-Saharan societies, sex between live male and female actors is as taboo in theater, and even in ritual, as it would be in the public market. Live theater or ritual acts involving sex usually are single-gender affairs. Pairs or groups of all men or all women mime heterosexual intercourse, camouflaging their actual genders under elaborate costumes. But with puppets, just about anything goes. Even when the racy puppet behavior comes in the guise of cautionary tales, the didactic frame largely provides an occasion for fun. For example, miniature lovers atop Gelede "masks" in Nigeria demonstrate the pitfalls of sexual passion by kissing or copulating.

This is not to say that sex has never gotten puppets into trouble. The hero of Spike Jonze's 1999 film *Being John Malkevich* (with puppetry by Phillip Huber) was hardly the first puppeteer to get blackened eyes because of his erotic shows. The Song dynasty official (and philosopher) Zhu Xi tried to ban puppet theater, partly because it could promote immorality. Seventeenth-century English Puritans included puppets in their condemnation of the stage as prurient, and a century later Spanish authorities denounced the popular hand puppet Don Cristobal for encouraging lewd behavior.

French Colonial authorities in Tunis, shocked by obscene Karagöz plays, shut down the shadow theater. But, on balance, puppets have had vastly broader permission to perform sex acts than live actors have had.

Puppets actually have some advantages as sexual actors. True, constructed performers cannot generate the electricity of live skin on skin, since they have none. But because their sexuality is so unexpected, it has the power of surprise. Audiences also are less apt to become distracted by feeling embarrassed for the puppets, or wondering if their mothers are in the front row. With constructed actors, spectators do not try to guess whether the performers actually are aroused or in which sense they are "performing" the acts.

Moreover, players crafted from wood, fabric or Celastic can be custom-made using materials, shapes, and mechanisms that enhance their parts. In fact, when nude and near-nude humans dance alongside puppet versions of themselves in Philippe Genty's *Do Not Forget Me* (1992), the live actors seem poorly designed, sensually flat compared with the performers whose features were planned explicitly for their roles. Some sub-Saharan puppets have genitalia as their dominant features. Penises can be longer and thicker than legs, and vulvas can extend halfway to the female characters' waists. Puppets of the Hausa people of Niger include some carved-wood gentlemen who must lean backwards to balance their immense

Curious creatures in Philippe Genty's *Breath* (1981). As they morph through various shapes, rocking, bouncing, leaning on, prodding, and penetrating one another, these blobs suggest various species, body parts, and emotions. But if what they *are* remains equivocal, what they are up to is not.

OPPOSITE: A seductress in Philippe Genty's *Dérives* (1989) controlling a population of puppet and human men. Naked beneath her trench coat, her lips permanently puckered, this orange-haired doll moves through her stage-world like a sexual beacon—looking as though she was made to lead precisely the life she does. Which, of course, she was.

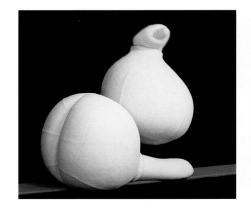
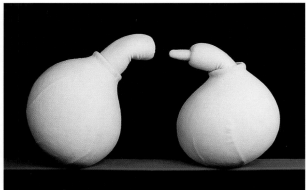

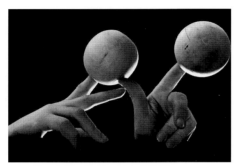

A love scene by Sergei Obraztsov using the simplest of puppets: two-inch, unadorned spheres on the tips of his index fingers. This skit dramatized Vladimir Mayakovsky's poem "Attitude To A Lady."

A lecherous old coot and his prey in Teatre ¾ Zusno's production of *Gianni, Jan, Johna, John, Ivan, Juan, Jean*. But, no, on second look, it is not that at all. Four hands plus one arm create this puppet prank.

appendages and women with vaginas the size of buttocks.

Puppets even have erotic tricks all their own, devices with no human counterparts. In *Uccelli, The Drugs of Love*, Roman Paska presented a panoply of sexuality, including foot-high actors groping incestuously under skirts and a miniature couple copulating in a wash basin. In one sequence, a puppet removed her clothes until she had bared even the joint mechanisms of her wooden body. No live actor could become that naked. Perry Alley Theater's sexual farce "Share and Share Alike" (part of their 1997 trilogy *Strange Love*) followed the bedroom antics of a most peculiar ménage-à-trois: a hand-puppet woman with big, cherry-nippled breasts; her hand-puppet inamorato; and the man's vestigal conjoined twin—a weird multi-pronged appendage (the puppeteer's gloved hand) protruding at the puppet's groin and standing erect to impress the lady.

In both puppetry and sex, fantasy is a great ally. When puppets combine with sex, they can engage a double dose of imagination. Erotic performers need not even be representational. One of Yves Joly's most famous pieces involved a gloved hand removing a series of gloves from another hand, until, finally, both were stark naked. (Caught red-handed, they got busted by black-glove police.) The Argentine puppeteer Mane Bernardo performed a similar erotic routine into the early 1990s. Hanne Tierney's *Incidental Pieces for Satin and Strings* (1991) included a lovemaking scene between two cloths. These lengths of pink satin and black lace had no identifiable body parts or even gender, but their activity was unmistakeable.

PUPPET SEX, like the human variety, comes in many temperaments—from naïve, to erotic, to ridiculous, to raunchy. At one extreme, constructed actors can approach carnal knowledge with childlike innocence. Sergei Obraztsov's staging of *The Divine Comedy* (1961), by Isidor Shtok, featured an Adam

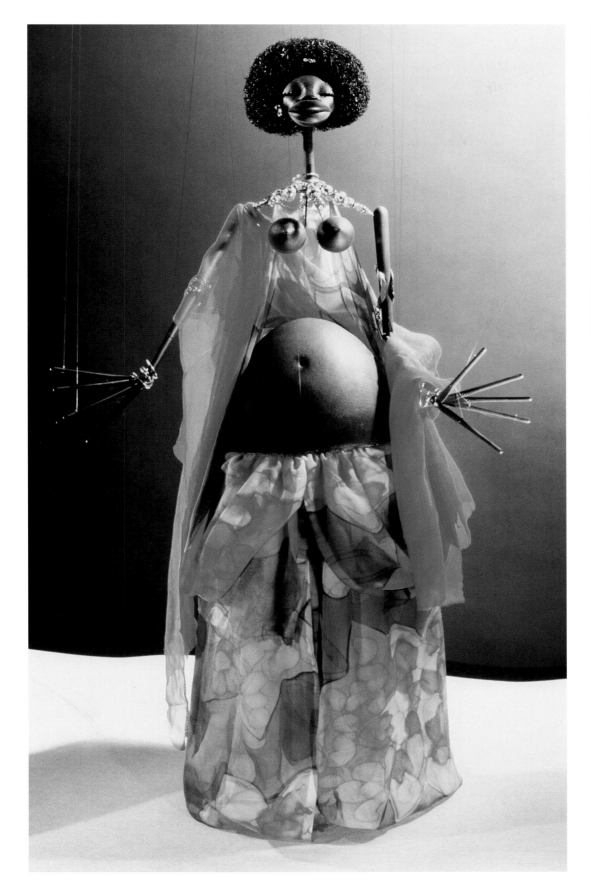

Salome rubbing her sexy body of metallic cloth against a John the Baptist made of steel in Hanne Tierney's 2000 version of Oscar Wilde's *Salome*. The contact creates light sparks and a tingling rustle. The metal coil suggests not only the cold, hard character of John the Baptist but also the prison enclosing him. And as the column rises and contracts back to the floor, it takes the shape of Salome's sexual desire.

Albrecht Roser's Black Belly Dancer. Much of the kick in her act comes from the marionette's witty movement, as four seemingly unconnected spheres capture the gestures and sensuousness of an exotic dancer.

and Eve with simplified anatomies in a world of crayola colors. Based on drawings by Jean Effel, this was an Eden of prelapsarian wonder.

Puppet belly dancers and strippers have long graced polite, even family entertainment. Bil Baird's anatomically exaggerated marionette Bubbles LaRue made her debut in 1942 and continued to take it off in public through the conservative 1950s in such fancy venues as New York's Persian Room. The Salzburg Marionettes' cast includes an exotic dancer who drops to her knees, swaying and undulating into a backbend. Even in conservative Egyptian society, puppeteer Ramzy Fahmy Mishriky has animated a marionette belly dancer that moves at the wrists, ankles, elbows, knees, shoulders, waist, and so

forth. The Israeli David Ben Shalom also performs with a stringed exotic dancer.

Almost always, the fun of these puppets lies in their technical ingenuity and playfulness rather than eroticism. It is not easy, after all, to make a marionette belly-dance let alone get undressed. Karagöz dancers have an extra hinge at the hip that allows them to undulate. The Romanian Tandarica company's 1964 *Í and Dead Matter*, staged by Margareta Niculescu and Stefan Lenkisch, featured a willowy dancer whose torso was just a single length of rope.

Some puppets' chief raison d'être is amorous tenderness or pure eroticism. The Brazilian Grupo Contadores de Estórias' *Maturando* (1987), an exploration of sensuality,

shows a puppet arousing herself to an orgasm. In *Optic Fever* (2001), Theodora Skipitares's jointed shadow puppets, inspired by Greek vase paintings, engage in tender and passionate foreplay and play. Massimo Schuster creates a fiercer sexuality in *The Mushroom* (2000). To conjure the scene of his lover copulating with his enemy, the narrator-protagonist slings the two figures wildly around the stage lassoed together in a rope.

Some contemporary performers have explored the odd eroticism between the puppeteer and the puppet, between the artist and the artist's creation. The puppeteer in *Maturando* seems almost a caring partner to the puppet woman he manipulates. The rela-

tionship can be more literal. One of Robert Anton's tiny characters made passionate love to Anton's bare hand. This puppet-puppeteer sexual electricity often has a bi-polar charge, showing the artist both in love and in mortal struggle with the creation, as the dream attacks the dreamer. In the Odin Teatret's *The Castle of Holstebro*, directed by Eugenio Barba, actress Julia Varley two-steps and swirls with a dapper, tuxedo-clad skeleton (a puppet she manipulates), perhaps aware that she is dancing with death, perhaps not. The life-size alter-egos that try to rape and kill the puppeteer in Nicole Mossoux's *Twin Houses* (1994) are not only her nemeses, but her lovers. As the constructed body attached to Mossoux moults and trans-

A young monk wrestling with the lover he abandoned. In *Kiyohime Mandara* (1987) solo performer Hoichi Okamoto and his life-size puppet literally cast off successive selves in a wordless dance until their final, fatal encounter. Based on an old Japanese tale in which a spurned lover became a serpent and killed her betrayer, the work, according to Okamoto, conjures worlds of unconscious emotion. Okamoto founded his solo Dondoro company in 1974.

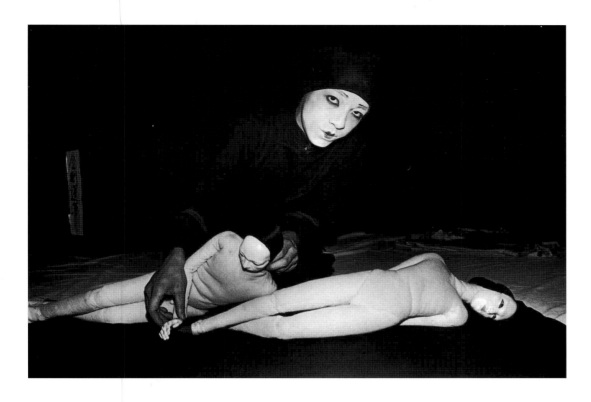

LEFT: Winston Tong performing *Bound Feet* (1977), an erotic fantasy with puppets. To explore the eroticism of pain, Tong feminized his face with white powder and red lipstick, then manipulated the cloth and porcelain dolls in tender lovemaking that focused around the woman's tiny, tortured, bound feet. Here, the puppeteer looks up as if suddenly remembering the audience that has been spying on his reverie.

BELOW: Basil Twist's feet in stiletto heels and Stickman, an fifteen-string, twenty-two-inch-tall basswood marionette that has become his signature puppet. At an S&M cabaret organized as a lark by a group of artists in 1995, Stickman became a foot-fetishist and Twist a dominatrix, periodically kicking or stepping on the marionette as it fondled his foot.

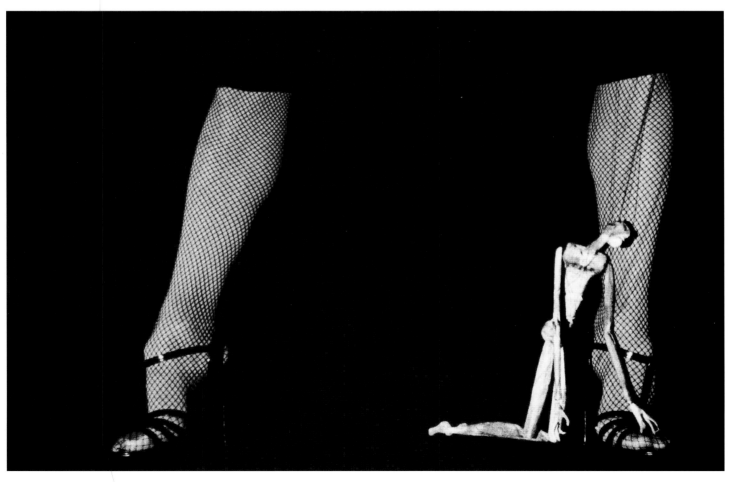

forms, the interaction slides toward an intense, sometimes violent eroticism.

A GREAT DEAL of puppet sex, not surprisingly, is comic. After all, however imaginatively alive puppets may be, the idea of inanimate objects having sexual urges let alone groping and thrusting in sexual passion is preposterous. An otherwise unremarkable X-rated scene, such as the pair of twenty-somethings in bed in the Broadway musical *Avenue Q* (2003), can be hilarious when it is done by puppets. And constructed actors' range of physiology can make their liaisons uniquely outlandish. Karagöz, with his comic-book-proportioned body, is fabulously mismatched with the shadow plays' shapely courtesans, sexpots with nipples poking out from plunging bodices. Live actors could hardly have performed the bizarre seduction-murder in Julie Taymor's 1988 *Juan Darièn* between a jaguar in human disguise and a transvestite with a pistol for a penis. Similarly, only a puppet canine could have handled the action and dialogue in Lee Breuer's *Ecco Porco* (2002), which features a live actor having phone sex with his dog.

In fact, sexually inclined puppets form a worldwide dynasty of bungling and deluded wooers. Pushy women are a favorite target. One of Obraztsov's most popular hand-puppet skits, set to music from Bizet's *Carmen,* featured a señorita clad in red with black lace, wagging rubbery arms as she loomed over a cowering Don José. That lady was modest, though, compared with other sex-crazed puppet crones. One Javanese *wayang* clown has flabby breasts, a too-toothy grin, and unflappable confidence in her sexual allure. Bruce D. Schwartz's hand-puppet farceurs included a libidinous shrew whose vociferous advances sent the devil himself fleeing for his life.

Puppeteers also dish it to the gentlemen, offering up a panoply of lecherous old coots and clumsy suitors. The elderly man panting away with his young wife in a Japanese puppet play nearly 1,000 years ago has modern compatriot

descendents, including a besotted old fool who unwittingly procures young lovers for his wife in a puppet farce on Japan's Sado Island. The eighteenth-century Italian Giovanni Bertelli, famous for bawdy and scatological puppetry, often featured the idiotically infatuated old codgers of commedia dell'arte. The Turkish Karagöz is forever hatching sexual intrigues that backfire leaving him naked in the street, having been caught spying in a bathhouse, outsmarted and forced out of doors by a courtesan, or undone in some other botched scheme. Even the wholesome Kermit the Frog, in a cameo appearance on a Muppet Show pilot (called "Sex and Violence"), tries to put the moves on a voluptuous dance partner saying "Well, uh, I might be able to get you a job on an educational show for kids."

Niceties of taste often succumb to gleeful outrageousness. The English Mr. Punch mouths smutty come-ons to every female he sees—like a mongrel chasing cars, except that he knows what to do if he catches one. Petrushka, the Russian national hand puppet, fulfills his conjugal duties on stage with great verve. In Julie Taymor's *Liberty's Taken*, brothel patrons appear as shadow-puppet silhouettes performing duo and trio acts.

Karagöz's gargantuan member has been misused as everything from a bridge support to a horse-hitching post. In Africa, puppets perform seductions and even rapes as farces. One puppet comedy of the Ibibio in southern Nigeria shows a man's rape of his chaste, if flirtatious, daughter-in-law, presenting every bit of the action in elaborate detail. Typically, the audiences for such intentionally outrageous shows include men, women, and children.

Some puppet sex is *not* for family audiences. Henri Rivière's Chat Noir cabaret, renowned for shadow plays of bible stories and Napoleonic epics, also presented *Pierre Pornograph,* a display of sadomasochism in silhouette, in 1894. The Mamulengo hand puppets of northeastern Brazil still climax their shows in the wee hours, after women and chil-

Young lovers in *Softly* (1980) by the Grupo Contadores de Estórias. In an endangered paradise of Amazonian jungle, one-foot-high Indians in tiny hammocks eat fruit and make love. Infused with a radiant sensuality, this episode is one of a trio of wordless scenarios showing Amazonian peasant life. The Brazilian company was founded by Marcos and Rachel Ribas.

Miss Piggy, one of a long line of eros-driven, romantically challenged puppets, delivering an illustrated lecture on ideal frog physique.

dren have gone home, with all-male-puppet orgies, performed by impressively endowed nudes. The contemporary American puppeteer Jim Gamble's dramatis personnae include a male stripper with a light at his genitals. Australian Philip Millar's rock opera *Tyrannosaurus Sex* stars a singing penis named Bob, who has a nightmare about a monstrous phallosaurus.

Puppets are naturals for expressing sexual fantasies of domination, both of controlling and of being controlled. At the tame, if slightly bizarre, end of the spectrum, some American World War II servicemen received pictures from puppeteer Herb Scheffel of one "Trellis Divine," a pin-up marionette. Or, reversing roles, early twentieth-century postcards, mainly in France, showed nude or minimally clad women cuddling their little Polichinelle, a French cousin of Punch.

Oskar Kokoschka used puppets and dolls to play out pathologies that ricocheted off both extremes of domination. On one hand, he wrote *Sphinx and Strawman,* a play for "automatons," showing a man become a helpless marionette through his sexual fixation. On the other, he commissioned a life-size replica of Alma Mahler, briefly his lover and then, much longer, his obsession. It was rumored that he took this submissive version of his mistress with him on carriage rides and to the opera before she met her demise by decapitation.

Constructed actors also hold their own in X- and XXX-rated theater. After all, besides being anatomically made to order, porn puppets

"They're Easy to Handle When You Know How"—an indulgent marionettrix handling her man in a 1948 pin-up by Gil Elvgren. America's foremost pin-up artist during the 1940s and 1950s, Elvgren painted several images of puppeteer-beauties controlling little guys on strings. Originally a calendar picture with a self-portrait where Santa now stands, Elvgren modified the image for this yuletide beer ad.

are totally compliant no matter how unseemly the act. Graphically sexual puppetry has a long history in the West. An impresario of erotic mime told Socrates that he made his real money doing puppet performances, presumably with the same sort of content. A seventeenth-century traveler in Russia wrote he was appalled to find public puppet shows that presented men copulating with women, other

men, and large mammals. (In this case, according to the witness, the hand-puppet shows were modeled on the contemporary sexual behavior.)

From time to time, artists have established theaters specifically dedicated to naughty puppetry. The Erotikon Theatron, on La Rue de La Santé in Paris, was a twenty-one-seat cabaret that lasted from 1862 to 1863. Its participants ranged from relative amateurs to luminaries of

A self-portrait by Oskar Kokoschka, holding his made-to-order Alma Mahler. Kokoschka found his puppet Alma disappointing, with "polar-bear fur" rather than the silk skin he had specified. Nonetheless, he provided her with a maid, who dressed her and washed her lingerie. (One can only guess why the lingerie needed washing.) In the end, Kokoschka threw a champagne party for the doll, where she was manhandled until her head fell off. Then he threw her in the trash. Kokoschka also had less pathological involvements with puppetry. He created shadow figures for an Indian folk tale at Vienna's Fledermaus Cabaret using the color palette of Oriental miniature painting.

the theater, art, and music worlds. Georges Bizet was resident pianist, and the puppeteers included the renowned puppet satirist Louis Lemercier de Neuville and Louis Duranty, a novelist who became famous for his Guignol theater in the Tuileries. Erotikon's specialty was puppet misbehavior, trashing all sorts of pompousness and propriety. For its first show, it advertised star actors of the day performing on sets painted by Michelangelo. And thirty-four years before Alfred Jarry's Père Ubu created shock waves by uttering "merdre" ("ppsshit") on stage, Erotikon performed a play subtitled *"Signe d'argent,"* vulgar slang for the same thing. *The Marquise, or Shit* offered the spectacle of an aristocratic lady not only being sexually serviced by her servant but also craving and eating excrement.

Often, pornographic puppetry has a high ratio of outlandishness to smut. Contemporary American puppeteers have presented such spectacles as a lesbian melodrama performed entirely by hussied-up dildos, and a yard-long penis puppet that opens up alligator-style.

There even is a small body of XXX-rated puppet films. Henri Xhonneux's *Marquis* (1990), with art direction by Roland Topor, is a picaresque travesty set during the French Revolution. The leading roles are the Marquis de Sade and his sole prison companion, his penis—played, of course, by a puppet. Only a constructed-actor penis could have the necessary stature and stability, let alone carry off the dialogue and facial expressions. Meanwhile, around the Marquis de Sade and his pal, other characters' sexual antics careen toward the ridiculous. One of *Marquis*'s climaxes, for example, involves a horny Bastille warden and a humongous, cooked langoustine. Some films go way past *Marquis* into hard core, including at least one movie made by a leading director of human-actor porn.

WITH THIS—as with Kokoschka's constructed paramour—puppets have pretty much sprung over the top. But the trajectory toward the outrageous seems to be a natural path for puppets. And sex is far from the only sphere where they act out.

A Karagöz suitor specially designed so that his pants come down at the right time—or more often from his standpoint, the wrong time. Karagöz *celebi* characters are fashionable young gents who go a-courting, flower bouquet in hand and, sometimes, erection in pants.

CHAPTER 7

And Violence

WHAT POLITICAL CANDIDATE WOULD NOT BE incensed? At a big rally, the ragged half-wit he has bribed to praise him just stands there nodding and mumbling into the microphone. When sotto voce threats yield no results, he starts to harangue her. Then he belts her one. He whacks her around with his hat. Then he hits her with a chair. In full frenzy, he rips her leg off at the hip and starts to wallop her with it. As shreds of her insides fly around, he yanks off her other leg and strangles her with it. Finally, he loses interest and moves on.

Puppets such as this burlap victim in *The Dream of Your Life* (2000), by François Lazaro's Marseilles-based Clastic Theater, have often been the performers of choice for snuff roles. Even in live-actor theater, characters subject to serious violence may be played by constructed performers. In medieval Christian religious pageants, Herod's henchmen slaughtered dolls filled with red liquid rather than the local children. When plays showed the torture of saints, some productions used a trick platform that could flip over, switching the live actor with a life-size puppet better able to tolerate flaying, searing, de-tonguing, stretching, quartering, and other torments popular with spectators.

In short, one reason puppetry so often waxes violent is that it *can*. When the history and legends a society chooses to perpetuate involve brutality or gore, as they often do, puppets are a logical casting choice. What other actors could perform the Sicilian puppets' version of the chivalric epic *Orlando Furioso*, in which characters are impaled, decapitated, cleft head to groin, sliced front to back, blown up, and eaten alive? To perform *The Mahabharata* and *The Ramayana*, chief sources for the Southeast Asian *wayang kulit,* puppets are built to disassemble upon impact. The special x-ray vision of shadow puppetry even lets spectators see spears inside the bodies they pierce. When live actors play the same stories, they generally use stylized, symbolic action to present the carnage or else have narrators describe it. Stunt puppets also handle the spectacular deaths in northern Brazil's rural Mamulengo hand-puppet shows, including full and partial decapitations.

STILL, PUPPETS' ABILITY to withstand violence cannot in itself explain their extraordinary propensity for it. In nearly every part of the world, constructed actors treat audiences of all ages and classes to scenes of corporeal atrocity. Hand puppets in southern China have been whacking and stabbing one another with spears and swords probably since the 1500s. The first puppet images in medieval Europe—in a twelfth-century woodcut from Strasbourg and mid-fourteenth-century miniatures for *The Romance of Good King Alexander*—all show characters armed with swords or truncheons

Judy showing her young English audience how to settle a marital spat in this detail from an 1862 illustration by Edward H. Wehnert for *Great Fun for Our Little Friends*.

OPPOSITE: A climactic scene in the fifteenth-century *The Martyrdom of St. Apollonia*. Although painter Jean Fouquet does not reveal stage secrets in this miniature, the saint probably is on a trick pallet. With their victim firmly bound to the top, the torturers would briefly hover over her to block the audience's view, then flip over the board, allowing a dummy tied to the underside to take over the saint's ordeal.

going at one another. By the early fifteenth century, the puppet repertory included spectacles of diminutive warriors destroying whole towns. In eighteenth- and nineteenth-century Europe, little constructed actors demolished one another in street booths, at fairs, in wealthy homes and, probably, in royal venues.

Certainly puppet savagery assuages the human appetite for brutality without the immediate deleterious effects of acting out these impulses on living beings. Puppet violence also provides a means for jingoistic muscle-flexing, for showing that one has the best country, ethnic group, religion, value system, whatever, without massacring thousands of other people in the process. Violence permeates live-actor theater too, of course. But it is more pervasive in puppetry, where it can be much wilder and, at the same time, more palatable.

This said, puppets' brutality can be surprisingly unnerving, and not only because puppets can play more appalling atrocities. Knowing that the performers are not alive, audiences do not activate emotional defenses, the mental filters that screen out or distance what would be

unbearable to see. Nonetheless, viewers do suspend disbelief and buy into the stage reality. So the full horror that puppets can muster may catch spectators unaware, without the armor they would have donned for similar episodes in live-actor theater. The rape in El Periférico de Objetos's *Gesell Chamber* is so unsettling in part because the audience has been lulled into a sense of safety watching baby dolls enact a play.

A GREAT DEAL of puppet violence is more playful than serious. It invites audiences to share not so much in vicarious sadism as in a prankster's fun at breaking things. The barbarity is irreverent rather than vicious, and often so over-the-top that it bounds clear over the edge of horror into farce.

Comedy based on clobbering people has always been puppets' specialty, their stock in trade. Even good-natured puppetry often includes ludicrously violent humor. In Jim Henson's pre-*Sesame Street* television commercials, puppets were blown up or bonked with mallets for choosing the wrong brand of bread or, in one case, protesting the violence in the

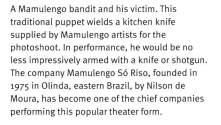

A Mamulengo bandit and his victim. This traditional puppet wields a kitchen knife supplied by Mamulengo artists for the photoshoot. In performance, he would be no less impressively armed with a knife or shotgun. The company Mamulengo Só Riso, founded in 1975 in Olinda, eastern Brazil, by Nilson de Moura, has become one of the chief companies performing this popular theater form.

commercials. A 1980s West African social-work manual suggested using slapstick puppet shows to educate audiences about domestic violence, and included an illustration of a hand puppet literally batting her husband's head off.

One widespread puppet-farce atrocity is vivigestion, eating live creatures. A popular traditional Chinese hand-puppet routine (often performed by the late Yang Feng, a fifth-generation puppeteer, who was based in Seattle) shows a tiger chowing down his overconfident handler. In sixteenth-century Istanbul, shadow shows at a royal circumcision included a dragon devouring live humans and a cat's gustatory delectation of a mouse. The cat routine has survived into modern Karagöz. Shadow theater, again, can give

spectators the bonus of following the continuing action *in ventro*—as in Julie Taymor's *Juan Darièn*, where audiences saw an unfortunate cobbler's ordeal inside the stomach of a jaguar. Mummenschanz added a new twist by having a gluttonous character eat itself, stuffing its entire body into its mouth.

Since comic servants participate in the *wayang* fights, battlefield carnage sometimes comes in forms most undignified. A minor character may get flattened beneath a rotund clown or asphyxiated by a close-range fart. In one battle routine by the Balinese dalang I Wayan Wija, a flying arrow plucks the head off a combatant, whose truncated body wobbles for several seconds before flopping over; the arrow zooms onward with the head in tow, making several passes across the screen, until it

The *Mahabharata* hero Bima using a severed head to club an enemy demon in *Bima Suarga*, performed circa 1980 by Larry Reed's Shadowlight Theater.

Mortal Danger—Sergei Obraztsov's Russian version of a traditional Chinese hand-puppet routine depicting a bad day for the tiger-tamer.

hits another soldier, replacing his head, which plops onto the ground.

Some ridiculous puppet aggression is pure testosterone spree. Oversize phalluses on Indonesian shadow-puppet clowns and minor monsters in past times often could be detached and wielded as clubs. Semar, the secretly powerful servant-clown in Javanese *wayang Mahabharata*, sported a penis that was the ultimate weapon when hurled in battle, a kind of pre-fission nuclear missile. Some macho Mamulengo gents in Brazil use their impressive phallic members to whap opponents. The Turkish Karagöz also has sometimes wielded a weapons-grade penis, which could be removed and used to beat Greeks, Armenians, Jews, and anyone else foolish enough to share his screen.

Even George Bernard Shaw loved puppet carnage, although he was generally a pacifist and his own dramas were sophisticated satires for live actors. His lifelong attraction to constructed performers began in childhood, from watching them getting bashed: "Nothing delighted me more," he once wrote, "than when all the puppets went up in a balloon and presently dropped from the skies with an appalling crash on the floor."

ONE OF SHAW'S favorite characters—in fact, the most beloved and long-lived theatrical figure in live-actor or puppet theater in Europe, the Middle East, and the Americas—is an unrepentant ruffian puppet whose chief *modus operandi* is bludgeoning his victims, typically in unprovoked attacks. The English and American character Punch, a devil-may-care serial killer, is perhaps the most blithely sociopathic version of this rascal, but he has many foreign cousins with a familial resemblance: a huge, usually hooked nose, often a hump-back, a sartorial preference for red, and a propensity for whacking people to death.

The three-dimensional branch of the family, mainly hand puppets, includes Italian Pulcinella, French Polichinelle, Spanish Don Cristóbal, Portuguese Dom Roberto, Austrian-

A Sicilian marionette soldier from Palermo caught in one of the hazards of puppet warfare.

Mr. Punch's techniques for handling a wailing baby and dealing with a pesky magistrate in illustrations from *Aunt Louisa's National Album*, published in Britain circa 1870.

Karagöz, from Turkey, in the awkward predicament of having been turned into a goat.

German Kasperle, Dutch Jan Klaassen, Romanian Vasilache, Hungarian Vitéz László, Russian Petrushka and Czech Kašpárek. Shadow-puppet members of the clan include the Turkish Karagöz, Greek Karagiozis, Syrian Karakos, Saudi Arabian Karakoz, and Iraqi Quarakoz, plus a few other Arabs and Slavs. Aragos, the Egyptian cousin, is both a shadow puppet and a hand puppet. Kindred spirits, if perhaps not blood kin, include a host of Asian mischief-makers: the Chinese Guo Gong, who traces his forebears to the sixth century; South India's Vidūṣaka (possibly a grandfather to Southeast Asia's complex clown clan); and Korea's merry, cherry-red exhibitionist Hong Dongji.

These little troublemakers have been such audience favorites that many puppeteers over the centuries scarcely dared to put on a show without them, whether they belonged in the story or not. The famous eighteenth-century English puppeteer Martin Powell showed Punch and his wife dancing inside Noah's ark during the Great Flood. In France, Polichinelle often delivered a prologue for classier shows and sometimes entered the action as well. The German Kasperle became a regular member of Don Juan and Dr. Faust's households. His Czech brother Kašpárek starred in *Faust* and a (loose) translation of Shakespeare's *Hamlet*. (For some of these appearances in classical theater, the mischief-maker reinvented himself as a marionette—inherently a more refined player—and became more smart-aleck than killer.) Karagiozis turned up as a messenger in serious heroic dramas.

Because Pulcinella-Punch-Karagöz generally played below the social level that historians recorded, his early genealogy is guesswork. Like his Asian counterparts, he clearly goes

Petrushka, from Russia, a character that developed from early nineteenth-century Italian puppets performing in Russia's fairgrounds.

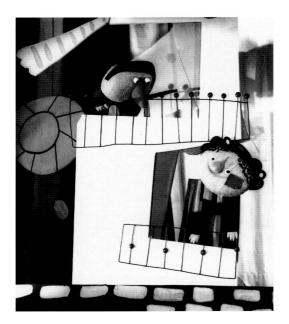

ABOVE: Spain's Don Cristóbal, cudgel in hand, eying his young, unwilling bride in *The Three Wives of Don Cristóbal* (1965). Adapted from short plays by Federico García Lorca, the show was directed by Margareta Niculescu for Romania's Tandarica Marionette and Puppet Theater using a mixed cast of puppets and live actors. Lorca had revived the dying Don Cristóbal tradition in the 1920s with several short plays. He staged the first in his home in 1922 with music composed and performed by Manuel de Falla.

RIGHT: Vitéz László, from Hungary, uncharacteristically unarmed as he negotiates with the devil. Vitéz László's usual bludgeon of choice is an oversize (human-scale) frying pan.

Bil Baird's mid-twentieth-century Punch and Judy, based on engravings by George Cruikshank published in 1828. Cruikshank had modeled his illustrations on the puppets of Giovanni Piccini, an Italian who had introduced the now-classic Punch and Judy scenario to London (and renamed Punch's wife, previously called "Joan").

back centuries if not millennia. In fifth-century B.C.E. Greece, troupes that played both mime and puppet shows featured a live-actor clown with a hook nose, a hunchback, and a big truncheon at the ready—in other words, a live-actor Punch. If the Greeks' puppet repertory paralleled their live shows, as often happens, then the little sociopathic rogues, by whatever name, may be as old as Aeschylus. This conjectural lineage continues in the third century B.C.E. on into the second century C.E. with *phylakes* and then Atellan farces, little slapstick burlesques in

southern Italy that included buffoons like those in the Greek mimes—and that, again, *could* have had puppet versions. But then, for a thousand years after the fall of Rome in the fifth century, the type falls from view.

The documented genealogy of Punch and his cousins begins in the fifteenth century, in southern Italy, with the emergence of commedia dell'arte. This form of improvised farce using stock characters became popular in both masked-actor and puppet versions. And it included a hook-nosed buffoon, Pulcinella, who

provided the name, though neither the personality nor grotesque style the clan later developed. In France, the Italian clown mutated into "Polichinelle," a violent rascal with an ill-proportioned physiognomy, bright-colored clothing, and a great big baton. This cruder version of the zany traveled across and beyond the continent, mainly during the eighteenth and nineteenth centuries.

Crossbreeding with local clowns and adapting to local tastes, the character developed regional variations. The Turkish Karagöz is forever getting bright ideas that land him in complicated pickles (making him as much like the commedia's Arlecchino, or Lucy Ricardo, as like Pulcinella), while the Hungarian Vitéz László is a simple lout who wouldn't know an idea from a plate of spaetzle. Don Cristóbal is often older, has (ill-gotten) wealth, and, like all good Spanish heroes, can bristle about his honor, a concern of little concern to the penurious German Kasperle. The Egyptian

Aragos, for all his sociopathic tendencies, has a kind streak, something foreign to the English Punch.

Still, the clan shares a basic dramatic, as well as facial, profile. Although, like commedia characters, they have different biographies in various plays, they are usually social underlings. Whatever their weapon of choice—broomstick, truncheon, frying pan—it is always at the ready. And while they attack authority figures with special gusto, they also are wont to assault friends and family.

Perhaps these villains' most curious feature, though, is that no matter how monstrous they may be, the audience generally roots for them. When a nineteenth-century English performer tried presenting a more moral puppet show, with Punch getting his comeuppance, audiences would have none of it. In fact, these violent rapscallions often become folk heroes. Punch and Kasperle, on their puppet stages, fought on their respective sides in World War II.

Kašparek in the middle of the action in the Czechoslovak-American Marionette Theater's *Don Juan, or The Wages of Debauchery* (2003). Here he offers his smart-alecky opinions as his boss tries to bribe a religious ascetic to blaspheme.

The classic English Punch and Judy scenario offers a clue to this appeal. Punch defenestrates his baby, bludgeons his wife to death, fatally beats a neighbor's servant, a doctor and sundry others, then impales the magistrate and hangs the hangman. While this behavior is not exactly heroic in the traditional sense, it is monumental in its own way: Beyond merely violent, it *violates* every law, every boundary of civilized behavior. These brutes are a poor man's Faust or Tamburlaine or Don Giovanni—someone bold enough to overstep all limits, break every rule, exceed what humans are meant to be and do.

Moreover, unlike those classier characters, Punch gets away with it. After his killing spree, Punch comes face to face with the devil. The high-brow heroes all lose the game when supernatural forces kick in (if they have not already been defeated by humans). Not so Mr. Punch. Continuing his winning strategy of battery with a blunt object, he fights the devil—and kills him. In many scenarios, Punch then comes up against the ultimate challenge, the character Death. In some versions, he parries and negotiates with Death to a draw; in others, he whaps Death to death. Although things don't always work out quite so well for the whole clan— Petrushka and Karagöz often get the short end of the stick—most of these guys get away with murder. In sum, beyond the outrageous, irreverent slapstick that is their trademark, the Pulcinella clan are the baddest and boldest of all theatrical protagonists, leaving the heroes of the Western tragedies, Hindu epics, and just about everything else looking like ninnies.

As DEDICATED BREAKERS of both pates and taboos, puppets have naturally been called upon to embody ritual pandemonium when ceremonial occasions require it. They have often figured in the sanctioned misbehavior of Europe's Carnivales, Feasts of Fools, and other festivals that temporarily upend the normal order of things. They take part in comparable observances in Southeast Asia and Africa.

But those officially sanctioned performances are a sideline. In or out of season, with or without permission, puppets will have a go at the prevailing rules. And they defy the most basic social mores. The popular Korean clown Hong Dong-ji not only shows up buck naked but pees all over the audience with his squirt-gun penis (perhaps a vestigial fertility rite, à la the Japanese *noroma* comic Kimosuke, but a social violation nonetheless). Obese servants in *wayang kulit* are forever passing gas. Puppet naughtiness continues right up to contemporary television. On Comedy Central's *Crank Yankers*, Muppet-like characters enact and lip-synch recorded crank phone calls. Triumph, the obnoxious rotweiler "insult-puppet" on Conan O'Brian's late-night show, abuses people for their physical appearance and ethnicity. Triumph's anti-French comments during a visit to Canada in 2004 even sparked protests in the House of Commons.

A venerable facet of puppet impertinence is roasting sacred cows, including high culture. The traditional title for "Punch and Judy" players is "Professor," in itself a swipe at highbrows. Puppet shows of Paris's eighteenth-century fairgrounds regularly lampooned performances at the Comédie Francaise and the Opéra. Jean-Baptiste Lully's successful opera *Phaëton*, for example, inspired half a dozen small-stage parodies, including one called *"Polichinelle Phaëton—or The Clumsy Pig."* In nineteenth-century England, when the great Sir Herbert Beerbohm Tree was playing *Henry VIII*, Mr. Punch set up just outside the theater with "Henry the Twenty-eighth," bringing Punch's wife-dispatching tactics to Henry's marital issues. In another play, Punch paid hommage to an opera hero's battle with a lion by duking it out with a pig.

Indecorous and ribald puppet satire also became regular fare at turn-of-the-twentieth-century cabarets in Paris, Berlin, Barcelona, Munich, and other cities. Michel de Ghelderode raised hackles with his 1933 military epic for puppets, *The Siege of Ostend,* featuring slapstick, scatalogy, and nonsense language. Even Edward Gordon Craig, for all his rhapsodizing about the transcendent deathlike beauty of übermarionettes, wrote a puppet travesty of *Romeo and Juliet* that included such elevated action as Romeo's leg falling off with a clunk.

Shakespeare remains a favorite for puppet spoofs. American puppeteer Bill Mack for years set up his castelet outside the New York Shakespeare Festival's Delacorte Theater, offering ten-minute versions of whatever was playing inside. To sum up Shakespeare's Byzantine gender scrambling in *As You Like It,* Mack's Sebastion mused to the "lad" (actually Sebastian's disguised sister), "I had a sister once, but she was a girl." Lasse Akerlund's

sausage-dinner version of *Macbeth* also carries forth this tradition of puppet roasts.

Puppets' association with children, far from a handicap, can add an extra dimension of outrage, of innocence perverted, to puppets' misbehavior. Peter Jackson's puppet film *Meet the Feebles* features evil twins of the *Sesame Street* crew, foul-mouthed little hippos and frogs that mainline drugs, projectile vomit, and gun down their fellows. Greg the Bunny, who briefly had his own adult sitcom, looked like a child's stuffed cuddle-toy. He just didn't talk like one.

Puppets' rule smashing sometimes goes past the far end of comedy, to the point where pandemonium turns into apocalypse. When the-

Marvin Suggs and his Muppephones, an outrageous little xylophone created for the Muppet Show by longtime Henson collaborator Frank Oz. The little furballs yelped "ow" on pitch when Marvin bonked them with the mallet.

Frank Einstein: Rewired (1993), Green Ginger's spin-off from Mary Shelley's *Frankenstein*. Even in this show for family audiences, Green Ginger infuses nose-drip humor with ludicrous horror, including a severed hand in a jar. This Welsh company, founded in 1978 by Terry Lee, also performs street theater.

A twelve-foot-high Gerber baby wearing earphones and usually running old movies in its eye-sockets in Squat Theater's *Mr. Dead and Mrs. Free* (1981). With nothing but popular culture blasting in its head, this trash-brained baby helped to convey Squat's vision of a doomed society. Like most of Squat's New York work, the show was staged in a storefront with the view periodically opened to the street.

ater artists want to show a universe in which the center just does not hold, they often turn to puppets. The Hungarian expatriate theater company Squat, based in New York in the 1970s and 1980s, used puppets for some of its wierdest and most disturbing visions. Its *Pig Child Fire* (1977) featured a hulky (puppet) pig excreting a live actor. Contemporary British puppetry includes whacked-out irreverence that waxes dark to the point of sinister. The recluse hero of *Snuffhouse Dusthouse* (1990), by the Faulty Optic company, lacks legs not, as viewers naturally think at first, because leglessness is a puppet convention, but because his mother lopped them off when he was a kid. In his lair jury-rigged from trash, cockroaches on treadmills produce electricity and any visitor is an enemy. In the Welsh company Green Ginger's *Bambi—The Wilderness Years*, Walt Disney's big-eyed fawn has become a street urchin scrambling to survive in a sleazy, brutal society.

The end of civilization was home territory for Jan Švankmajer, whose puppet-laced films included a version of Punch and Judy (1966).

His ravaged-looking characters, presented in fractured images in ruptured time and space, become emblems of disorder itself being further shattered. In Švankmajer's *Don Juan* (1970), horror tangles with absurd humor. One wooden puppet spurts blood when stabbed, but another, when sliced open, just shows his bare-wood construction material. Other filmmakers, including the Brothers Quay, have used constructed performers to render nightmarish, sometimes apocalyptic visions.

Alfred Jarry's Père Ubu, an exemplar of the demise of civilized life, began his career as a puppet. Fifteen-year-old Jarry and his co-author schoolmates first created Ubu in 1888 as a lampoon of their physics teacher, using the "Théâtre des Phynances," a troupe of puppets they had made. Jarry's three *Ubu* plays present the barbaric reign of an invented usurper king of Poland—a brutish, greedy, vainglorious, generally nauseating anti-hero for the twentieth century. Loosely travestying *Macbeth* with other chopped chestnuts thrown in, the plays savage even basic logic. With stage directions such as "he makes a bloodbath of Poles," "he lengthens himself," and "a wave breaks over everyone,"

A modern ingénue shares a peanut with her date, in *Rico and Dolores* (1992), by the American performance artist Joan Evans. Glued to her television show, the woman fails to notice that the rodent is gnawing off chunks of her body. For Evans, this is a vision of the end of civilization.

Pierre Bonnard's 1910 charcoal sketch of the puppet workshop. Alfred Jarry appears in the middle of the trio on the left. Bonnard depicts himself sitting at the table sculpting a puppet.

Alfred Jarry's own "veritable portrait of Monsieur Ubu," a woodcut for the first edition of *Ubu Roi* in 1896.

with characters that get impaled, cleft in half, and flushed down toilets, *Ubu*'s world, like Punch's, is a natural for the puppet stage.

For the play's 1896 live-actor premiere at Paris's experimental Théâtre de l'Oeuvre, Jarry stressed to the director, Aurelien de Lugné-Poë, that *Ubu* should retain the character of puppet farce. (That show used masks and sets by painters Pierre Bonnard, Paul Sérusier, Edouard Vuillard, and Henri Toulouse-Lautrec, as well as Jarry.) Afterward, Jarry and friends returned to the drawing board to reinvest *Ubu* with freewheeling absurdity that only puppets could bring. Their first public presentation (following several private showings) was in 1898, at the Théâtre des Pantins using characters designed and built by Bonnard.

Père and Mère Ubu had to wait two thirds of a century for a major, successful puppet-stage show of their Royal Lownesses. In Stockholm, puppet master Michael Meschke was looking to capture the sense of rupture and violence that

imbued the contemporary world. In 1964 he staged Jarry's *Ubu*. For Meschke, whose Polish-Jewish family had fled to Sweden in the 1930s, the play's message about government terror gone amuck was an especially crucial one.

Since Meschke's production, *Ubu* has often been used as a vehicle for addressing the issue of idiotic violence. One of the most important Ubu productions was by Catalan artists Joan Miró and Joan Baixas, who collaborated on an *Ubu* from 1975 to 1977. Miró's designs drew on the local tradition of giant body puppets, placing Ubu's exuberant brutality uncomfortably close to home. In 1987 William Kentridge and the Handspring Puppet Company created *Ubu and the Truth Commission*, using Jarry's *Ubu* as a lens to view South Africa's apartheid regime and its aftermath.

Puppet mayhem has thus entered into the political fray. In fact, puppets' tradition as political players is probably as venerable as their history of wreaking havoc.

Père Ubu (played by Allan Edwall) with his subjects in Michael Meschke's 1964 Marionetteatern of Stockholm production. Franciszka Themerson, who had illustrated an edition of *Ubu,* designed the puppets as white cartoon figures outlined in black. All but Mère and Père Ubu were flat, from four inches to ten feet high and operated from behind. Père and Mère Ubu were three-dimensional—she a sloppy, lumpy body-puppet and he a grotesquely padded actor.

RIGHT: *Ubu Roi*, a 1966 lithograph by Joan Miró. The artist had been fascinated by the character of Ubu ever since exploring Jarry's play with fellow surrealists half a century earlier. He had filled four notebooks with visualizations of Ubu, even inventing additional adventures for him. This 17" x 26" lithograph contains seeds of Miró's later puppet designs, particularly in the conception of Ubu himself.

BELOW: Joan Miró (with paintbrush) and Joan Baixas (at rear) working on *Death to the Tyrant* (1978), based on *Ubu*. Baixas, previously a painter, co-founded Putxinellis Claca in 1968 to explore puppetry. Miró, whose only prior designs for the stage had been more than thirty-five years earlier (for the Ballets Russes), was among several visual artists Baixas approached to collabrate, and Miró suggested they work on *Ubu*. They began the project in 1976, when Miró was over eighty. They saw *Death to the Tyrant* in part as a funeral for the despot Francisco Franco, just one year dead at the time, and as a commentary on petty daily tyrannies—of a landlord, a bureaucrat, a patriarch— that add up to a kind of pervasive violence.

An erector-set guillotine at work in the 1984 *Ubu* by Massimo Schuster, designed by Enrico Baj. This Ubu world was a society at the brink, where people were no different from out-of-control, lethal machines. *Ubu* was the first of five collaborations between Schuster and Baj, including an opera, *The Blue-White-Red and the Black* (1989), with music by Lorenzo Ferrero and libretto by Anthony Burgess, for La Scala in Milan.

CHAPTER 8

Politics

PUPPETS ARE INVETERATE POLITICAL ANIMALS. And like many politicians, they can play on both sides of the fence. Governments and religious authorities have sometimes kept constructed actors among their retainers to adorn festive occasions. In eighteenth-century Istanbul, turbaned giants on barges floated past Sultan Ahmet III during royal celebrations. In the same period, Franz Josef Haydn, serving as the Esterhazy court composer, wrote a puppet opera to flatter the visiting Austro-Hungarian Empress Maria Theresa. Oversize puppets adorned many of the Soviet Union's parades on May Day and anniversaries of the Revolution. Smaller-scale puppets also have endorsed and flattered those in power. After a 1968 coup d'état in Mali, for example, tiny versions of the new president and his motorcycle escort performed on a *sibondel*, a miniature stage worn atop the head.

Governments also have commandeered puppets to serve specific agendas. From the start of Russia's Bolshevik regime, constructed actors disseminated the official line in such crowd-pleasers as *The Burning of the Hydra of Counter-Revolution* (1917) and *Petrushka the Fidget: For All Bourgeois a Threat* (1917). Like Soviet artists in all genres, puppeteers were required to fight against the bourgeois decadence of "formalist" art by toeing the aesthetic line of simple realism. Even Sergei Obraztsov

could break the rules only gingerly, notwithstanding his international renown, his established loyalty to Communism, and Stalin's personal favor.

Similarly, the government of Nazi Germany ordered that all theater, whether with live or constructed actors, actively further the party's mission to glorify the Aryan "race." Although puppeteers sometimes could hold Hitler's theater police at bay simply by playing traditional Kasperle farces, Kasperle himself became Nazified. He appeared as a government spokespuppet in propaganda posters, political cartoons, and ads for businesses serving the war effort. Kasperle even underwent a cosmetic makeover after the Reichinstitut für Puppenspiel decided his big nose looked too Jewish. (They actually x-rayed puppet heads to check his racial pedigree.) New, more Aryan Kasperles featured blond hair and a ski-slope nose.

Puppets performed partisan work for the Allies in World War II as well. In England, Punch raised his bludgeon to fight for the Union Jack. The puppeteer Percy Press made Punch an English soldier, and the hangman he hanged was Hitler. Obraztsov staged a miniature Axis summit with Mussolini as a bulldog, Hitler as a German shepherd, and the Vichy France leader Pétain as a poodle, all barking and yapping.

OPPOSITE: A *Spitting Image* version of Margaret Thatcher wielding her chief instrument of state, a meat cleaver, used here for debraining.

BELOW: A portrait puppet of General Charles de Gaulle by the Bozo people of Mali. This unarticulated, painted wood marotte dates from World War II, when France's government-in-exile had its base in Africa. Some sub-Saharan puppets, including portraits like this one, honor the regime in power. Local chiefs sometimes animate their sculpted staff, a symbol of power, using it like a marotte.

Frida Kahlo and Diego Rivera with a Judas effigy. Mexican Catholics have burned Judas puppets since the early days of Spanish conquistadors and missionaries. The practice may derive from a Carnival auto-da-fé, burning a straw or rag heretic. In the New World, locals dressed the Judases like Spanish rulers and made their spectacular (gun-powder aided) demise a celebration, even packing the Judases with treats that flew into the crowd. Banned in the mid-nineteenth century, this folk art was rejuvenated a century later, with Kahlo and Rivera among its champions. Contemporary Judases, generally papier-mâché over a reed frame, may represent the devil, policemen, politicians, or fashionably dressed social elite.

After World War II, many puppets either returned to their old government jobs or got new government jobs. In the Soviet Union, both live and constructed actors again promoted the Bolshevik program, including socialist realism. Leaders in the newly independent Indonesia used shadow puppets to promote a national confederation and teach citizens how to participate in this new kind of government.

For puppeteers in post-war Communist China, government service was *de rigeur*. During the Cultural Revolution of the 1960s and 1970s, puppets (and live performers) not directly performing as indoctrination tools were destroyed. New modern-dress shadow puppets played factory workers and peasants. Later, they demonstrated the virtues of one-child families. Opera troupes, whether with puppets or live players, performed only the eight approved model revolutionary operas.

Effigies have been used to make political statements, often attacking absent enemies. These demonstrations run the gamut from being sponsored by governments to being in opposition. The Iranian regime presumably supported the Teheran demonstrators who savaged an effigy of Uncle Sam in February 2002 after George W. Bush had labeled Iran part of an "axis of evil." In October 2000 effigies of Israeli Prime Minister Ehud Barak and U.S. Secretary of State Madeleine Albright were torched by Palestinian refugees in Lebanon, expressing sentiments with which officials in Beirut no doubt concurred. The Indian government may have been less sanguine about Tibetan exiles setting afire a constructed double of Chinese leader Le Peng in New Delhi in January 2000. Certainly, the rebellious American colonists who hanged a dummy representing a British tax agent

The Rat, a prominent New York labor activist, on the job. The thirty-five-foot tall rodent and its half-size cousin, shown here, frequently appear at labor actions. The Rat's most famous encounter occurred in 1999, when a security guard outside the CBS offices tried to stab it to death—and the police arrested the rat's handler as well as the rat (took it as evidence, they said). After a campaign to "Free the Rat," a judge ruled that its presence at demonstrations was covered under first amendment rights to free speech. Or, to put it more grandly, puppets are protected by the U.S. Constitution.

The Pakistani president, General Pervez Musharraf, being savaged in effigy in April 2000 during a demonstration by Hindus protesting the recent killing of Sikhs in Kashmir.

English children watch Winston Churchill thwack Hitler in a September 1941 showing of *Punch and Judy Goes to War*.

China, anti-government sentiment was so much a part of popular puppetry that one insurgent reportedly traveled around arranging puppet shows to gauge unrest and recruit local malcontents. Royal spies in twelfth-century Sri Lanka studied the arts of song, dance, and "leather figures" so that they could insinuate themselves as moles among performers and sniff out rebellious types. Two of the earliest surviving puppet plays from Europe, in Ben Jonson's *Bartholemew Fair* (1614) and Cervantes's *Don Quixote* (1606–1615), mock religious authorities.

The tradition continues. In southern Europe through the mid-twentieth century, itinerant players infused traditional stories with topical barbs aimed at government, business, and the church. Korean puppets satirize corrupt officials, decadent aristocrats, and hypocritical monks. The popular Indian jester Vidasuka and the Javanese *wayang golek* clown Semar both break the story frame to address spectators about current affairs.

One of constructed actors' assets as protest performers is that authorities frequently cut them some slack. Even performing out in the open, dissident puppet theaters often have something like a court jester's license to criticize. In early nineteenth-century Rome, live actors were required to submit scripts for pre-approval, but puppets were not, even though their satires regularly mocked the pope and featured senile, lecherous cardinals. In fact, royal jesters sometimes used puppets for their riskier bits, animating a *marotte*, an all-in-one puppet, mock-scepter, and noise-maker.

In Europe, puppets' greater freedom of expression has in part been a happy byproduct of being considered trivial. Between the sixteenth and nineteenth centuries, they enjoyed dispensation-by-neglect all over the continent. Even when governments banned live theater—in Antwerp (1585) and Puritan London (1642)—or restricted it to a very few licensed companies—in Paris (1680), Brussels (1700), and London (1737)—the authorities often did not bother to

in 1765 did not ask their English governor for approval.

Political puppeteers need not necessarily immolate their characters or hack them to pieces to grab attention. In one 1980s Italian Carnival float, a titanic Ronald Reagan sat with knife and fork in hand, dining on the booty as European leaders an eighth his size rode beneath him on torpedos, carrying his pallenquin and doing his dirty work. Outsize puppets often add panache and photo ops to political demonstrations and union picket lines. A block-long, ravaged-looking woman floating above the streets of Paris in December 1993 drew publicity for the marchers' demand for stronger UN action in Bosnia. Outside the 1999 World Trade Organization summit meeting in Seattle, protesters carrying upside-down marionettes landed a slot on the evening news and a picture in the *New York Times*.

IN FACT, PUPPETS have generally been less likely to serve the mighty than to skewer them. Live-actor theater also may jab and stab, but political satire, even out-and-out sedition, has long been a specialty of the small stage. In ninth-century

attack puppet shows. In some cases, puppeteers were limited to outdoor performances, but otherwise left largely unconstrained. During periods when live actors in Rome could play only during Carnival season, little *burattini* carried on year-round. And in nineteenth-century Spain, shadow puppetry was the only theater allowed during Lent.

Sometimes puppetry escaped regulation by positioning itself outside the definition of "theater." In France spoken dialogue was the acid test for "theater": sung or narrated performances were exempt from the rules. Since Europe's puppets had often used narration rather than dialogue anyway, the practice just became more frequent. Sometimes a voice distorter—a "swazzle" held in the mouth—sufficed to ward off government controls, rendering puppets different enough from live actors (or, simply, beneath official concern). Having to use a swazzle was hardly a handicap, since many puppeteers across Europe and the Near East used voice squawkers anyway for characterization and comic effects. Finally, pushing against these regulations in order to taunt authorities became a part of the show.

When officials in seventeenth-century France and eighteenth-century England *did* harrass puppeteers, the instigation often came from disgruntled live-actor troupes that had been banned or that were licensed and trying to quash competition.

Puppets have at times presented extremely nervy work right out in public. In 1867 Erotikon veteran Louis Lemercier de Neuville staged an allegory criticizing Napoleon III's government, not just publicly but in front of Napoleon. The nineteenth-century Czech puppeteer Jan Nepomucky Last'ovka performed incendiary material, then talked his way out of trouble by blaming his puppet, Kašpárek. Werewere-Liking used puppets in her Ki-Yi Mbock theater in Ivory Coast for the very dangerous business of attacking corruption.

ALL THIS SAID, at times and in places throughout history, authorities have tried to censor and squelch puppet shows either because they considered the performers nogoodniks or because the shows were challenging those in power. And so puppeteers have resorted to various sorts of stealth. Dissident puppets make use of

BELOW LEFT: A *wayang klitik* of a Dutch officer in Indonesia. In Southeast Asia puppets representing colonialists usually were big-nosed European types. In West Africa, where the French imported Vietnamese as low-level functionaries, the foreign-overseer puppets often looked Asian. In post-independence Africa, those figures came to represent any oppressor or exploiter. *Wayang klitik* are shallowly carved wooden *wayang* manipulated much like *wayang kulit*, except in *front* of the screen.

BELOW RIGHT: Fred Schneckenburger's 1951 Kasperle puppet commenting on the day's news in "We Read the Papers." This Kasperle/Harlequin shrank, literally, under the weight of events, regaining normal size only after destroying the newspapers. Schneckenberger called another character "The Smashed-in Face—a face that no longer exists because the war destroyed it." That figure had only half a head but displayed a medal on his chest.

live-actor theater's full arsenal of subversive tricks. Puppets living under foreign occupation often use local dialects and slang to shoot defiance at the unsuspecting butts of their opposition. In 1920s French Indochina, Cambodian shadow puppets of top-hatted, big-nosed westerners seemed benign to people who could not make out the dialogue—about forced labor, tax extortion, and the frigidity of French women. In Mali, before the French abolished impressed labor in 1945, Bamana men on conscripted road-construction teams staged protest puppet farces in the local language in full view of their clueless foreign overseers.

Dissident puppets, like live actors, have also camouflaged their messages within plays that authorities would not likely flag and monitor as potentially subversive. Polish players began to include patriotic material on their szopka Nativity stages in the mid-nineteenth century in defiance of the Austro-Hungarian and, later, Russian occupation regimes. Until well into the 1990s, Czech artists under foreign-imposed governments helped to maintain their national heritage by performing banned stories in puppet shows for children. Turning classics and other innocent-seeming plays into political allegories became a well-developed ruse in Soviet satellite countries. For example, *Cirkus Unikum* (1978) by the Czech Drak Theater, portrayed the revolt of circus performers against an evil ringmaster.

Besides strategies for dissent that they share with live actors, puppets have special tricks and advantages. Puppet theaters can gain much political mileage from being small. A portable theater can reach a wide public. Also, a little theater can more easily be made on the cheap, within the means of people who have neither money nor access to mainstream venues. Most important, though, a small-scale puppet show can be strategically inconspicuous and can clear out quickly if necessary. A hand-puppet stage can be packed up and out of sight within seconds. Police cannot censor performances or arrest performers they cannot find.

Clandestine puppet shows have sometimes been fabulously audacious. The show with sadomasochistic-priests that was betrayed to the Spanish Inquisition is one example. In 1792 doomed French aristocrats secretly staged executions of miniature revolutionary-court judges: a scale-model mahogany guillotine chopped off their wax heads, releasing a gush of red liquid. A few decades later the French writer Stendhal saw puppets in Naples doing dangerous political satire in the relative safety of a private drawing room.

Even when the authorities do find a puppet show that offends them, they may not be able to sniff out the offenders. One intriguing story of puppet subterfuge involves a mysterious Madame de la Nash, who surfaced in London in 1748. Dodging theater licensing laws by calling her puppets "breakfast room" entertainment, she offered ferocious political and artistic parodies. After her little theater was found out and shut down, she disappeared forever—without the authorities ever learning that Madame de la Nash was an alias of the well-known satirist Henry Fielding. Not only had Fielding's puppet plays already rankled government officials, it was Fielding's live-actor burlesque of the prime minister that had triggered the shutdown of most London theaters in 1737.

In recent years, Sicilian television newscasters have used the anonymity of a puppet for protection from the Mafia. After a journalist covering organized crime was murdered, a hand puppet named Paolino took over the beat of reporting about the mafia and mafia-friendly politicians. (The death threats that Paolino receives do not faze him.)

Despite their advantages, puppet rebels all around the world have at times been silenced. In China the Manchus' ban on Cantonese performances after the Taiping rebellion of 1894 explicitly included the small stage, since both puppeteers and live actors had been among the rebels. The French paid uncharacteristic attention to satiric puppet theaters in the mid-nine-

A section of *The Tower of Medieval Sciences* (1989), a kinetic sculpture of carved wood, scrap metal, and glass by the Russian artist Eduard Bersudsky. This ten-foot-high piece is one of several contraptions Bersudsky made between 1978 and 1989 showing people and rats toiling away, often under the watchful eyes of Lenin or Stalin. Because his work complied with neither the form nor the spirit of Soviet official dictates for art, he kept it closeted in his one-room Moscow apartment until *glasnost*. In 1989 theater director Tatiana Jakovskaya added music and gave the mobile sculpture a more theatrical presentation. Bersudsky and Jakovskaya now continue their work in their Sharmanka gallery in Glasgow, Scotland.

teenth century both on home ground and in their North African colonies. They closed any that displeased them. In turn-of-the-twentieth-century Warsaw, when szopka shows became too transparently patriotic for the Russian occupiers, they revoked the right to perform. A half-century later, roadside puppeteers in Senegal so blatantly promoted opposition parties that the government outlawed the performances.

Getting shut down is not the worst that can happen. It takes little imagination to guess how the Spanish Inquisition handled people involved with the kinky clergy puppet show. In northern Italy during the eighteenth and nineteenth centuries, street performers caught lampooning the pope, the Austrian occupiers, or local VIPs were jailed. Some intrepid souls, including a famous Milanese hand puppeteer Il Romano and a satirist Ghetanaccio, no sooner were released than they resumed their shows and were rearrested, repeatedly. In Russian-occupied Warsaw in 1793 someone convinced an innocent nicknamed Sheepskin to guillotine

miniature versions of Polish collaborators in front of the army chief's house. The fall-guy was whipped.

Contemporary puppeteers have been no less vulnerable. Avant-garde theater director Eugenio Barba's oversize Mr. Peanut puppet, a skull-head atop a black suit, was attacked by club-wielding police as it performed outdoors in Pinochet's Chile. Actress Julia Varley, on stilts inside the body puppet, was beaten to the ground. In June of 2000 Theatre Junction, a prominent Pakistani puppet troupe, had its play *Bunch of Lies* shut down in Lahore by a mob of party loyalists who also assaulted and tortured the troupe leaders. During the U.S. Republican National Convention of 2000, Philadelphia police made a pre-emptive strike on a warehouse where "puppistas" (puppet activists) were preparing for a protest march. The puppets included 138 oversize skeletons representing people executed under then-Governor George W. Bush, and giant peanuts carrying money bags and labeled with names of corporations and the

Punch clouting Jesse Helms, chairman of the U.S. Senate Foreign Relations Committee, in a 1977 performance of *Mr. Punch Reads the Newspaper*. The sketch, improvised to each day's news, formed part of *Works in Regress* (1994), by Preston Foerder. Punch batted Helms for his ultra-conservative policies—including opposition to government funding for the arts. Two years later Helms denounced a television puppet for preschool children, accusing Tinky Winky of subversively destigmatizing homosexuality.

amounts of their campaign contributions. The police not only destroyed all the puppets but arrested more than seventy puppeteers, holding them in "preventative detention," and reportedly beat some of them.

THE HISTORY OF dissident puppetry in Europe is replete with the antics of its favorite brats, the Punch/Pulcinella/Polichinelle/Kasperle/Karagöz clan. These characters always have peppered their acts with irreverent ad-libs, and often these have been topical. Sometimes their political acts are simply anarchic. During the French Reign of Terror, Polichinelle set up his own miniature guillotine not far from the real one and had his head lopped off again and again. But their nose-thumbing and head-thwacking have also been mixed with focused protest and advocacy—occasionally in government service, particularly in wartime, but more typically

championing the underdog. Even when the puppets have appeared in relatively classy venues, their sympathies have been with the oppressed. In the licensed London puppet theater that Charlotte Charke opened in 1738, Punch regularly starred in political satires. In one farce by Henry Fielding about the brutality of the sex trade, Punch (in drag) played a madame, clobbering whores and johns alike.

The shadow-puppet branch of the rascal clan has been especially brazen. Until the late nineteenth century, when political satire was banned from Turkish puppet plays, Karagöz derided not just crooked businessmen and mercenary soldiers but government officials up to and including the Sultan. In lands under Ottoman occupation, puppeteers turned the traditional villains in all their stories into Turks. And well into the twentieth century, Karagöz's cousins in Algeria, Tunisia, and Libya used de-

The Terrifying Night of the Unfortunate Baroness Ecologia de Creys-Malville or *The Vampires of Creys-Malville* (1981). When a problematic nuclear power plant opened in Creys-Malville, France, the Compagnie Jean-Guy Mourguet in Lyons staged this Guignol horror show of politics and ecology. Here Chiracula (conservative President Jacques Chirac, at left) and M. le Marchais (Communist Party leader Georges Marchais) prepare to suck the blood of the conservative ex-president Valery Giscard d'Estaing, while Mitteratu (Socialist former president François Mitterand) looks on. Jean-Guy Mourguet is the fifth-generation descendant of Laurent Mourguet, creator of the original Guignol. Chiracula has become a regular member of Guignol troupes.

RIGHT: A cartoon by puppet-film artist Jiri Trnka (who began his career in Josef Skupa's theater) showing Spejbl and Hurvínik in a concentration camp with an ominous chimney in the background. Trnka also made political puppet films, including *The Hand* (1965), a condemnation of totalitarian government. Created while Czechoslovakia was under Soviet domination, the film was banned for twenty years.

BELOW: Josef Skupa with his stand-up comedy duo, Spejbl and Hurvínik. Spejbl (at left) was a parrot-brained defender of authority and rules, while his son Hurvínek was full of ideals and questions. The pair's increasingly topical repartee became so vexing to the Nazi occupation government in Prague that one collaborator denounced Spejbl and Hurvínik as Jews (news to Skupa). Skupa performed underground until his arrest in 1944. Surviving the war, though in broken health, he was given his own theater, renamed the Theater of Spejbl and Hurvínek.

tachable phalluses to beat miniature French Colonial officers.

In the early nineteenth century in Lyons, France, the tribe got a new member destined for a political career. Laurent Mourguet created a character he named Guignol. Like the Punch clan, Guignol was irreverent and had a penchant for whacking people. But Guignol diverged from the typical family profile. Supposedly a self-portrait, Mourguet's puppet had a small nose and a sweet smile. Moreover, he was kind of an okay guy. He usually had some excuse, however flimsy, for beating his victims, and he was generous with the next-to-nothing he had, niceties rare among his cousins. Other French puppeteers adopted Mourguet's new character and within decades Guignol had replaced Polichinelle as the national puppet hero. The name "Guignol," which Mourguet had made up, became synonymous with puppet.

Tradition has it that Guignol championed the silk workers of early nineteenth-century Lyons, who had grown impoverished as the demand for silk fell off with French aristocrats' heads. By 1852 puppet shows were upsetting authorities enough to provoke a law requiring pre-approval of an unalterable script. Even these no-doubt sanitized plays show Guignol as a voice for the common Lyonnais constantly being misused by bigshots. In some shows, he even ran for office. Apart from a few periods when he was just benign entertainment for children, Guignol has continued to take on abusers of money and power and to join protest marches—for example, against the building of a nuclear plant in 1981. Modern Guignol companies often include contemporary French politicians and the pope.

Other populist puppet rascals have been little Robin Hoods performing felonious income redistribution in plays that combine social criticism, melodrama, and farce. German-speaking puppets have played valiant crooks loosely based on the historical characters Heisl, a

Bavarian animal poacher, and Carl Stülpner, an eighteenth-century poacher and army deserter, both of whom had been hanged. Slovak and Polish puppets helped to immortalize their preferred good-hearted thief, Janosik. In Italy, near the turn of the twentieth century, the multi-generation Luigi Lupi troupe, which still performs (with puppet-handlers Luigi VI, VII, and VIII) was among the earliest to celebrate the bandit named Musolino. Across the world, bunraku heroes often play on the wrong side of the law to rescue their love or their honor.

In the late nineteenth and early twentieth centuries, European political puppets found a

Tinka's New Dress (2000), a tribute to Josef Skupa by Canadian puppet artist Ronnie Burkett. Burkett staged the play on a revolving carousel (an homage to *The Three-Tiered Carousel*, a comic allegory satirizing Hitler, which Skupa wrote with Frank Wenig and presented in 1937). *Tinka* showed puppeteers variously resisting or collaborating with an unnamed repressive regime and included satiric stand-up marionettes somewhat in the manner of Skupa's Spejbl and Hurvínik.

new niche in artists' cabarets. The initial program at Eleven Executioners, in Munich, in 1901 included a puppet show mocking Kaiser Wilhelm II's imperialist ambitions. Krakow's cabaret the Little Green Balloon opened in 1905 with a comic patriotic szopka (and was savvy enough, unlike its Warsaw counterpart, to hold the Russian censors at bay). The Noise and Smoke cabaret in Berlin, Four Cats in Barcelona, and others also featured puppets with a propensity not only for the indecorous and ribald, but for politics.

The Nazi dominance of Europe leading up to and during World War II prompted many puppeteers to perform resistance work clandestinely in a potentially deadly cat-and-mouse game with authorities. Czech artists created an especially lively underground puppet culture coordinated by Jan Malík, performing secretly in basements and private homes. The most important of these puppeteers was Josef Skupa, whose satiric duo Spejbl and Hurvínek became increasingly political in the 1930s and early 1940s. Dozens of Czech puppeteers, including Skupa, landed in Nazi prisons and concentration camps.

In wartime Poland, the anti-Nazi company Sztuka ("Art") managed to tour during 1942–1943, offering a szopka nativity in which the three magi were Roosevelt, Churchill, and the Polish general Sikorski. The Fairytale Hut puppet theater in Italy performed through World War II, peppering innocent-sounding shows with blatant anti-Mussolini jibes. Amazingly, even prisoners of war and concentration-camp inmates managed to stage political puppet shows. Polish captives in Mühlberg presented such szopkas as the "Prisoner of War Nativity," in which a four-headed Herod had the faces of Axis leaders and Stalin. And inmates of the Nazi death camp at Dachau staged a puppet *Faust* in which Himmler was presented as the devil and one camp official was a witch.

A generation later, during the tense years leading up to the USSR's demise, some puppeteers were front and center (ahead of politicians) in challenging the authorities. One 1989–90 show by Lithuania's Sepos Theater depicted Karl Marx as a big red book with arms and a beard, usurping God's place in heaven.

Ravaged agents of the secret police in *The Mushroom, or Public Confession with Guaranteed Corpse* (2000), by Massimo Schuster, based on a text by Bulgarian poet Tzvetan Marangozov. Schuster played the narrator, a spy unable to escape his job. For the other characters, Joan Baixas burned and gauged styrofoam heads, to which Schuster added a few sticks, shirts, and bright-colored mop buckets. Pictured here, right to left, are the narrator's Irish girlfriend, two minders, and Brigitte Bardot, who makes a cameo appearance in the story.

The outlaw hero Cangaceiro. This popular Brazilian Mamulengo bandit is an armed thief who usually steals from the rich and gives to the poor, but also, when the fancy moves him, robs the poor and keeps the loot. Mamulengo heroes often are criminal champions of the people. Puppets that play police, soldiers and land-owners have nasty countenances and the characters usually meet nasty ends.

The following year, he used quasi-bunraku puppets and narrators to present *Antigone*, Sophocles' disquisition on civil disobedience against despots.

Some of Europe's most political live-actor stage artists have incorporated puppets into their theater. Nobel Laureate Dario Fo's ferocious political comedies have included all sorts of constructed performers. In his 1968 *Grande Pantomima with Flags and Small and Medium Puppets*, the character Fascism, a giant rubber-mouthed grotesque, spawns smaller-scale oppressors, including a king and queen, a general, a bishop, and a character called Capitalism. In Fo's version of the Stravinsky opera *A Soldier's Tale* (1978, La Scala, Milan), the state is a huge gaunt marionette which various interested parties manipulate and keep from collapsing.

IN THE UNITED STATES, politically engaged puppet theater emerged in pockets during the first half of the twentieth century, partly in response to the socially unbalancing boom of the 1920s and then the Great Depression. From 1925 to 1933 on New York's immigrant-packed Lower East Side, Yosl Cutler and Zuni Maud, Jews from Eastern Europe, ran the Yiddish-language Modicut puppet company in a former clothing factory. The troupe, which achieved international recognition, performed folk tales, left-wing political comedies, and satires of Yiddish art theaters. Modicut's of Herbert Hoover had a rotten apple for a head. Its character "Vol Strit" (Wall Street) conspired with world leaders to boost the economy by starting a war.

The short-lived Vagabond Puppeteers travelled through rural New York State for six weeks during the summer of 1939. The troupe consisted of the future folk-singer/activist Pete Seeger (then twenty years old), three friends, and twenty-two homemade puppets. Focusing on local concerns, such as the need for dairy farmers to organize, they played in union halls and in the open air, including along a picket line. Seeger supplemented the puppet skits with

Michael Meschke's reminder at the 1972 Olympic Games of an injustice at the Stockholm Olympics sixty years earlier. Native American Jim Thorpe, the first athlete to win both the decathalon and pentathalon, had been stripped of his gold medals because he had once earned two dollars a game in a sandbox league, and thus was deemed a professional athlete. Meschke's street procession in Munich included puppets not only of Thorpe (at right, running) but also of Sweden's King Gustav V and an Angel of Peace that had appeared in the opening ceremonies in 1912. (The Olympic Committee restored Thorpe's standing in 1982 and returned the gold medals to his family two years later.)

Another Sepos skit presented Stalin and Hitler in a Punch and Judy whackabout "negotiating" for control of Lithuania.

Many of Europe's most prominent and inventive puppeteers of the past several decades, including Joan Baixas and Massimo Schuster, have incorporated politics into their work. In Stockholm Michael Meschke followed his 1964 black-and-white *Ubu* with other shows on social or political themes. In 1973 he directed *The Life and Death of the Bandit Murieta* by the Chilean dissident poet Pablo Neruda.

Uncle Tom's Cabin, the most famous Abolitionist play, performed in 1936 by the Jubilee Singers, a troupe of eight African-American singers and puppeteers with the Buffalo Historical Marionettes. The Jubilee Singers performed before white as well as black audiences and also had a weekly radio show. The 200-member Buffalo Historical Marionettes, founded by Esther Wilhelm, was part of the Depression-era Federal Theater Project, which employed thousands of out-of-work stage artists between 1935 and 1939 (and which Congress defunded in response to its activist work).

protest songs. African-American puppeteers, meanwhile, began to counteract minstrel caricatures. Some tackled issues of race. Two troupes of black puppeteers in the 1930s Federal Theater Project staged *Uncle Tom's Cabin*. The Jubilee Singers in Buffalo, New York, also did a play about Eli Whitney, whose invention of the cotton gin reinforced slavery. Via puppets, these African-American artists were playing white characters—quite a turn around from the minstrel model of white performers in black face.

By the 1960s in the U.S., the civil rights struggle and the Vietnam war had spawned a new political engagement, and puppets joined in. The key figure was artist Peter Schumann who started the Bread and Puppet Theater in 1962 on New York City's run-down Lower East Side. He mingled puppets and live actors, some of them masked, and used a rough papier-mâché and tempura-on-bedsheets style that has become his signature. Schumann typically incorporated Christian symbols, and at every show the company broke bread with the audience, sharing loaves that Schumann had baked. Schumann also began to mount deliberately

ragtag antiwar demonstrations and street processions, usually with music and puppets, in Washington, D.C., and New York. Based in northern Vermont since 1974, the company hosts large gatherings each summer and continues to create puppet theater on themes such as homelessness and exploitation of the Third World.

Part of Bread and Puppet's legacy is the raft of political puppeteers who found their own voices working there. Paul Zaloom started out with Bread and Puppet in 1971 and still works with them on occasion. His own deadpan-lunatic, politically acerbic theater varies in form, but often he animates a tableful of selected trash to perform a story. Great Small Works, composed largely of Bread and Puppet members and alums, creates socially engaged "toy theater." Minneapolis's Heart of the Beast Puppet and Mask Theater, founded in 1973, also has Bread and Puppet roots. Using masked and unmasked actors, three-dimensional and two-dimensional puppets ranging from small to gigantic, and anthropomorphized objects, it stages plays, parades, and circuses, focusing

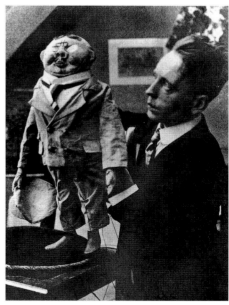

John Heartfield with a "conservative citizen" from *Simply Classical, or The Tax Furies*, at Berlin's Noise and Smoke café in 1919. Writer Walter Mehring warped Aeschylus's *Oresteia*, which Max Reinhardt was directing next door at the 3,000-seat Grosses Schauspielhaus, into an ominous allegory of contemporary Germany. Mehring made Electra and Orestes into fanatical nationalists, and the antagonist Aegisthus into a spineless democrat. Apollo, who in Aeschylus's trilogy resolves the conflict, became Woodrow Apollon. Artists Georg Grosz and John Heartfield designed the actors.

Uncle Sam taking a break during a Bread and Puppet Theater demonstration in Washington, D.C., to protest the war in Vietnam.

LEFT: The Bread and Puppet Theater's figure of Archbishop Oscar Romero of El Salvador (the company's only portrait puppet) embracing his flock. *The Crucifixion and Resurrection of Archbishop Romero* celebrated the activist priest who had advocated for the poor despite threats from right-wing death squads, and was murdered in his church in 1980. This performance took place during a 1984–85 Bread and Puppet tour of Central America.

Paul Zaloom demonstrates President Ronald Reagan's latest Star Wars technology in *The Future* (1984). The trash-bin dome over Zaloom's head makes him an astronaut. He aims a broken toy gun at a hubcap space station, demonstrating the "star-wars-kill-the-other-guy-billion-dollar-lazar-zap-thing."

on issues of ecology and social justice. The Underground Railway Theater, a quarter-century-old company based near Boston, has used three-dimensional and shadow actors to address such issues as the Ku Klux Klan and the plight of contemporary Central American refugees.

As in Europe, some of the most prominent puppeteers in America regularly focus on political and social concerns, even if politics is not their preeminent agenda. Theodora Skipitares's performance pieces have centered on class bias in urban development, the collateral-damage casualties of scientific progress, and the abuse of women in the sex trade and in prison. Janie Geiser's theater also ranges widely in theme and form, but she returns again and again to stories about an individual, usually a woman, lost and imperiled in a world that is uncaring, venal, or destructively stupid.

MUCH OF Latin America has traditions of populist puppetry. In Mexico, Mireya Cueto creates

socially engaged puppetry in poor urban communities. Escobar Duarte, a nun who works in the slums of northern Brazil, uses masks and puppets to counter racism. Nicaraguan theater companies have used masks and puppets to dramatize issues of land reform and the plight of street children. Members of Bread and Puppet, the Underground Railway Theater, and other companies have also worked with troupes in Latin America.

IN WESTERN AFRICA, Mali's most renowned puppet artist, Yaya Coulibaly, maintains traditional puppetry, including satires mocking social fads and venal behavior. But he also creates new works with a more cutting political edge. His little actors have performed plays about the treatment of West African soldiers by colonial France in the two world wars and about political corruption.

South Africa has, not surprisingly, been rich territory for political puppetry. Since the early 1990s, the Handspring Puppet Company and the painter, filmmaker, and animator William

Kentridge have reworked classics, including *Woyzeck*, *Faust*, and *Ubu*, to address the country's social crises. Gary Friedman, a white native of Cape Town (who recently emigrated to Australia), has produced a wide range of activist puppetry. His Punch and Judy takeoff, *Puns and Doedie—Puppets Against Apartheid*, launched in 1981, featured a former sewer-department worker turned member of parliament. The cast also included President P.W. Botha, Archbishop Desmond Tutu, Margaret Thatcher, and Ronald Reagan. In one episode, Botha looked

for "Afronauts" to establish new "homelands" for blacks off the planet. Following the end of Apartheid, Friedman's constructed performers worked mainly in film and television. In his *Puppet Election: 92*, a little green-skinned TV news reporter presented major issues and even interviewed the candidates—the actual candidates, not puppet copies.

FRIEDMAN'S TELEVISION puppets were part of a widespread infiltration of political puppets into that medium. For more than a decade starting

A dissection—or, perhaps, vivisection—in Theodora Skipitares's *Under the Knife: A History of Medicine.* Skipitares's work usually combines original texts with archival texts that she unearths. Here, the sixteenth-century anatomist Andreas Vesalius recalls learning that physicians may cut open still-breathing criminals to study the body functions. Another scene quoted a woman's harrowing account of her mastectomy without anesthesia, because pain was believed a necessary part of the cure.

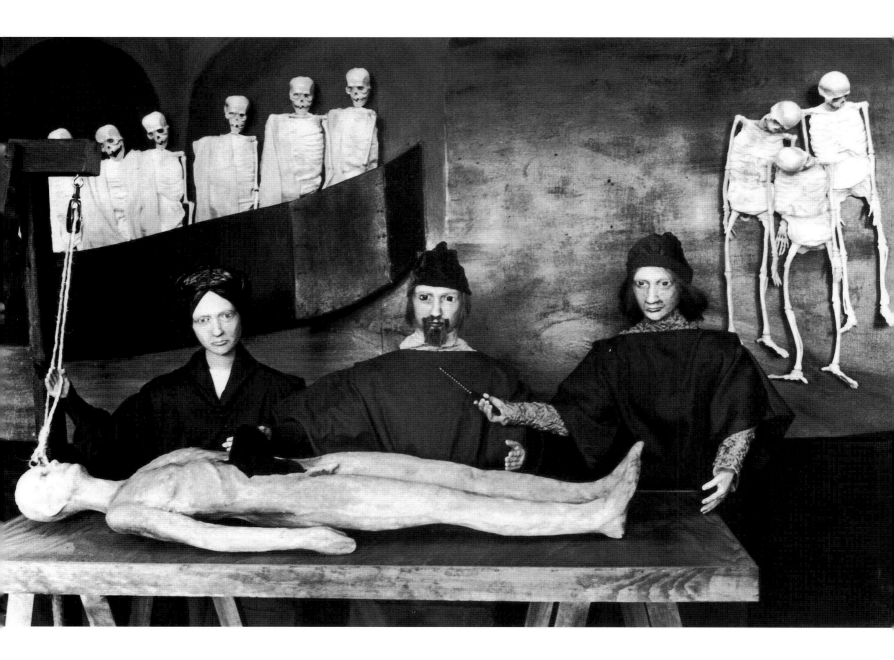

Haunted by violence, a woman prepares to flee at the beginning of Janie Geiser's 1994 *Evidence of Floods*. After her escape, the woman's abuser both stalks her and frames her for murdering him. Audience members follow the woman's story on a sequence of miniature stages. Geiser, who heads the puppetry program at the California Institute of the Arts, works in a wide range of forms. Often she uses ultra-simple, unarticulated, flat wooden or sheet-metal actors. Her films mix flat puppets and animated illustrations.

in the mid-1980s, Roger Law and Peter Fluck created the weekly *Spitting Image* show in Britain. Their satire was rarely subtle, and they aimed their weapons low. Latex versions of Margaret Thatcher wielded a whip or meat cleaver. After O.J. Simpson's acquittal for his ex-wife's murder (but before Princess Diana's death), a horse-faced Prince Charles burbled to O.J. about how he admired his "work."

Similar shows developed around the world, including *Les Guignols d'Info* (*The News Puppets*) in France, *Kukly* (*Puppets*) on Russia's NTV, and *Rubbery Figures* in Australia (named for a famous characterization of the national budget). Political caricature puppets also got television

series in Spain, Portugal, Israel, Mexico, New Zealand, and Indonesia. Although the ratio of potshots to serious criticism has differed among the shows, none of them has set the deference bar very high. Regular characters on the Israeli show *Ha'chartzufim*, for example, have included not only caricatures of (then) Palestinian leader Yasser Arafat and Israeli Prime Minister Benjamin Netanyahu but also gossiping cockroaches under Netanyahu's sink. Some of the programs have been variants of the model. The *Rubbery Figures* portraits are mainly small, one-handler puppets. In Mexico, the puppet skits are interspersed in the actual evening news. In Indonesia, traditional *wayang* portray the politicians, drawing connections between characters in the Hindu epics and contemporary figures.

Some of these political puppet shows became wildly popular. *Spitting Image* was such a must-see that a tape of the Sunday program was rerun Monday mornings in the House of Commons. *Kukly* was for years the most watched television show in Russia, and *Ha'chartzufim* was the most popular show on Israeli TV.

Pedictably some of the subjects did not appreciate the portrayals. The British royal family threatened to sue when *Spitting Image* presented Prince Andrew as a centerfold with "Cumberland spicy" sausage links adorning his groin. But they backed off, perhaps anticipating the display of evidence in court.

Other TV satires did spark legal action. When a French priest went on trial for child molesting, *Les Guignols d'Info* had a field day: Week after week, audiences watched a puppet version of the Abbé savor unsavory acts, while his attorney, M. Collard, acted as the devil's advocate (literally) and the priest's minion. The priest, who received a ten-year prison sentence, and Collard both sued the *Guignols*—Collard for a symbolic one franc, the Abbé for one million francs. The *Guignols'* attorney argued that France had a long tradition of puppet satire. In a decidedly ambiguous verdict, the court found for the plaintiff—but awarded only one franc in damages to the priest as well as M. Collard.

For the creators of *Kukly*, the stakes became higher. In 1995 Boris Yeltzin's chief prosecutor launched a criminal investigation in an effort to intimidate the puppets. Five years later, having been warned to keep their President Putin puppet off the show, the Kukly aired a Putin-less episode in which characters continually referred to a leader too terrible to look at, while they discussed the Russian war in Chechnya. When *Kukly's* producer was jailed in June 2000, the next show—five days later—included the dropping of an iron curtain.

Ubu and the Truth Commission (1998) by the Handspring Puppet Company and William Kentridge. *Ubu* provided the framework for a troubling view of South Africa's confess-and-be-pardoned hearings and the impunity conferred on perpetrators of atrocities. Jane Taylor's script incorporated testimony from the Truth and Reconciliation Commission's sessions. Here the apartheid government's bureaucracy appears as a voracious briefcase-cum-alligator.

BELOW AND OPPOSITE: Boris Yeltsin and Bill Clinton puppets with their manipulators in a 1998 episode of *Kukly*. Yeltsin is offering Bill Clinton practical advice at the time of the sex brouhaha. Clinton should lie, of course, but say something more plausible than that he has had *no* extramarital liasons. Also, he ought to clean troublemakers out of the news organization and put in his own people—a tactic Yeltsin describes as "personnel policy." And, the bottom line, Clinton should call in tanks. After all, Yeltsin says, "are you the commander in chief or just a guy from Arkansas?"

CHAPTER 9

And Other Public Service

Puppets' contribution to the body politic has many facets. Almost universally throughout history, they have participated in child rearing. Puppets have a unique rapport with very young people. For both groups, the border between fantasy and reality is porous. And both groups can blur the distinction between what is sentient and what is inert. As performers, puppets offer child spectators guided excursions into imagination. As toys, they let youngsters try out different identities and behaviors without real-life consequences. In addition, they can provide inspiration and apprenticeship for future artists. Many important figures of live-actor theater, including Johann Wolfgang von Goethe, Constantin Stanislavski, and Frederico García Lorca cut their theatrical teeth putting on puppet shows as children.

But child care is just one dimension of puppets' social service work. They have routinely participated in education, health care, commerce, and even law enforcement. Plus, they have helped to transmit and conserve culture.

Puppets tutor adults as well as children. Language instruction is one of their specialties, perhaps because they help to ease self-consciousness as well as drudgery of memorizing. For at least half a century, puppetry has been included as a pedagogical tool in teacher-training courses for adult literacy and immigrant language instruction around the world.

Teaching history is another puppet forte partly because puppets can be made to look like the historical figures they impersonate. And, oddly, they can sometimes be more believable in their roles than flesh-and-blood actors can. Once an audience has taken the imaginative leap to accept a constructed actor as alive, it takes little more to believe that the actor is Cleopatra, Abraham Lincoln, or Mahatma Gandhi.

As teachers and child-care workers, puppets have responded to changing technology, moving into film, television, and computer animation. Bil Baird created some of the earliest educational puppet films, including one series that featured a rod-puppet French instructor named Monsieur Patapouf. South

An early twentieth-century Christmas postcard showing a girl's delight in her new pantin. These little puppet toys were such a craze at times among children and young women that guardians of the social order began to view them askance. In the mid-eighteenth century, pantins were banned for a time, allegedly out of concern that their use by pregnant women could produce newborns with their legs all akimbo.

OPPOSITE: An early critter from Macy's Thanksgiving Day Parade. Macy's launched its parades in 1924 as a kind of circus procession with elephants, camels, bands, and floats. Three years later, the store asked puppeteer and designer Tony Sarg, who also created Macy's animated Christmas window displays, to invent huge balloon characters as the parade's focus. The initial upside-down marionettes—including a dragon and a toy soldier—came primarily from Sarg's imagination, but also included the cartoon figure Felix the Cat. Later balloon beasts have mainly incarnated popular cartoon characters.

Chinese children playing with marionettes in a painting from the Ming Dynasty (1368–1644). This distinctive control mechanism is still used in China.

Africa's Handspring Puppet Company has developed multimedia puppet programs to teach science.

The Muppets of *Sesame Street*, which began broadcasts in 1969, gave children such a leg up in reading and arithmetic that many early-grade school curricula were adjusted upward. (Other Muppets, meanwhile, were teaching lessons in salesmanship and corporate creativity to IBM employees in a series of films commissioned by the company.) On French television, the little puppets Chapi and Chapo wove educational material in each episode of their childrens' show, which began in 1974. More recent additions to the ranks of puppet instructors include a feline family based in a library in *Between the Lions* and a

team of "Space Puppets" with expertise in English grammar.

Puppets have also taught religion. Southeast Asian shadow shows enacting *The Ramayana* and *The Mahabharata* transmit not only the stories of the Hindu epics but social values. The dalang puppeteer-priests act as moral guides as well as entertainers. Puppets serve in Western Christian ministries as well. Scores of books tutor Sunday school teachers on using puppet shows in their classrooms. Instructors can purchase readymade sets of bible-character puppets as well as pint-size, hip, born-again believers ready to act out their faith. Preprinted fabric panels feature cut-and-sew hand puppets of Adam and Eve, Jonah and the whale, and Noah with pairs of elephants, bears, and lady-

World's Fair in 1934 and a candy-munching Ghanean hand puppet named Sweettooth in the 1980s, have helped to engage generations of young audiences for lessons about oral care. Nurses in 1960s Hong Kong staged shadowplays with cardboard puppets to teach about food safety and hazardous toys, and in sub-Saharan Africa, nutritionists have long used miniature actors to alert mothers to the dangers of contaminated water. Escobar Duarte's mask and puppet shows in the slums of northern Brazil have included all kinds of public health campaigns. In the U.S., longtime Henson associate Leslee Asch's puppet show about nutrition, *Crunchy Colors*, has periodically been revived over three decades on the Floating Hospital ship. Even the Punch clan sometimes joins in the effort. In the Czech Republic, Kašpárek has costarred with Infectious Bacteria and Fly in a play about good sanitation and ventilation.

Puppets' court-jester-like license has allowed them to include sex education and family planning in their social-work portfolios even in cultures where such dicey subjects are practically taboo. In Benin, certain *gelede* puppets demonstrate proper sexual comportment, showing positions for intercourse and even ejaculating coconut-milk "semen." In Ahmedabad and Rajasthan, in western India, hand puppets get away with performing didactic skits on the sometimes explosive issue of birth control. Gary Friedman's Puppets Against AIDS have spread their message, including condom use, through much of southern Africa and parts of East Africa. In Islamic Java, *wayang* clowns sporting the old-fashioned jumbo penises have demonstrated how to put on a condom.

Since at least the mid-twentieth century puppets have also aided in psychological and physical therapy. As psychiatric diagnostic aids, puppets can help therapists to get information: Improvising with puppets, patients may reveal angers, fears, longings, and attitudes they normally hide. Counselers often suggest that

bugs. *The Eyes of Tammy Faye,* a documentary about the televangelists Jim and Tammy Faye Bakker, shows how their puppet acolytes helped to spread the faith.

Puppets often speak to immediate moral crises. For example, after the genocide in Rwanda and Burundi, UNICEF-sponsored puppet shows in a refugee camp urged nonviolence. To help counteract prejudice against AIDS victims, the South African *Sesame Street* added an HIV-positive Muppet to its regular cast in 2002. Characters from the Israeli and Palestinian versions of the show sometimes play together.

Community medicine is another puppet specialty. Miniature dental hygienists, such as the talking molar Jimmy Chew at Chicago's

Shari Lewis and her sock-puppet sidekick, Lamb Chop. An early entry in children's puppet television, Lewis starred in award-winning shows from the mid-1950s until shortly before her death in 1988. The daughter of a vaudeville magician, she learned ventriloquism from the African-American puppeteer John W. Cooper.

The Conquest of Mexico performed by puppets of El Teatro Campesino in 1978. Luis Valdez founded the company in 1965 to help organize migrant workers in California. For several years, the troupe performed in the fields with Cesar Chavez's fledgling farm workers' union and helped to raise consciousness and money for the cause. In 1968 Valdez expanded El Teatro Campesino's mission to include reflecting and affirming Chicano culture. *The Conquest of Mexico* used the style of traditional Mexican hand puppets to show Hernando Cortés' subjugation of the indigenous peoples.

The Brewery Puppet Troupe's quartet of doo-wop crows, the Crowtations, presenting the history of Harriet Tubman and the Underground Railroad. Founded by Brad Brewer in 1973, the troupe enacts well-known and less-well-known stories from African-American history. In 1999 they created a show about Lewis Latimer, the self-educated son of black slaves who became an inventor associated with Thomas Edison. The Crowtations also perform rap and motown and are favorite street players in New York's Central Park.

Local children exchanging greetings with a character manipulated by Yaya Coulibaly. The son of a traditional puppeteer, Coulibaly not only performs for entertainment but also as part of initiation rituals. His Sologon troupe, founded in 1980, has played throughout the world.

trauma victims, including children, use puppets to demonstrate experiences they would otherwise find impossible or unbearable to describe.

As treatment tools, puppets let patients attempt difficult social interactions through the buffer of a fake persona. Some patients who shun all flesh-and-blood companions make their first forays toward contact in this way. The Hungarian therapist Dr. Alain Polcz has described how children who refused all communication began to interact with, for example, a clueless little duck puppet that mistook shoelaces for a tasty snack of worms.

Group therapy with puppets takes place even in drug-treatment and prison situations. One program in Soweto, South Africa, used hand puppets to help inmates due for release role-play behaviors in real-world situations they might encounter outside. Group facilitators also use puppets with upscale clientele. The services of one major New York consulting firm

include a pricey program that guides Fortune 500 executives through puppet improvisations to help hone their managerial skills.

In physical therapy, puppets not only help to sustain patients' interest but can help to improve coordination. They have proven particularly helpful in speech therapy. Some reticent patients become able to vocalize when they shield themselves behind a puppet persona. Many stammerers get a respite from and, perhaps, help in managing their affliction when their speech is part of a theatrical performance (with or without puppets).

Crafted performers in some societies even are believed able, in the hands of experts, to prevent or diagnose illness. In parts of southern Vietnam, armed archers made from vegetation have the power to keep sickness from entering the premises. Southern India's bommalattam puppets (the ones suspended from the handler's head) also give ritual perform-

Marionettes in Togo performing a cautionary tale about safe sex and AIDS in the early 1990s.

Similarly, in the Japanese imperial court at Nara, small effigies were rubbed over the emperor's body each month to absorb any spiritual pollution, then cast into a river.

These processes can work in reverse as well. In ancient Greece if a man wanted a certain woman to be smitten with love for him, he could bind a small effigy and attach magic inscriptions. Contemporary African and Afro-Caribbean voodoo dolls can forward bodily ills inflicted on them onto a remote live target.

Puppets have also worked in law enforcement. In many societies, people charged with imposing order are given the anonymity of a disguise which sometimes is so radical as to be a body puppet. In Benin, walking stacks of straw, twice human height, patrol at night, maintaining order and even decreeing punishments for offenders. These forbidding supernatural watchmen from secret Zangbeto voodoo societies carry an aura of authority far more daunting than any civic policemen. Marionette miniatures of these sentinels not only entertain but serve as reminders of their power.

Puppets have played a role in commerce for centuries, mainly in advertising and public relations. In seventeenth-century Paris, Jean Brioché (the first puppeteer in France for whom biographical information survives) used his little players to draw patients to his toothpulling chair near the Pont Neuf in Paris. Guignol began his career the same way, as a shill to lure mouth-pain sufferers to Laurent Mourguet's surgical pliers.

Puppets have continued to serve as marketing tools. In the 1930s, MGM advertised a film around the United States via a truck that contained a little puppet stage. Miniature look-alikes of the actors presented what would now be called a "trailer." Companies have advertised consumer products by sponsoring puppet shows, interspersing commercials in the entertainment. Many such shows played at World's Fairs—including Chicago in 1934 and San Francisco and New York in 1939. In *The Chase and Sanborn Puppet Show* at the 1939 New

ances to fight off disease. In West Africa, miniature diagnosticians, usually carved from wood, reveal information about a patient's disease to traditional healers during ceremonies conducted for that purpose.

As far back as ancient Egypt, potent figurines also have been used to help cure illness. A 4,500-year-old papyrus describes how a clay crocodile was bound to the head of migraine sufferers to relieve their symptoms. Spirit-based medicine of this sort remains widespread in West Africa. In a voodoo hospital in Seko, Togo, potent stone or wooden images minister to patients suffering from physical ailments or spiritual disorders such as lovesickness. Local healers sometimes prescribe special carved figures for patients to harbor. If a sickness stems from malicious spells, these constructed medical aides can neutralize the malefaction, or if necessary the malefactor. Other medical puppets act as surrogates to accept transfers of sickness from patients. In Sri Lanka shamans lure disease into special constructed bodies, which they then send floating away down the river.

York World's Fair, marionette versions of Messrs. Chase and Sanborn bicycled on stage to advertise their coffee. During the same era "Fashionettes," super-model string puppets by American puppet master Sue Hastings, presented the latest fashions in *Harper's Bazaar*.

More recently, Jim Henson's Muppets worked predominently in television commericals during their early years, though Henson removed them from the commercial sales force when they became regulars on *Sesame Street*. Across the world, Rajasthani puppets promoting family planning also promoted Lifebouy soap.

Celebrity puppets have endorsed all manner of merchandise. Punch has lent his name and likeness to products from upscale Cuban cigars to household mops, and has advertised everything from candy to ladies' shoes. Kasperle has appeared in print ads for Volkswagen. Javanese *wayang* sell all manner of products in print and on television. And portrait puppets of live stars—from the Three Stooges to *NSYNC— not only have plugged the originals but have themselves been money-makers.

Another multi-million dollar marketing strategy is puppet mascots. Some are conceived from the start as puppets, such as the Pets.com dog and Bayer Japan's sock-puppet-dog veterinarian, Dr. Heart, which hawks flea and tick medication. Most, though, start out as characters in television or print ads or on product packaging, and then puppet versions spin off as premiums. By making Pillsbury's Poppin Fresh or the Snuggle Fabric Softener Bear or Jolly Green Giant vegetables' little Sprout into interactive playmates, marketers foster brand recognition and loyalty.

Some of puppets' service to their society is less tangible. Their prominence in so many public

A jointed cardboard Howdy Doody selling white bread. Howdy's celebrity-endorsement portfolio followed (and created) the tastes of his fans through grade school in the 1950s—including Wonder Bread, Blue Bonnet Margerine, Welch's Grape Juice and Howdy's own Ice Cream Cake Roll. Donald Duck and other Disney characters also took advantage of their fame to sell white bread, sugary cereals, and toys.

Ralph Lee's "Ghost of Tom" wafting through Greenwich Village during the annual Halloween parade. Begun by Lee in 1973 as a trick-or-treat entourage for his children, the event mushroomed into a yearly revel with twenty thousand participants and 1.5 million spectators. Lee, who bequeathed the Halloween parade to others after nine years, founded the Mettawee River Company in 1975. His dramatizations of myths and legends from around the world often involve oversize, visually spectacular puppets.

celebrations, including religious rituals, political events, and civic activities, helps create common reference points that forge the sense of belonging to a community. The oversize *gigantões* at Brazilian carnivals, the mobile animal-stage puppets of Mali's masquerades, and the upside-down marionettes of New York's Thanksgiving Day Parade become icons of a sort, reinforcing a sense of cultural identity and continuity.

Puppet theater may also be the oldest mass medium, creating and communicating shared references across divides of class, ethnicity, and geography. In Song Dynasty China, a thousand years ago, the very same puppet troupes played at court, in wealthy homes, at public tea houses, and in peasant villages. Many generations of illiterate Sicilian farmers learned stories of the Christian Crusades and chivalric tales from rod marionettes.

The conduit of information and ideas goes from the lower classes up as well as from the top down. Java's shadow-puppet buffoons, for example, have the ear of wealthy, powerful citizens, and can use their pulpit and jesters' license to inform those people about the problems that common folks face.

With its portability and adaptability, puppet theater has reached populations with little access to other forms of culture. Before electronic media, puppets often provided a window to the outside for isolated rural dwellers. Itinerant Karagöz performers regularly stopped at mountain villages in Turkey and on Cyprus, providing not just entertainment but up-to-date news. Mamulengo still plays a similar role in remote areas of northern Brazil.

For groups uprooted by war or other social or natural upheavals, puppets can provide cultural lifelines. Constructed actors have often entertained soldiers stationed in remote outposts. In fourteenth-century China, shadow puppets accompanied the Yuan troops on military campaigns to amuse them between battles. Greek Karagiozis master Sotiris Spatharis wrote about being called from his World War I soldiering

A portable puppet theater and a soldier in Yunnan Province, south-central China, in 1917.

duties in Thessalonika to play for officers and soldiers. Puppeteers also were at the trenches entertaining French, Italian, and German soldiers. During the second world war, Both Hitler and Stalin drafted puppets to perform behind and even at the front lines.

Puppet theaters also have been cobbled together in field hospitals and prison camps. Wounded Allied soldiers during World War II created puppet theaters to entertain one another. At Thereisenstadt, the Nazi "show" concentration camp outside Prague, an inmate named Freddy Hirsch ran a shadow theater for children, who made and operated their own cardboard puppets before being deported and murdered. Czech women imprisoned at the Nazi concentration camp at Ravensburg put together a puppet theater. Even amid the butchery of the death camps at Auschwitz and

Charles Tebbutt, a London cabbie, provides on-the-job entertainment with homemade puppets in his ingenius theater setup, circa 1937.

Birkenau in 1943, a Polish prisoner named Wakdenar Nowakowski wrote puppet plays and, it seems, managed to perform them.

Puppets often migrate with resettled immigrant populations, keeping their mother culture alive. The earliest European settlers in the Americas brought constructed performers from home. In sixteenth-century Mexico, the Spanish conquistador Hernando Cortés even took a puppeteer with him on a six-month gold-hunting expedition.

Half a millennium later, old Iberian folk puppets thrive in contemporary Latin America. The Argentinian performer Ariel Bufano toured in the late 1900s with a folding altarpiece-stage adapted from medieval Spanish puppetry. The huge-faced *gigantes,* or "fatheads," that still perform in Central and South America look just like *cabezudos,* the commoner-clowns of Spain's five-hundred-year-old Gigantes y Cabezudos festivals (though the figures have morphed into predatory bigshots, such as the Nicaraguan dictator Anastasio Somoza). "Papa" Agrippino Manteo carried Sicily's rod marionette tradition with him from Catania first to Argentina and then, in 1919, to the Lower East Side of New York City, where it thrived for three quarters of a century, passing from father to son. Trick puppets from Martin Powell's eighteenth-century London theater crossed the ocean with immigrants. They thrived in vaudeville, and some remain standard acts in the American puppet repertory.

A puppetry workshop for Nazi soldiers in 1940. Hermann Schultze (left) demonstrates the hand position for manipulating traditional Kasperle hand puppets. Well, not exactly traditional. Schultze's Kasperle has the Aryanized features favored by the Reichinstitut für Puppenspiel, for which Schultze, the repertory advisor, created anti-semitic play adaptations. His was one of many German puppet companies drafted to entertain troops.

Polichinelle aboard a troop ship in the 1850s. Using a horse stall as a castelet, Polichinelle demonstrates truncheon technique to French soldiers headed for battle in the Crimean War.

BAGATTELLARO

A Naples street puppeteer in an 1840 painting and his contemporary counterpart on a Cairo street in 2000. Despite the miles and the years that separate them, the shows they performed were probably as similar as their gear. The Egyptian had just packed up after performing an Aragos farce; the Neopolitan would surely have presented Aragos's cousin Pulcinella. Prior to electronic media, few cultural phenomena bridged geography and time as broadly as these popular puppets.

In fact, puppet theater is generally stable compared with other types of performance and so works as a cultural conservator. Chinese marionettes today use the same idiosyncratic paddle-with-hook mechanism pictured in Ming Dynasty paintings (see page 188). Itinerant puppeteers in contemporary Turkestan use a tent-castelet similar to one described by a seventeenth-century traveller in Russia and Iran.

To a degree, continuity is built into a theater of constructed actors. Unlike living performers, puppets can be maintained in their original form. Ones that become frail or creaky with age can be fixed or reproduced rather than replaced by an entirely different performer. When a puppet character transfers from one handler to another, it retains not only its performance history but its outward appearance and its anatomy, the mechanisms that determine how it can move. And so constructed actors can survive their handler's biological death. Josef Skupa's disciple Miloš Kirschner was able, with Skupa's blessing, to carry on with the satiric duo Spejbl and Hurvínek. And Michael Meschke was able to revive the *Faust* that his teacher Harro Siegel had created, using Siegel's original marionettes.

ABOVE: A traditional demon and a modern bandit in Thai *nang talung* shadow-theater. The weapons, clothes, and physiognomy of these painted leather puppets reflect their different eras, but the basic look of the traditional bad guy carries over to his contemporary counterpart. Like the old *yaksa,* the modern outlaw has bug eyes, a wide mouth, and long, pointed fingernails. The bandit's beard and eyebrows create a facial contour similar to the older puppet's. And his rifle takes the place of the demon's baton.

LEFT: Contemporary shadow puppets of Chinese workers. Although they portray very different subjects than their traditional forbears did, these figures maintain a link to the past by using the same basic visual and movement styles, including arm and waist hinges, as pre-Revolution shadow puppets. (See, for example, the endpapers.)

OVERLEAF: A traditional puppet in Buon Me Thuot village in the central highlands of Vietnam. In areas of North and Central Vietnam where ethnic minority cultures had been suppressed for decades, puppets and puppeteers emerged again as soon as they were permitted to perform. This well-endowed character appeared in 1993, as part of a showcase of traditional arts.

Kathakali puppets in Kerala, in southwest India. The local hand-puppet tradition, passed down through families for generations, became a miniature version of *kathakali* religious dance-drama around the eighteenth century.

In the West, where live-actor theater normally passes down only the dialogue from one production to another, puppet stages pass down not just words, but sets, costumes, music, blocking, phrasing, interpretation, and actors. Guignol today looks and acts substantially the same as Mourguet's version. An eighteenth-century Dutch Jan Klaassen and a modern English Punch could swap roles and hardly miss a beating.

Of course the puppets adapt and mutate as life around them changes. As the tourist trade in Thailand spawned bevies of sexy hostesses and entertainers, risqué ladies also began by the mid-twentieth century to show up in shadow plays. During the Cultural Revolution in China, when most traditional culture, from

clothing styles to family roles, was crushed, shadow puppets altered their wardrobes and their subject matter. Still, in both cases, the basic form of the puppets survived.

The originally Hindu *wayang* of Java even adapted to religious conversion all over Southeast Asia. Indonesian Christians took the format of *wayang* to make shadow-puppet images of Jesus, Mary, and Joseph for Nativity plays. More typically, though, *wayang kulit* kept the names, family ties, and basic shapes of the original Hindu characters when the theological environment changed. Characters from the Hindu epics are the chief players in shadow shows in Cambodia, which is Theravada Buddhist. In Indonesia and Malaysia, which are primarily Muslim, the Hindu *wayang kulit* has

survived despite the region's conversion to Islam, which forbids human and animal images. The puppets' Islamic faith sometimes figures in the story line. In one Javanese shadow play, the popular clown and incognito god Semar decides to make a pilgrimage to Mecca. When non-Muslim forces rise in opposition, a great jihad erupts, sparking the cosmic battle that climaxes every *wayang* performance.

In Africa, puppet breeds have thrived with little mutation for generations and even centuries. Most have weathered tremendous cultural changes including, in some cases, Christian and Islamic campaigns to annihilate such "idols." Malian bird puppets that an Arab traveler saw in the fourteenth century have descendants in the region today.

Puppet characters sometimes extend the artistic longevity of their flesh-and-blood counterparts. Live-actor commedia dell'arte waned in the mid-eighteenth century but the form remained lively on the small-actor stage for another 150 years. A family of commedia puppets even figures in Carlo Collodi's 1883 puppet classic *Pinocchio*. Europe's religious Mystery plays, nearly defunct in live-actor theater by the end of the sixteenth century, continued in puppet shows well into the nineteenth century and sporadically after then. If one includes movable crèches, first cousins to puppets, a lively tradition of constructed-actor Mystery plays can be said to survive to this day.

"Toy Theater," which became popular in nineteenth-century Europe, also preserved live-

Jesus center screen in *wayang wahyu*, Indonesia's Christian shadow puppetry. As in the traditional Hindu *wayang*, the forces of disorder and evil are arrayed to the puppeteer's left while the good characters (adorned with halos) are lined up to his right.

OVERLEAF: A puppet version of *The Passion* in Brussels. This 1982 production was staged by the seventh in the line of Brussels's "Toone" puppet masters—a non-hereditary dynasty begun in the 1830s and carried on by successive artists who have adopted the tradition and the name. From their medieval beginnings, Europe's religious pageants (both puppet and live-actor versions) mingled contemporary local types with the biblical characters. All Toone shows feature the mischievous free spirit Woltje (sporting his signature checkered jacket), who narrates, comments on, and sometimes participates in the action.

The box for a shadow-theater game set. While Europe's art cabarets, such as the Chat Noir in Paris, featured sophisticated, avant-garde shadow theater performances, this boxed game contained instructions and props for bringing the latest thing in theater into your own living room.

actor shows after those shows closed. Printers in several countries sold sheets with toy versions of current live-actor hits: tiny-scale black-and-white or color scenery plus portraits of the original actors dressed and posed for various scenes. The paper images could be pasted on cardboard, colored if necessary, and "tinseled" with metal foil, fabric, and leather for the characters' armor, clothing, and boots. (Some of these toy theaters, by Pollock's of London, still are being made and sold.) This pre-electronic Masterpiece Theater enabled home audiences

to see the great Edmund Kean performing as Richard III, Macbeth, Shylock, Brutus, and Lear, long after the shows had closed. When Loïe Fuller was wowing turn-of-the-twentieth-century audiences in Europe and America with "dances" of incandescent light on her diaphanous scarves, a toy version let home puppeteers recreate her show, even shining light through the floor, as Fuller did. Decades before the advent of photography, let alone film or video, paper puppets were conserving the great theater of the day for posterity.

A Greek Karagiozis toy theater. These characters, meant to be cut out and hinged with knotted cord, include (left to right) the devil, an Orthodox priest, the Vizier, and Karagiozis's sons Skorpios (facing right) and Mpirikokos.

BELOW: A nineteenth-century French toy theater sheet. The characters here include Polichinelle (far left), the devil (center top), Harlequin (to the devil's right), Pierrot (far right), and other stock characters.

CHAPTER 10

Crossing Between Worlds

ALTHOUGH PUPPETS' FUNDAMENTAL GENIUS lies in their ability to come alive, some of their most awe-inspiring feats involve being dead. For Gordon Craig, the special appeal of an "über-marionette" was that it could incarnate existence beyond the flesh-and-blood world. It could offer a "glimpse of that spirit which we call Death." His new brand of actor, he said, "will not compete with life—rather go beyond it. . . . it will aim to clothe itself with a death-like beauty while exhaling a living spirit." This alive/dead bi-valence is puppetry's unique charge.

Straddling mortality, puppets have often been the performers of choice for plays that cross the life/death divide. In some cases, playwrights conceive such works with puppets in mind. For example, Maurice Maeterlinck specified that marionettes should perform his 1894 *Death of Tintagiles*, a nightmare about the sacrifice of an innocent. Other times, the casting choice comes from the director. August Strindberg wrote *A Ghost Sonata* for live performers, but Roman Paska's 1994 staging with the Swedish Marionetteatern smudged the play's murky life/death border even further by double-casting live actors and puppets in the same roles. Here was an apt ensemble to play Strindberg's restive phantoms and morbidly alive wretches.

Puppets from bygone times, or that recall bygone times, can serve to conjure a world that no longer exists on earth. The old-fashioned actors that Czech puppet master Věra Říčařová animates and the ravaged, phthisic characters in Jan Švankmajer's puppet films seem to be testifying from their own afterlife, evoking the era when they were alive.

ARTISTS HAVE SOMETIMES highlighted puppets' life-straddling stunts by juxtaposing constructed performers with live ones in unexpected ways. Often, the puppets outshine their human costars. In the Czechoslovak-American Marionette Theater's *Rusalka, the Little Rivermaid* (1984), director Vit Horejš wrought metaphysical havoc by casting his baby daughter in a cameo role among the puppets. Little Sarazina's features appeared so understated next to theirs that *she* seemed like the interloper, the fake. On the other hand, artists may challenge the illusion of the puppets' aliveness in order to emphasize the mystery of real life. In *Bird Bear* (1986) Lee Nagrin showed dolls being mauled, and then brought a live finch into the same space—suggesting the fragility and sacredness of living beings.

Live/non-alive issues have, like virtually everything, been fair game for puppet sport. Punch and Judy professors traditionally cast a real dog alongside their puppets. Toby would bark or chomp on cue and retrieve Punch's defenestrated baby from in front of the booth.

OPPOSITE: Song-and-dance skeletons in Frank Paris's *Dance Macabre*. Besides these dapper twenty-eight-inch-tall plastic hoofers, Paris's revue featured an assortment of ghouls, including fan-dance skeletons that performed with ostrich-feathers. During the mid-twentieth century, Paris's marionettes played at Radio City Music Hall and Madison Square Garden and on early television's variety shows. Paris made the original Howdy Doody marionette, which was replaced following a dispute over spin-off rights.

Silent witnesses in the Théâtre du Soleil's *Terrible but Unfinished Story of Norodom Sihanouk, King of Cambodia* (1985). These figures by sculptor Erhard Stiefel represent a cross-section of Cambodian society from peasants to royalty—and suggest the victims of Cambodia's wars and the Khmer Rouge genocide. Ranged in high, shallow niches around the walls of the Cartoucherie theater, observing as their country's catastrophic history unfolds on the stage, they recall figures that look out from the high mountain graves in Sulawesi (see page 219).

Old-style puppets evoking a lost era in *Piskanderula* by the Czech artists František and Věra, presented in New York in 1996. Arrayed about the stage, these denizens of the past seem almost like spirits hovering about a graveyard and then, one by one, coming alive. Founding members (chief designer and a main puppeteer) of the Czech state puppet theater Drak, František and Vítek and Věra Říčařová left that company in 1981 and now create their own installations and presentations in a small workshop/theater outside Prague.

OPPOSITE: Ilka Schönbein with a ghastly figure in *Metamorphoses of Metamorphosis* (1994), a solo street performance by Schönbein's Theater Meschugge, based in Germany. Wordless vignettes evoke the terror and despondency of Central Europe's Jewish ghettoes, with puppet characters that include a lecherous rat, a predatory spider, and a raven.

Neville Tranter in a tug-of-war straddling the border between life and death in a 1992 performance of *Manipulator and Underdog*. Here the puppet to which Tranter imparts life is trying to kill him.

Among the most popular trick puppets across centuries and cultures have been corpses and skeletons that collapsed in pieces and then miraculously reassembled and scampered off.

GENERALLY, THOUGH, breaching the border between the inert and the living is no laughing matter. It is taboo. And it is treacherous. From popular legends, to fiction, to religious teachings, people who imbue matter with life usually pay dearly for it. Even Carlo Collodi's Pinocchio wreaks all kinds of mischief for Geppetto, the kindly old woodcarver who made him. Usually, the consequences are more grim. The out-of-control golem of Prague and Dr. Frankenstein's homicidal monster imperil the whole society.

Sigmund Freud posited that the ambiguity between automatons and living creatures gave people a profound sense of unease, of the "uncanny." In fact, puppets crossing into life is a frequent subject of horror films, such as *Magic*, about an evil ventriloquist dummy, the Chucky movies, featuring a doll possessed by a serial strangler, *Attack of the Puppet People* and the *Puppet Master* series. The composer Charles Gounod made his 1872 "Funeral March of a Marionette" sound so spooky that it became the

theme music for Alfred Hitchcock's television mystery series.

Even good-natured puppets that come alive bode trouble. A thousand years ago, the Japanese considered it ominous if Buddhist statues began to cry, sweat, or grow hair. In modern times, puppeteers in China's western Fujian region follow prescribed steps to keep the *chou* clown marionettes from coming to life, leaving their storage cases and causing mayhem. Similarly, should the benevolent, sacred *barong landungs* of Bali come alive with no one animating them, priests must spring into action to appease them back to dormancy.

Because puppets are so potent, people who handle them often possess special religious authority and abilities. Balinese *dalangs* are considered priests as well as entertainers, and their performances frequently are part of temple festivals or blessing ceremonies. The artists of *nang talung* shadow theater in southern Thailand also are in touch with elements of magic, with certain characters being especially powerful. In Niger and Nigeria, puppeteers have supernatural gifts that enable them to pierce their own or a spectator's tongue or eyes, eat glass, or sit on a sharp, pointed stick. The

A plucked performer in *Zooedipous* (1999) by the Argentinian company El Periférico de Objectos. Looking at Sophocles' tragic hero through the lens of Kafka, the show plays at the border where the inorganic, the living, and the dead all challenge one another. The cast includes not only live actors and puppets but chickens and insects, variously alive and dead, on stage and in projections. A dead chicken's entrails are read for prophecy—but dead chickens also, as here, are manipulated like puppets.

most magically endowed of these artists reputedly can bring puppets to life and change humans into monkeys.

Another testimony to the formidable power of puppets is the fervor with which they have sometimes been killed. Anecdotal accounts of puppeticide in Western culture go back more than two thousand years. A Greek explorer about 100 B.C.E. reported that Celtic tribes routed malevolent forces by torching colossal wickerwork dummies, which had been imbued with anima by being crammed with live prisoners. In 1601 some Belgian constructed actors accused of immorality were burnt as heretics (and the wife of the puppeteer was condemned as a witch).

IN MANY CULTURES, crafted beings straddle the living/non-living divide by serving as substitute bodies for spirits whose original bodies have died. These replacement bodies may be life-size or miniature, may have movable limbs or not, and may resemble the deceased or follow a conventional style. Sometimes they incorporate the person's clothing or bones to attract the spirit or make it feel at home. Or the entire corpse may be doctored so that it can be moved like a puppet. Into the nineteenth century, some Catalan fishermen reportedly would take the corpse of a departed friend to the local inn for a final game of cards, manipulating it through the necessary moves. The use of retrofitted or newly constructed bodies to house spirits occurs among societies as geographically disparate as the Maori of New Zealand, the Batak on Sumatra, the Babwende in West Africa, and the Kwakuitl of North America's northwest coast.

One common function for such after-market bodies is at funerals. During this transition between earthly and post-earthly life, the

Pale, life-size mannequins haunting *The Dead Class* (1975) by the Polish painter and director Tadeusz Kantor (leaning on the back row). In Kantor's holocaust-stamped theater, puppets such as these, tossed or lugged around by spectral-looking live actors, were apparitions of destroyed lives. In his manifesto, "The Theatre of Death," Kantor wrote, "The MANIKIN in my theatre is to become a MODEL that mediates a strong sense of DEATH and the condition of the Dead. It is to be a model for the Live ACTOR."

Si galegale funeral puppets from Sumatra. Among the Batak people of Lake Toba, these articulated effigies moved by wires perform to appease the spirit of a man who died childless. Traditionally, the skull of the dead man, decorated with soot and fruit, was the puppet's head, and this composite body went through the required rituals. More recently, the *si galegale* has come to incarnate the deceased's non-existent son, and the skull has been exchanged for a painted wood head. The "son" performs mourning rites to keep the dead spirit from plaguing the living.

deceased often needs a physical presence in order to participate in the sendoff rituals. Afterward, in some cases, the constructed body remains among the living. There it may serve as a remembrance or it may provide permanent quarters for the spirit, either continuously or on its periodic visits. Among Melanesian peoples in coastal New Guinea, families keep and pray to the funerary statue, a wooden body with the deceased person's skull for its head. One of this *kowar*'s eye sockets is filled, letting the spirit keep tabs on terrestrial goings on. Turks in parts of Central Asia harbor *kugurcak* ("puppets") of dead relatives, to which they proffer affection and food.

Often spirits of the dead use puppet bodies not just to keep an eye on the living but to par-

ticipate in the ongoing ritual life of their society. Ancestors can be an imposing presence at ceremonies in puppet bodies either left from their funeral or specially constructed. Among the Tolai people of New Britain, a female ancestor appears at funerals and other important occasions as a humongous figure with a cone-shaped head and a body made of leaves. In traditional Kwakuitl initiations, a nearly life-size ancestor effigy is draped over the body of the initiate, who wears it like a necklace: The live person's head pokes through the puppet's rope belly, letting the ancestor's wooden arms and head dangle down in the front, and its legs hang down in the back.

Instead of remaining among the living as a pied à terre for the spirit, the constructed funerary figure may transport the soul of the deceased into its afterlife. Often, the spirit's two physical bodies—the cadaver and the ritual body—are buried together. Additional constructed attendants may accompany the deceased into the tomb, that is, into the next existence. In ancient China, the entourage for important people ranged from simple straw *yong* figures used three millenia ago, to articulated wood and clay versions a few centuries later, to the retinue of thousands of detailed, life-size terra-cotta soldiers and horses buried in Xi'an, China, with a third-century B.C.E. emperor.

When Egypt's pharaohs and VIPs entered the afterlife in mummified or constructed bodies, they too brought along hundreds, even thousands, of followers made of wood or faience. Many of these servants were simple, stylized *ushabti* figures, but others were crafted in detail and placed in elaborate settings to perform specific tasks. The tomb of Meketre, a high official under late eleventh- and early twelfth-dynasty pharaohs circa 2000 B.C.E., includes two dozen miniature boatloads of attendants fishing, baking, weaving, tending cattle and so forth. Meketre's storehouse manager Wah was buried near these boats, perhaps so he might continue to oversee expenditures.

Some constructed funerary bodies are designed to transform in view of the mourners, modeling the dead person's transfiguration from an earthly state to some different kind of existence. They may be made from perishable grasses and fruits that will decay back into nature much as the corpse will. Often, temporary

A dead man in the Lower Congo making his farewell rounds. Through the early twentieth century, the Babwende people constructed gigantic *niombo* figures for very important or wealthy citizens who had died. The corpse was dried over a fire, swathed in hundreds of yards of cotton cloth, raffia fabric and blankets, then decorated with the appropriate facial features and clan tattoos. Just before burial, the *niombo* danced its way (with the help of carriers) through the important locations of the person's life.

A Fon woman in Benin looking after dead twins. When one twin dies, the mother continues to nurture it using a small wooden substitute body. Once both twins have died, they are kept together in the form of carved-wood figurines. This woman is looking after the *hovi* twin dolls of her father and his twin brother as well as a twin statue she found and took under her care.

bodies are cremated, sending the spirit to its next abode in the form of smoke. Marco Polo wrote of paper dolls being burned at a funeral in China in 1280—either modeling the deceased's change from a corporeal to an invisible state, or sending company to the dead one. In contemporary Vietnam, the Viet and Tay people burn paper effigies of the deceased along with paper replicas of household goods for use in the afterlife, items such as bicycles and more recently cell phones. Shops in overseas Chinese communities carry paper clothing, running shoes, and kitchen appliances to be sent as smoke to dead relatives.

Puppets may model not only transformation of humans to their post-earthly state, but also the annual dying back and rebirth of the land. Until recently, human-shaped effigies representing winter were drowned in rural Poland and burned in Hungary each year to end their seasonal tenure. Among native North Americans, Hopi Corn Maidens and snakes perform at planting time. And during Kwakuitl winter ceremonies, the head of a string puppet is replaced with a small bird.

BESIDES ACCOMMODATING the dead, puppets provide temporary bodies for all manner of other spirits, demons, and gods. Their chief area of work besides fertility is protection, safeguarding humans and their spiritual allies. Formidable wooden guardians flank the doors of many Asian temples to keep out malevolent beings. Among the Tlingit of southern Alaska,

A perishable puppet by the Coatimundi company, from the 1970s. The lady has a dimension of genuine aliveness because it is clear that, like all living things, she will die. Made of such ephemeral materials as flower petals, she will barely outlive a performance. Coatimundi was founded in Mexico in 1972 by French artists Jean-Claude Leportier and Catherine Krémer, then relocated to Provence in 1981. The company works with puppets, automatons, animated objects, masks, and mime.

A family enjoying afternoon tea in Michoacan, Mexico, on the Day of the Dead. Each year on November first and second, Mexicans bring out skeleton mannequins and puppets, from tiny to lifesize, fancifully decked out in tableaux that mimic daily life. The skeletons create a hospitable environment for the dead, who visit their families during the celebration. In this nominally Christianized, pre-Columbian ritual, the living offer flowers and food, including skulls made of bread or sugar. For at least a century, the skeleton figures have often been satiric, a tradition fostered by woodcut artist Jose Guadalupe Posada.

Burning bulls carry passengers to their next, incorporeal existence in a 1983 cremation in Peliatan, Bali. The remains of the dead, in this case three people, wrapped in cloth, are placed inside bulls made of basketry and paper. Amid prayers and offerings, the animals are set ablaze, taking their charges into the world of spirits in the form of smoke. Because cremation ceremonies are expensive and must take place at certain auspicious times, the dead often wait for years in temporary graves before being exhumed for their journey onward.

a shaman's gear included painted wooden figurines with human hair and, typically, extra faces or eyes to keep away evil spirits. These guardians would taste the shaman's water for any signs of supernatural infection and after the shaman's death might remain with the corpse to deflect hostile beings. Among Christians, the potent objects have generally been more stylized and emblematic. Crucifixes, St. Anthony medals, and other amulets and icons can effect communication with or draw protection or mercy from supernatural beings.

Spirits also inhabit puppets for divination. In Sierra Leone, supernatural forces cause certain puppets to lurch or lean in coded gestures that experts in such matters can interpret. In Congo during the first part of the twentieth century, *Galukoji*, carved heads at the end of an accordion-gate mechanism, had the power to finger criminals by springing out at the mention of their names.

In many religions people literally take divinity inside themselves by means of puppets—ingesting icons endowed with potency. For the feast of Huitzilopochtli in ancient Mexico, an

effigy of the god, made from seeds and blood, was divided and eaten as part of the ritual. In sections of eastern India and Tibet, sacrificial cakes called *gtor-ma*, made from barley flour, butter, and water, are shaped to represent certain deities. Medieval Christians similarly used sanctified flour to bake bread in the shape of religious figures, continuing the practice for centuries even after an eighth century synod banned it. At Easter in parts of Italy today, Christians eat a *colomba*, a cake shaped like a dove, an embodiment of the Holy Ghost. And in Communion rituals, the faithful ingest wine and wafer ritually transubstantiated into the body of a god. Gingerbread men, eaten at Christmas, may be vestiges of a related ritual.

SOMETIMES, RATHER THAN supplying physical accommodations for an incorporeal spirit, puppets provide a means for humans to control beings that are out of their physical reach. The ancient Greeks and some of their fourth century B.C.E. neighbors restrained hostile gods, spirits, or humans by "binding" a small effigy—tying a statue's hands and feet, gagging it, or confining it in a jar—and inscribing or enclosing a written spell. Voodoo believers in West Africa and Haiti, as well as contemporary wiccan cults, perform similar rituals. Burning of effigies may derive from this sort of practice.

Puppets also convey the concerns of humans to supernatural powers. Among the Senufo of West Africa, wooden figures inside

Life-size *tau-tau* at the entrances to cliffside graves in Toraja in southern Sulawesi. These post-death bodies are made from several pieces of jackfruit tree wood, jointed to facilitate the *tau-tau*'s active participation in funeral ceremonies. After the corpse has been put into a cliff-side cave, a *tau-tau* dressed as the person did in life provides ongoing accommodations for the spirit, watching from a balcony by the entrance to the burial chamber, with one arm reaching out toward the living.

An eighth-century "host" figure from Teotihuacan in central Mexico. Terra-cotta statues like this one, found at pre-Columbian burial sites and other caches around Mexico and Central America, seem to have housed spirits. The hollow sculptures with removable chest panels contained tiny (two- to four-inch-high) figurines of people and, sometimes, gods.

A Tlingit shaman in 1905 holding a pair of rattles in the form of ravens. The ceremonial masks, puppets, and animal-shaped rattles of many Northwest Coast Native Americans become inhabited by spirits during rituals.

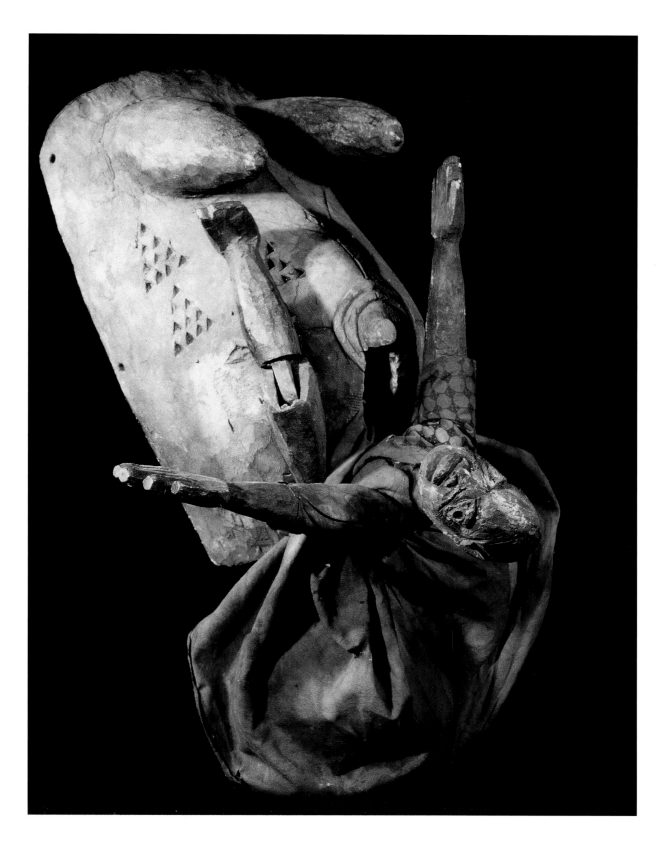

A Yoruba face-puppet giving birth to a smaller puppet. In this carved-wood creation from Nigeria, the face puppet's body corresponds to the puppeteer's facial features—breasts placed like eyes, the navel at the nose, and vagina at the mouth. The crossing of metaphysical boundaries here is doubled, or squared: inert matter endowed with life creates *another* life. Puppets spawn puppets in various cultures. One Native American shaman mask, for example, hatches a bird from the top of its head.

Rampaging *nafiq* characters at a late twentieth-century Senufo funeral in Ivory Coast. For the Senufo, the main task of funeral masks and puppets is not to host the deceased in the world of the living but to chase the dead person's spirit away to its afterlife abode. The multi-day event involves a series of formidable "masks," some of which actually are body puppets. *Nafiq,* the largest, is a quasi-buffalo up to fifteen feet long, with two men and a roaring noisemaker inside.

A St. Veronica statue in procession in Latin America. Effigies of saints carried in religious processions, particularly in southern Europe and Latin America, are respected, greeted, and implored by the faithful along the route. The cloth that St. Veronica carries, imprinted with the image of Jesus' face, is believed to have a vitality of its own, so that the figure of Veronica has a double layer of potency.

ABOVE: An early twentieth-century kachina doll, a "spirit being" of the Zuni people from western New Mexico. Kachinas are pictured on kiva walls and pottery dating back to the thirteenth century. Traditionally, a kachina doll was given to a child by a *kokko*, the spirit being of an ancestor who appeared at winter ceremonies as a masked-dancer kachina. This sixteen-inch-high *siwolo*, or buffalo kachina, with movable arms, carries a lightning stick in his left hand and originally held a rattle in his right hand. Since the 1930s, kachinas have been commericalized into souvenirs and collectable art.

TOP RIGHT: A miniature shaman of the Tlingit people of North America. This five-inch-high wooden puppet was part of a mid-nineteenth-century shaman's gear. With its own masks as well as a special headpiece and hat (not pictured here), it may have been left with a patient as a post-treatment amulet. It is adorned with paint, animal skin, human hair, beads, and tacks.

OPPOSITE: Spirits and humans mingling in the audience for a Balinese shadow play in a 1937 painting of a temple festival by Ida Bagus Made Tibah. In the foreground a man with a sacred dagger subdues a demon, while all around the courtyard tree branches seem to coil, almost like serpents.

OVERLEAF: Heroes and demons at the edge of existence in the Javanese shadow theater. As the *Mahabharata* hero Bima battles the giant Suratimantra, they wash in and out of focus, emphasizing their liminal nature on the cusp between the physical and the incorporeal. These puppets are in the style of Surakarta, central Java.

spirit houses transmit messages to beings that exist on another plane. Haitian Voodoo dolls tied to trees similarly deliver human communications to supernatural addressees. Europeans, from ancient times through the modern era, have offered their gods wax images of themselves as a kind of sacrificial offering, sometimes using a full-body effigy, sometimes just a replica of a body part that was ailing. So many of these *ex voto* figures hung from the ceiling in one Florentine church in the early seventeenth century—some six hundred life-size figures plus many smaller ones—that the place became a safety hazard, with artificial bodies and limbs periodically crashing down onto worshippers.

SOME CULTURES consider shadow puppets to exist at the intersection between the human and spiritual worlds. They inhabit the borderland between what physically exists and what does not. Viewers watch dramas enacted by characters, sets, and props that have no concrete substance, that are nothing but the absence of light from an area on a screen. While most puppets provide a corporeal pres-

ence for an imaginary or invisible being, shadow puppets incarnate beings that can live on a plane of pure spirit. Balinese and Javanese *wayang kulit* are said to play for earthly and supernatural audiences at once. That those puppets are mainly denizens of the night, when all manner of spirits prowl, makes them especially well positioned for this multi-level audience.

Incorporeal actors have been fashioned from light as well as from shadow. Early people may have used shiny mirror stone to cast shimmering images of supernatural presences. The Balinese *dalang* I Wayan Wija recently used a similar technique in *Shadow Bang* (2003), with puppets made in the traditional *wayang* style but from mirror Plexiglas. For this experiment with the Bang on a Can company, Wija's coconut-oil lamp both cast shadows of leather puppets and threw reflections of Plexiglas figures onto multiple screens. As he bent the slightly flexible plastic puppets, the images stretched and twisted with eerie otherworldliness. On a single stage, physical beings, shadow presences, and characters of disembodied light crossed into and through each other's worlds..

CHAPTER 11

Living on the Edges

Finally, then, what is a puppet? And what is not a puppet? Where are the boundaries that separate puppets from masks, amulets, dolls, statues, automatons, and illustrations? No matter how close in or far out you draft those limits, some creations straddle them, and some puppets have outposts beyond them. Normally, a kitchen fork is not a puppet—but in Lasse Akerlund's *Macbeth,* a fork plays Macduff. An amorphous shimmer of light is not, normally, a puppet—but in Ping Chong's *Kwaidan,* a pale blue glow plays a ghost. Trying to fix the limits of puppetry is a hopeless exercise. The borders are misty. And porous. And elastic.

And interesting. The territory around the edges of puppetry teems with fascinating in-between and cross-breeds. This book has already touched on a few of those murky borders: Masks and costumes disguise the handler, whereas puppets are beings distinct from the manipulator (more or less); the continuum from amulets and ritual objects to puppets involves belief versus suspension of belief and a human versus supernatural target audience. Mainly, though, the previous chapters have played fast and loose with the boundaries of puppetry. This final chapter will explore some of those edges and some of the life in the borderlands.

DOLLS

In post-antiquity Western cultures, the difference between dolls and puppets has seemed simple enough: If the figure moved via external strings or rods or a manipulator's hand inside it, it was a puppet. If it moved through direct hands-on manipulation, it was a doll. Or, using an alternate criterion, if it performed for an audience other than the person controlling it, it was a puppet. If it performed only for the benefit of the person playing with it, it was a doll.

But a little scrutiny smudges both these criteria. The dressed-stick-figure spies that Massimo Schuster hurls about in *The Mushroom* are certainly puppets: They are constructed actors performing a play for an audience. But Schuster operates these puppets mainly by direct hands-on manipulation. In Japanese bunraku, the operator who moves the character's feet uses the same hands-on technique. So mode of manipulation cannot be the acid test for puppet versus doll.

What about performing for an audience versus for oneself? Few people would dispute that a child entertaining herself with hand puppets of Kermit and Miss Piggy is playing with puppets. But how is her play with Barbie and Ken or the Teenage Mutant Ninja Turtles different from that—apart from mode of operation, already shown *not* to be the determining factor? True, children often posit a

An ivory doll from the sarcophagus of Crepereia Tryphaena, a Roman child of the second century C.E. This doll is an especially fancy one (Crepereia's family was wealthy), but even ordinary Roman girls often had dolls. On her wedding night, a girl would dedicate her doll to Venus. If she died before marriage, as Crepereia did, the doll remained with her after death. This doll's hands, feet, and head (possibly a portrait) are more finely carved than the body, which presumably would have been hidden under clothing.

OPPOSITE: "Pierrot Writing at a Desk," a musical automaton created circa 1895 by second-generation automaton-maker Gustave Vichy. Writing by the light of an oil lamp, Pierrot falls asleep, and the light goes out. He awakens and rekindles the lamp, turns his head, blinks, and resumes writing.

close personal bond with their baby dolls, but they likely do not do so with the Ninja Turtles. And ventriloquists posit a personal relationship with their puppets.

Perhaps puppets tend to come alive only when someone actively animates them, whereas dolls keep their imagined life even when they are alone. A baby doll tucked into bed stays asleep—that is, stays alive—even when its handler goes out to play, whereas a Mr. Punch hand puppet lying on a table may be inert matter. And perhaps, for this reason, dolls can simply hang out, but puppets tend to engage in active scenarios, including speech. But in all these respects, many figures usually called dolls act more like "puppets" and vice versa. Finally, the familiar Western divisions between puppets and dolls are as much arbitrary habits as meaningful distinctions. In many languages, a single noun identifies both: French *poupée*, Italian *pupi*, and Russian *kukla* all can mean both "doll" and "puppet."

STATUES

A statue is inert, whereas a puppet is imaginatively endowed with life. That border seems clear enough, yet many figures slide back and forth or inhabit an equivocal middle ground.

Just about any object *can* become a puppet by being cast as a player in a scenario. To wit, Lasse Akerlund's cutlery Macduff, Preston Foerder's cellulose-sponge frog prince, Paul Larsen's 1902 radish and beet tragedians, or, moving out of the kitchen, the Tam Tam company's pliers ballerinas and Paul Zaloom's plastic-shrub George Bush. Transforming everyday objects into puppets has become so workaday that performance artists have teased spectators with performing objects that stubbornly remain nothing but objects. Stuart Sherman would stand before an audience presenting and rearranging oranges, neckties, whatever—which steadfastly remained just oranges and neckties being moved around.

While any statue, figurative or abstract, *can*

be used as a puppet, some statues have proclivities for it. Life-size, three-dimensional figures of people or animals have an obvious advantage in seeming alive, especially if they are arranged in tableaux. Some even mingle with spectators, either infiltrating the universe of the viewer or establishing their own environment and pulling the viewer in. George Segal's life-size portrait mannequins neither move nor pretend to become alive. But apart from being chalk-white and motionless, these imposters are plausible inhabitants of the spectator's society. Glimpsed quickly, they can seem to be fellow humans. The sculpted inhabitants of Red Grooms's "Rukus" installations mostly remain stationary, but gallery visitors sitting alongside Grooms's constructed subway riders in the

walk-through *Ruckus Manhattan* (1975) have more of an I-thou relationship than one usually has with sculpture. "Puppets" or not, these figures flirt with imaginative aliveness.

Smaller-scale or larger-than-life mannequins in tableaux sometimes play at the edge of puppetry, especially if the characters are movable. They can almost seem frozen in one stop-action frame of an activity. Early twentieth-century statuettes from a miniature Sino-Vietnamese funeral now pose mid-procession in a museum case in Aix-en-Provence, France. But the eight individual pallbearers carrying the palanquin and the large contingent of silk-clad mourners are caught at one of many possible moments. They could just as well show the next instant or one ten minutes later. Folk

Alexander Calder's miniature circus, now frozen in one moment in New York's Whitney Museum. The dozens of animals, tightrope walkers, trapeze artists, weight lifters, and clowns are crafted from twisted wire plus wood, cork, and metal. Calder did solo performances with his circus starting in the 1920s and for decades afterwards. Some of his later ideas, including kinetic sculpture and stabiles, may have had their germs in his circus.

Miniature scenes crowning New Year's costumes in Switzerland's Appenzell Canton. The little tableaux of everyday life take on an odd kind of vitality as these "Shelli" and "Rolli" masqueraders go from house to house dispensing good wishes in return for food or money.

RIGHT: A late nineteenth-century mechanical crèche from Provence in southern France. Controls for all the characters connect to a clockwork apparatus in the base. As usual in the region, the Nativity scene is surrounded by the bustle of contemporary village life and local characters, including a knife-sharpener and a washerwoman.

artists in northeastern Brazil sculpt and paint groupings of inches-high clay characters—a patient and doctor in an examining room, masqueraders at a local festival, itinerant farmworker families lugging their meager belongings. These figurines can be manipulated to enact a continuing story, bringing them to the brink of puppetry.

Some tableaux actually *are* puppet companies posing off-season as sculpture, that is, fixed at one frozen moment of their show. Alexander Calder's miniature performing circus now appears as a stationary museum display. Hanne Tierney's puppets, tied into one configuration from their show, appear as installations in art galleries and museums. The puppetry in their blood tinges their character even when they are still.

A fixed grouping also can sort of come to life when the whole scene is moved about. Some traditional winter-celebration masks in northern Europe have miniature tableaux on the top. For a fête honoring St. Nichloas in Améland, Holland, inches-high children frolic with a sled on a head-top stage. The figures do not move individually but the whole scene gets a dynamic feel from being worn, animated by a live dancer. Similarly, although few of the demons, birds, and serpents on Northwest Coast Indian rattles move, they get a kind of aliveness from the rattle's motion.

In Christian societies, the most common sculpture installation is the Nativity crèche, a tradition begun by St. Francis in 1223. The first Christmas crib, variously reported as using live actors and sculptures, may have included at least one puppet: A witness reported that the "lifeless" Christ child in the manger miraculously became alive. By the eighteenth century, crèches included dozens of free-standing people and animals. Usually clay, plaster, or wood, crib figures sometimes were spun from glass or shaped from bread dough.

And some came to be animated. Most simply, the three kings would be repositioned each day moving from the outer edges of the scene

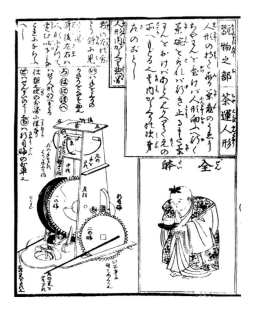

A tea-serving automaton in Hosokawa Hanzo Yorinao's three-volume *Illustrated Miscellany of Automata*, published in Japan in 1796. The doll brought a cup of tea to a guest and then, when the guest returned the empty cup, turned and walked back to the host. Automatons were so in vogue in eighteenth-century Japan that a prominent playwright and maker of mechanical dolls, Takeda Izumo, created his own theater for them in Osaka. The great bunraku playwright Chikamatsu sometimes wrote for Takeda Izumo's automaton theater. And Takeda helped to develop new mechanisms for the puppets and scenery of bunraku.

to the manger. Sometimes, though, the full cast of unarticulated figurines was moved around to perform the Christmas story. Certain crèche figures, then, were given movable limbs or props. Some of these, particularly in Poland and southern France, were internally strung with the control cords emerging at the bottom and going through slots in the crèche floor. Other crib figures developed into stringed marionettes. Where exactly along this continuum crèche figures crossed from statues into puppets is hard to say.

AUTOMATONS

Some internally-strung crèches in late eighteenth-century France developed another variation: all the controls for all the figures were rigged to a single clockwork mechanism. This brought them into another border territory: the ground where puppets meet automatons.

Automatons, that is, figures that run *auto*, on their own, have been popular since ancient times in Europe, East Asia, and the Middle East. A fifteenth-century B.C.E. statue of Memnon, in Egypt, reportedly issued melodious sounds and moved its feet at sunrise and sunset, all without any visible help from humans. In the third century B.C.E. Philo of Byzantium made mechanical people and animals that could gesture, pour liquids, fly, or sing by means of mechanical, hydraulic, or pneumatic devices. In third-century C.E. China, miniature jugglers, acrobats, wrestlers, and masqueraders, all powered by water-run machines, performed for commoners and royalty. Other inventors and engineers, including the thirteenth-century Mesopotamian Ibn Al-Razzaz Al-Jazari, created and documented all manner of mechanical marvels—used sometimes to illustrate scientific principles, but often to entertain royalty. The ninth-century B.C.E. Byzantine Emperor Theophilus held court in a throne flanked by mechanical roaring lions and shaded by a tree made of silver and gold that harbored mechanical singing birds.

Some eighteenth-century automatons achieved international celebrity, including a duck by artist-inventor Jacques de Vaucanson that could flap its wings and digest grain. Other famous automatons of the time played musical instruments, wrote letters, or served drinks. To this day, constructed creatures that seem to move on their own—from windup monkeys, to robotic pet dogs—delight and fascinate. Artists such as Nam June Paik and Mark Sussman have created performance works for entirely remote-controlled actors.

The distinction between puppets and automatons might seem straightforward. Puppets operate via direct human manipulation; automatons are machines. So, for example, string marionettes of the three Magi are puppets. But a mechanical crèche, with one gizmo moving three dozen people, sheep and oxen, is an automaton. Mr. Punch bashing pates in a portable castelet is a puppet. A miniature executioner beheading John the Baptist every hour in an eighteenth-century German clock is an automaton.

But the border is by no means clear. An internally-strung Thai puppet, clearly a *puppet*, has a dozen-plus cords threaded over tiny pulleys, emerging at the bottom and tied to little rings. Geza Blattner's internally strung puppets, with one more level of complexity, had their string-ends rigged to wooden piano-type keys. Continuing further toward machines, some nineteenth-century English peep shows had each internally strung character operated via a hand-crank. Showmen even hooked up several figures to a single hand-crank. Sometimes, instead of turning the apparatus manually, the handler ran everything with a wind-up spring. Similar setups have been run by one or more motors—and, now, those mechanisms may be run by a computer. Where along this progression puppets become automatons is a judgment call.

A figure's *puppetness* (to use the Russian master Sergei Obraztsov's term) probably has more to do with *whether* it takes on vitality than with how it does so. Even machine- or computer-controlled figures can become imaginatively alive. The wildebeests that seem to stampede toward the audience in *The Lion King* actually are mounted on half a dozen horizontal cylinders parallel to the stage front at varying distances behind it. As the cylinders rotate in place, they bring each row of puppets up from behind again and again. Certainly a complex mechanism—and certainly puppets. Constructed actors also can be remote-controlled, as characters were in sections of *The Great Muppet Caper* and subsequent Muppet films. But Kermit and friends do not stop being puppets for having microchips rather than human hands inside them.

An odd subspecies of automatons is *fake* automatons—devices operated by a live handler, but made to seem mechanical to wow audiences with the engineering genius supposedly involved. Many Japanese karakuri ningyo dolls that perform atop pageant cars have concealed humans pulling their strings or levers and turning their cogs. And some of the most famous putative automatons of eighteenth- and nineteenth-century Europe, including chess players and fortune-tellers, were notorious counterfeits with hidden live operators.

ILLUSTRATIONS
Over the centuries, illustrated storytelling has developed into puppetry—in India, Southeast Asia, East Asia, and Europe. The evolution

An animated Christmas window at Lord & Taylor department store in 1952. The American puppetry pioneer Tony Sarg, who designed Macy's window displays (and created its giant Thanksgiving parade puppets), began in 1935 to make mechanically animated scenes for the store's Christmas windows. Mechanized store-window displays soon became a New York Yuletide tradition. Here mannequins of contemporary children watch as turn-of-the-century dolls come alive in a carnival scene: As the gilt Ferris wheel slowly turns, the dolls in their swinging gondolas wave and hold up toys. The ribbon banner reads: "To laugh aloud like a child again, and see the world as you did then—this is the gift of Christmas."

A picture-storyteller with his scroll in Bihar in eastern India—probably an itinerant player performing in exchange for rice or a bit of money. Paintings like these, in story-board frames, may have developed into shadow puppets.

RIGHT: A southern Italian *cantastoria* in an anomyous 1830 colored chalk lithograph. Appropriately, these ragged performers are presenting "Cantastoria of the Madonna of Carmine," about the Virgin Mary's help to the needy.

OPPOSITE: A Cambodian *nang sbek thom* story-illustration puppet presenting a scene from the *Reamker* (the Khmer *Ramayana*). Initially these characters appear in separate one-person illustration puppets: Preah Ream (Prince Rama), in one picture-puppet, comes upon what looks like, but is not, the corpse of Neang Seda (Sita), his wife. Those two puppets are whisked out of sight, and this one emerges showing both characters in a single puppet, as Preah Ream cradles the supposed Seda. These *nang sbek thom,* similar to traditions in Thailand and parts of India, perform only the *Reamker.* Cambodian *nang shek toch* uses smaller single-character puppets, more like Javanese and Balinese *wayang kulit.*

from painted images to constructed actors involves intriguing in-between species.

Traditions of storytelling with pictures exist throughout the world. In India by the fourth century b.c.e. and possibly hundreds of years earlier, itinerant showmen displayed paintings while telling stories, probably about gods and demons. Illustrated narration seems to have moved from India through Turkey, Central Asia, and Mongolia to China, where *chuan-pien* picture scrolls are documented in the T'ang period (618–906 b.c.e.), and Java, where *wayang beber,* performance scrolls twenty inches high and up to three yards long, are documented by the early fifteenth century. Traditions of illustrated storytelling in Japan, Tibet, Iran, Syria, and Palestine all survived well into the twentieth century and some continue to thrive. In Europe, performers were presenting picture narrations in Italy and Germany by the sixteenth century, and in France and Spain by the

seventeenth. Similar entertainments probably existed in England.

These forms evolved into puppetry along several paths. In parts of India and in Thailand and Cambodia, large paintings were broken into smaller units with one or two characters and their immediate surroundings. The pictures appeared in sequence, showing events that a storyteller narrated. At some point, these figures came to be made of leather carved in intricate patterns, and to be shown mainly as shadows. Where this sort of dynamic story-illustration survives, in India and Southeast Asia, for example, it is invariably referred to as puppetry.

In some places, individual characters broke free of the background setting and even developed movable parts. Sometimes characters skipped the intermediate step of small-group illustrations and simply walked off the picture scrolls. In Java, for example, characters pulled

La Cantastoria della Mad.ª del Carmine

ABOVE LEFT: A character starting to break free from the picture in a *tolu bommalatta* shadow puppet from Andhra Pradesh in southeast India. In this scene from *The Ramayana*, Sita's arm (articulated at the shoulder, elbow, and wrist) reaches clear out of the puppet frame as she drops an ornament to let Rama know she has been abducted. This kind of evolutionary link between story illustration and individual-actor puppets still is used for climactic moments.

ABOVE RIGHT: A nineteenth-century *tolu bommalatta* shadow puppet independent of his surroundings. The carved buffalo-hide puppets in Andhra Pradesh are often more than five feet tall.

OPPOSITE: Illustration puppets and individual characters share the screen in *Sunjata* (1989) by Amoros et Augustin of France and Ki-Yi Mbock Theater of Ivory Coast. The scene puppets here give the effect of a wide-angle lens, giving a broader vista of the action.

free of the *wayang* beber cloth to move individually, becoming *wayang kulit.*

Single-character puppets and scene "puppets" have often shared shadow screens with one another. Medieval Egyptian Mameluke figures included individual characters, such as a tea-seller hinged at the waist and a camel with movable legs, and also multi-character composites, such as ships filled with sailors. Contemporary Balinese *wayang kulit,* played mainly by articulated individual characters, incorporates group and scenery puppets, such as clusters of warriors in chariots.

In central and eastern Java, characters that had broken free of the story cloth sometimes developed a third dimension. These include the bas-relief *wayang klitik,* used mainly in East Java, and the fully three-dimensional *wayang golek.*

European story-illustrations evolved into puppets slightly differently, by plumping up into three dimensions straight from the painting. Picture-storytellers typically used posters containing a sequence of images. These sometimes fattened up into bas-relief or even high-relief sculptures, pulling away from the picture plane. Finally characters broke free and began to perform in front of the cabinet. To this day, Sicilian rod-marionette companies post picture-synopses virtually identical to the old-style story boards outside their theaters, which may suggest that they evolved from that early form.

The flow from illustration to puppetry continues in new guises. Since the early nineteenth century, illustrations in books have been animated with figures that move, transform, and pop into 3-D via hinges, pull tabs, wheels, strings, rivets, springs, and paper-folding technology. Munich artist Lothar Meggendorfer, often considered the inventor of pop-up books, was also a puppeteer. And the pioneer of American puppetry, Tony Sarg, designed movable storybooks that included free-standing props, such as a tiny pouch of gems for his *Treasure Island.* Many twentieth-century pop-ups have had multi-layer fold-out settings and bent-paper three-dimensional animated charac-

ters. The space capsule in a pop-up *Astronauts on the Moon* and a Christ in the pop-up *Jesus Lives!* catapult clear out of the book, several inches off the page, as they lift off on their respective missions.

Taking the final step into puppetry, some pop-up storybooks come complete with cardboard or cloth characters that readers can ferry through the sets. One series of Disney books included finger puppets of Winnie-the-Pooh, Donald Duck, and Mickey Mouse, designed to poke through a hole on every page. Another *Winnie-the-Pooh,* published in 1993, had five different fold-up toy theaters and came with a pouch of little cardboard actors. A book called the *Dolls' Open House,* published in 1956, opened out into a three-dimensional house and lawn, with free-standing characters, multiple changes of clothes, and movable patio furniture. The connection between picture storybooks and puppets is so strong that some illustrated childrens' books depict their characters as hand puppets or as marionettes, complete with strings.

Puppeteers have occasionally copied movable-book techniques. Nancy Loehman Staub staged an *Ugly Duckling* in 1973 using book-style pull-tabs. American puppeteer Penny Jones presented a childrens' show *Peppi the Pop-up Dragon.* In an early version of Lee Breuer's *Peter and Wendy*, the Darlings' house, made of white paper, folded up from the floor as if pages of a pop-up book had been turned. The Mexico City-based Teatro Tinglado created a yard-wide pop-up book in *The Repugnant Story of Clotario Demoniax* to show large-scale scenic events, such as a conflagration.

FILM AND ANIMATION

Some artists have created imaginary beings by projecting images made of light onto all manner of surfaces and forms. The Bauhaus artist László Moholy-Nagy's 1920s contraptions threw moving shapes made of colored light all around—a precursor to later artists' work that would bring moving light-shapes to the brink

Ghost Mock Sonic (1994), a video installation by the contemporary American artist Tony Oursler. By projecting moving faces or parts of faces onto all manner of surfaces, Oursler creates unnerving, oddly dynamic presences. Here, the body is made from a tripod, glass bottle, cloth, and styrofoam.

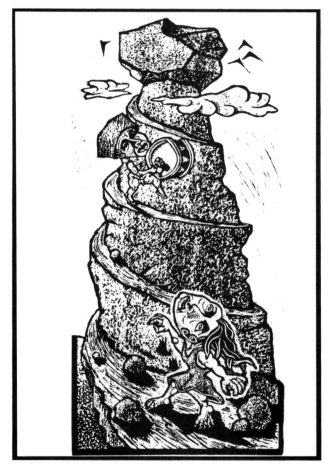

A woodcut by Jay Bolotin and automatons for his "mechanical opera" *Limbus* (2001). Haunted by a freak accident that had been reported in the news, Bolotin had created woodcuts to express the catastrophe latent in the cosmos seconds before a fifteen-ton boulder struck a house. Then he began to pull these images off their paper into three-dimensional, moving sculptures. The wooden figures, up to twelve feet tall, were manipulated remotely and shared the stage with two live singers. Bolotin also composed the music for *Limbus*, which premiered at the Opera Theater of Pittsburgh, directed by Jonathan Eaton.

OPPOSITE: A singer-storyteller using a tryptych of illustrations—or, perhaps, puppets—in a mezzotint by the late seventeenth- early eighteenth-century Dutch artist Jacob Gole. The figures in the nine-frame storyboard are either relief sculptures or, possibly, free-standing puppets. Certainly the group at the center-bottom frame seems to be separate figures.

BELOW: Theater Drak's 1974 production of *Till Eulenspiegel*—playing with the old mode of illustrated storytelling. Two actors narrated the tale while some fifty puppets (sculpted by František Vítek) acted it out in front of bas-relief storyboards. This 1974 production of *Till* was directed by Drak's artistic director Josef Krofta. Founded in 1959, Drak is based in Hradec Kralove, East Bohemia.

of imaginative life. The dreamscapes in Rudi Stern's Theater of Light blend computerized sequences of abstract images with stylized silhouettes of animals and humans.

Other artists have projected still or moving pictures of real people onto mannequins or moving surfaces, creating fleeting apparitions or trompe l'oeil actors. In Robert Lepage's *Elsinore* (1995), a one-man riff on *Hamlet,* Lepage shared the stage with images projected onto large screens that sometimes moved. The first "actors" to appear in Squat Theater's 1986 *Dreamland Burns* were white bas-relief sculptures with movies showing on them, creating the illusion of live actors. In his 1977 *Rumstick Road,* the late Spalding Gray projected an image of his late mother, a suicide, onto a living actress. The film features overrode the physical ones, and the dead woman appeared—offering a new slant on puppets' traditional job of giving the dead a usable body. For the Grands Ballet Canadiens de Montréal's 2001 production of

Queen of Spades (2001), the Brothers Quay created a gigantic, diaphanous apparition of a dead countess by projecting video onto gauzy scrim.

Beings made with projected light, like all constructed actors, can distort or ignore biological models. Meredith Monk has projected her own face onto a big round cloth-covered cage covering her head. Nam June Paik's 1990 video-sculpture tribute to his friend Joseph Beuys included a grouping of nine video monitors stacked into a vaguely human shape and all displaying a film or animation of Beuys's head.

STOP-ACTION FILM technique can be applied not only to subjects that can be photographed, but to drawings. At the dawn of motion pictures in the 1880s, the Frenchman Emile Reynaud created moving images from sequences of drawings. Forty years later, the American illustrator Walt Disney made this genre of animated cartoons so popular that some of its stars remain among the most famous personalities in the world.

BELOW AND OPPOSITE: Slow-motion film images of Meredith Monk's face projected onto an oversize head-screen in *16mm Earrings* (1980). Monk placed the cage over her head, then rotated it until its cloth-covered back came around front and became a projection screen. Behind Monk, below, is another scene from the show—a shadow film of a doll being burned in a room that is a miniature of Monk's. (The scenes were juxtaposed only in a 1998 installation at the Walker Art Center in Minneapolis. They did not appear together in performance.)

An animated illustration by William Kentridge showing a torturer showering off the filth of his day's work in Handspring Puppet Company's *Ubu and the Truth Commission* (1998). The production combined live actors, puppets, and animated film.

Animation can be both lower- and higher-tech than the Reynaud/Disney model of painted film frames. Artists drawing and re-drawing images in real time can effect a kind of animation-in-process. In his frolicksome ballet sendup *Swan Lake* (2000), the Russian director Ilia Epelbaum finger-painted a shimmering shadow animation of a swan on a pane of glass that had been splashed with water. A light beneath the glass cast the changing picture onto a screen. Basil Twist created a sort of real-time-animation chorus line for a 2003 toy theater show: Hidden behind the little stage, he painted a jaunty rhythm of parallel slanted strokes as the translucent white backdrop scrolled past. Then, on its second pass, he added a quick treble-clef curve onto each line, transforming the abstract pattern into a quasi-musical design, which suddenly gelled as Rockettes' legs.

As computers have eliminated the need for a dozen-plus hand-drawn cels per second, the art of animation has mushroomed. Some animation has used extreme stylization of character, setting, and visual perspective—all traditional hallmarks and specialties of puppet art. Invented universes such as those of Princess Mononoke and the Pokémon crew have their own fanciful brands of biology, physics, and style.

Computer animation also has moved in the opposite direction: toward trompe l'oeil realism. The mouse-star of *Stuart Little*, which *seems* to be a living being, is made up of electronic signals rather than DNA. Constructed actors can now be indistinguishable from ones that breathe. This new ersatz "life," poking away at the line between creatures and things, adds one more dimension to the peculiar taboo, unease, and thrill at the heart of puppetry.

Live and virtual performers sharing the stage via "motion-capture" technology in Merce Cunningham's 1999 *Biped*. Computer video artists Paul Kaiser and Shelley Eshkar had digitally "captured" the movements of two Cunningham dancers by means of dozens of sensors attached to the dancers' bodies. Kaiser and Eshkar then combined those recorded gestures with scanned charcoal strokes and wispy lines to make stylized human forms that executed the movements. On stage, evanescent digital performers gamboled across a scrim in front of their live cohorts, swirling, fluttering, changing color, wafting in and out of existence.

OVERLEAF: Joan Baixas painting a constantly transforming image—a kind of live animation—in *Terra Prenyada* (1997). On a clear plastic tarp covered with mud and lit from behind, he uses brushes, sticks, and his fingers to sketch, smudge, erase, and resketch an evolving story. Here, Baixas readjusts a woman's body-language as a man tries to pick her up in a bar. Soon vectors of speech will fly between them. Paca Rodrigo performs live abstract vocals for this wordless performance.

CHAPTER 12

Coda: Coming Full Circle

SOMETIMES THE GAME WORKS IN REVERSE: Instead of puppets pretending to be alive, live actors pretend to be puppets. This peculiar role reversal has come in various guises.

Live performers may cash in on certain puppet stars' popularity by playing live versions of them. In Turkey, human actors have staged Karagöz skits, costumed to ape the odd physiognomy and anatomy of the shadow-screen's Karagöz and his cohorts. The *Théâtre du Grand Guignol,* founded in Paris in 1897 by Oscar Méténier, began as a live-actor version of the Guignol puppet theater.

Or artists may take well-known puppet personae as raw material for their own live-actor works. In the ballet *Petrushka,* by composer Igor Stravinsky and choreographer Mikhail Fokine, dancers took the roles of the famous puppets. Martha Graham's comic dance *Punch and the Judy* (1941) presented a battling married couple, with Graham playing the wife. In his 1967 opera *Punch and Judy,* the British composer Harrison Birtwistle adapted the familiar cast and scenario into a ritualistic expression of cycles of destruction.

Sometimes, though, live performers do not merely play characters originated by puppets, but actually pretend to *be* puppets. Like the boy actors in Shakespeare's England playing women disguised as boys, humans play puppets that are playing humans. In parts of China

since the Song dynasty a millennium ago, children perched on the shoulders of adults have performed as "puppets in the flesh," copying movements from and sometimes sharing the stage with life-size rod-puppets. In certain Japanese kabuki plays, especially those adapted from the bunraku repertory, emotional climaxes

ABOVE AND OPPOSITE: A Javanese *wayang kulit* (leather puppet) and a very similar-looking *wayang wong* (human puppet). *Wayang wong* developed from live actors mimicking the performances of popular shadow and rod puppets. The human puppet here is the *Mahabharata* hero Arjuna as played by a prince from Yogyakarta, Java, circa 1920. The leather puppet is Dewasrani, a perfidious rival of Arjuna.

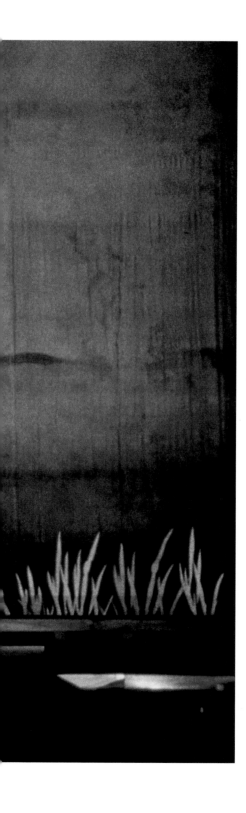

are presented as *ningyo buri,* that is, live performers acting like bunraku dolls, with black-clad "puppeteers" pretending to move them around.

Human faux-puppets have played in Europe as well. The eighteenth-century English actor-dramatist-producer Samuel Foote tried using cardboard figures on stage to circumvent the egos of live actors, but when audiences hated the experiment, he had live performers appear on stage behaving like puppets. Early Grand Guignol sometimes presented its actors as marionettes with strings fixed to their head and hands.

Live performers may act like puppets to make a political, social, or even metaphysical statement. In Jan Švankmajer's film *Don Juan* (1970) the main characters are played sometimes by actual marionettes and at other times by actors disguised as marionettes—making the play's moribund world seep from the patently make-believe into a world closer to the one the film's viewers inhabit. Dario Fo has had live performers move like marionettes, sometimes controlled by visible "manipulators," to show their subjugation or absence of will. In his 1994 staging of Rossini's *Italiana in Algeri* in Pesaro, Italy, an "ideal wife," a marionette built from vegetables, came to life: The actress who played the role was costumed to look like the puppet and mimicked its gestures. Fo played a drugged pope in *The Pope and The Witch* (1989) using mechanical movements to show his lack of control over his actions. The contemporary American director Richard Foreman had actresses in *Maria Del Bosco* (2002) move like mannequins to evoke the living-deadness of slavery to fashion and image.

Generally, though, the motivation for creating live faux-puppets is to heighten theatricality rather than to make a particular point. The device offers a system for setting stage behavior apart from everyday life. Using puppets as models, live actors find ways to perform that are more formal, comic, focused, extreme, or otherwise expressive than normal human behavior.

Faux puppets in the style of Japanese *ningyo buri* in *Drums on the Dike,* created and performed by the French Théâtre du Soleil in 1999.

The search for artistic form in theater has always been a tricky problem. While poets can shape language with tools such as meter, rhyme, and alliteration, and musicians organize sound-worlds with meter, modes, harmony, and polyphony, the raw material of theater is behavior. How can behavior be set in relief from everyday life, made more keenly expressive than everyday life, and given a pleasing artistic form without making it into fundamentally different behavior—that is, without distorting what one was trying to show in the first place? This conundrum has occupied stage artists since ancient times. Before the Greeks settled on masks to distinguish stage characters from real people, the theater pioneer Thespis reportedly tried covering his face with leaves or red-wine dregs. Classical French theater adapted its gestures from the stylized manners of the royal court. And around the world, over the centuries, live-actor theater traditions have achieved theatricality by copying puppets.

In a few cases, a live-actor theater has evolved directly out of puppetry, keeping the spirit and style of the original. In Java, the progression from painted story-cloth (*wayang beber*) to leather shadow puppet (*wayang kulit*) to three-dimensional rod puppet (*wayang golek*) continued with even more fleshed-out actors: humans, called *wayang wong* or *wayang orang*, literally, "human puppets." Those live "wayang" play the same repertory and, insofar as anatomy permits, copy the movement style of the puppets. In Italy, live actors performing *Orlando Furioso* have sometimes used a stiff-legged gait similar to that of the Sicilian marionettes.

Even when puppet traditions do not directly spawn live-actor theater, they may help to shape it: The human actors adopt or adapt a general aesthetic or specific traits from puppets. Turkey's live *orta oyunu* folk comedy seems to have traded influence back and forth with Karagöz puppetry for centuries. The indiginous *yoke thay* marionette stage of Burma, which dates from the eighteenth century, helped to shape the *zat* live-actor drama, whose perform-

ers still move in the mannner of puppets. As Japanese kabuki theater competed with the often more popular bunraku stage during the seventeenth and eighteenth centuries, its live actors adapted not only plays but, probably, stylization and broad gestures from the dolls. Some China scholars believe that the extreme make-up and movement style of traditional theater there reflects Song dynasty puppets.

Closer to home, puppets helped to re-theatricalize Europe's live-actor theater after it had been flattened by realism. Artists at the turn of the twentieth century drew on puppets indirectly and directly. Besides borrowing from non-Western live-actor stage traditions that were influenced by puppets, besides using actual puppets, beyond, even, creating live versions of specific puppets à la Grand Guignol, artists called for live actors to mimic the unabashed *theatricality* of puppets. Alfred Jarry announced before the infamous 1896 production of *Ubu Roi* at the Théâtre de l'Oeuvre that the (live) performers about to appear were "man-sized marionettes." Russia's seminal avant-garde director Vsevolod Meyerhold recommended that live actors learn their art from puppets—and not from just *any* puppets, but from the sort that "embrace a wonderland of make-believe" rather than merely copying humans. Plays by Maurice Maeterlinck and Paul Claudel were presented by actors using the broad stage movements and distorted voices of puppets.

Innovative American directors as well have asked actors to copy puppets as a way of heightening the stage reality and separating it from workaday life. In 1967 director/choreographer Jerome Robbins brought members of his repertory company to see the Little Players' *Romeo and Juliet*—and then told his actors, "That is exactly what I've been trying to get across to you people for months." Since the 1970s, actors in Richard Foreman's Ontological-Hysteric Theater have used stylized mechanical gestures and long freezes to help create a distinctive stage reality—the elegant, expressionist incar-

nation of his inner world. In Lee Breuer's "animations"—including *The B-Beaver Animation* (1974), *The Shaggy Dog Animation* (1978), and *Ecco Porco* (2000)—chracters often have been multiple-cast, incarnated both by puppets and by live performers acting like puppets. Playing Rose the Dog in *Ecco Porco,* actress Maude Mitchell even was suspended marionette-style by ropes.

THIS MAY BE the ultimate, ironic genius of puppets. Time and again, inert actors have breathed new life into the live-actor theater. So great is the power of puppets to show ourselves to ourselves that even flesh-and-blood actors, who would seem to have the advantage in imitating real people, have taken cues from constructed beings.

Finally, all art—in fact, everything human beings design—both reflects and helps to shape our sense of who we are. Puppets, with their peculiar ability to make us believe they are us, are surely among the canniest, and uncanniest, of human creations.

Life copies art as Jean Dubuffet outfits an actress to join the cast of still and animated figures in *Coucou Bazar* (1973). Dubuffet's hour-long dynamic tableaux included a hundred "practicables"—all in Dubuffet's trademark patterns of red, blue, and white painted on wood. The artist articulated the heaviest, which were on wheels, via mechanical contraptions. Puppeteers hidden behind lighter-weight figures carried and manipulated them. Finally, live actors masked and costumed to look like the constructed actors slowly came to life, choreographed in imitation of the puppets. *Coucou Bazar* was performed with music by the Turkish musician Ilhan Mimaroglu at the Guggenheim Museum in New York and as part of the Festival d'Automne in Paris. It had one other performance five years later in Italy.

Bibliography

Selected bibliography, selectively annotated.

GENERAL WORKS AND STUDIES COVERING PUPPETRY ON MORE THAN ONE CONTINENT

Anderson, Madge. *The Heroes of the Puppet Stage*. New York: Harcourt, Brace, and Company, 1923. A broad if quirky survey for general audiences, covering mainly European puppetry but also some Asian and African work. Still valuable notwithstanding references to "savage" peoples of Africa and the like.

Arnott, Peter D. *Plays without People: Puppets and Serious Drama*. Bloomington, IN: Indiana University Press, 1964. Largely a practicum and discussion of the author's work, but includes some European puppet history.

Baird, Bil. *The Art of the Puppet*. New York: Bonanza Books, 1973. A lavishly illustrated overview of European and American puppetry, with one chapter on Asia, through the mid twentieth century—by one of America's seminal puppeteers.

Baldwin, Peter. *Toy Theatres of the World*. Forward by George Speaight. London: A. Zwemmer, Ltd., 1992. Covers Europe and North America, with extensive b/w and color plates.

Baty, Gaston, and René Chavance. *Histoire des marionnettes*. "Que sais-je?" series on contemporary culture, #845. Paris: Presses Universitaires de France, 1972. Brief (123-page) survey of mainly European (some Asian) puppetry. No illustrations or bibliography.

Beaumont, Cyril W. *Puppet and the Puppet Stage*. London: The Studio, Ltd., 1938. Includes several hundred b/w photos of European and American puppetry of the 1930s.

Bell, John. *Strings, Hands, Shadows: A Modern Puppet History*. Detroit, MI: Detroit Institute of Arts, 2000. An accessible, balanced 116-page survey of European, American, and Asian puppet art. Well illustrated, in color, with puppets in the Paul McPharlin Collection of Puppetry and Theater Arts at the Detroit Institute of the Arts.

Benegal, Som, general editor, with John Carrau, Sina Kaul, and Chitra Chib. *Puppet Theatre around the World*. New Delhi: Bharatiya Natya Sangh, 1960. Forty articles about a variety of Asian and European theater.

Blackham, Olive. *Shadow Puppets*. New York: Harper & Brothers, 1960. Broadly based history and practicum of shadow puppetry by the director of England's Roel Puppets.

Blumenthal, Eileen. "Ritual Sex." *Puppetry International*, no. 14 (fall/winter 2003), 4–6. On use of puppets in tradional fertility rituals.

Boas, Franz. *Primitive Art*. New York: Dover Publications, 1955 (reprint of 1927 publication). A general study that focuses on the Pacific Northwest Coast peoples of North America.

Böhmer, Günter. *The Wonderful World of Puppets*. Translated from German by Gerald Morice. Boston: Plays, Inc., 1969. Essentially an exhibition catalogue for the superb Puppet Collection of the City of Munich.

Chesnais, Jacques. *Histoire générale des marionnettes*. Paris: Bordas, 1947. A historical survey, by a puppeteer, covering Europe, parts of Asia, and North Africa, with short portraits of two dozen specific traditions or individual artists.

Damianakos, Stathis, with collaboration of Christine Hemmet. *Théâtres d'ombres: Tradition et modernité*. Paris: Editions L'Harmattan, 1986. Essays on shadow theater including traditional Asian and Mediterranean forms and contemporary work. Some essays in English, others in French.

den Otter, Elisabeth. *Verre Vrienden van Jan Klassen: Poppenspel in Afrika en Azië*. Amsterdam: Kononklijk Institutvoor de Tropen, [1995] Companion volume of exhibition of African and Asian puppetry at Tropenmuseum, Amsterdam, 1995–96.

Emigh, John. *Masked Performance: The Play of Self and Other in Ritual and Theatre*. Philadelphia, PA: The University of Pennsylvania Press, 1996. Includes studies of New Guinea, Bali, and Rajasthan, with some discussion of puppets.

Fournel, Paul. *Les Marionnettes*. Paris: Bordas, 1995. Beautifully illustrated volume, originally published in 1982, with essays by experts in the various regions. Includes an alphabetical survey of major puppeteers.

Hillier, Mary. *Automata and Mechanical Toys*. London: Bloomsbury Books, 1976. Covers early automatons worldwide, with a focus on Europe.

———. *Dolls and Dollmakers*. New York: G.P. Putnams's Sons, 1968. Primarily about European dolls, with one chapter on Japanese dolls.

Holman, L. Bruce. *Puppet Animation in the Cinema*. New York: A.S. Barnes and Co., 1995. Covers Europe and the U.S., with some b/w illustrations.

Institut del Teatre Diputació de Barcelona. *Escenes de l'Imaginari: Festival Internacional de Teatre Visual I de Titelles de Barcelona. XXV Anniversari*. Barcelona: Institut d'Edicions de la Diputació de Barcelona, 1998. Companion to festival. Lavishly illustrated collection of essays on contemporary and cutting-edge visual and puppet theater. Trilingual (Spanish, Catalan, English).

Jenkins, Ron. *Subversive Laughter: The Liberating Power of Comedy*. New York: The Free Press, 1994. A study of performed comedy in Bali, Lithuania, South Africa, Italy, Japan, and America. Includes information on Lithuanian political puppetry and Dario Fo's puppetry.

Joseph, Helen Haiman. *A Book of Marionettes*. New York: The Viking Press, 1931. Mainly history, mainly about Europe, with one chapter on Asia.

Jurkowski, Henryk. *Aspects of Puppet Theatre*. Edited by Penny Francis. London: Embassy Press, 1988. Essays on various aspects of puppet theater, by a major historian of European puppetry.

Kominz, Laurence R., and Mark Levenson, editors. *The Language of the Puppet*. Vancouver, WA: Pacific Puppetry Center Press, 1990. Wide-ranging collection of essays.

Krauss, Rosalind E. *Passages in Modern Sculpture*. New York: The Viking Press, 1977. Discussion of twentieth-century sculpture in Europe and America. Includes performing objects made of light.

Mack, John, editor. *Masks and the Art of Expression*. New York: Harry N. Abrams, Inc., 1994. A geographically broad study, lavishly illustrated.

Maindron, Ernest. *Marionnettes et guignols*. Paris: Félix Juven, [1990]. Survey of European (focusing on French) as well as some Asian and North African puppetry from antiquity to the turn of the twentieth century. A hundred years old, but a classic resource.

Mair, Victor H. *Painting and Performance: Chinese Picture Recitation and Its Indian Genesis*. Honolulu, HI: University of Hawaii Press, 1988. Fine scholarly history of illustrated storytelling throughout the world. Extensive b/w and color illustrations.

Malkin, Michael. *The Power of Wonder*. Photographs by Richard Termine. Atlanta, GA: Center for Puppetry Arts, 1995. Exhibition catalogue for center's permanent collection.

———. *Puppets: Art and Entertainment*. Washington, D.C.: Puppeteers of America, 1980. Catalogue for exhibition at Center for Puppetry Arts, Atlanta, GA. Brief survey of world puppetry. Extensive b/w and color illustrations.

———. *Traditional and Folk Puppets of the World*. New York: A.S. Barnes and Co., 1977. Digestible international survey of traditional puppetry.

McCarthy, Kerry, editor. *African and African-American Puppetry*. Atlanta, GA: Center for Puppetry Arts, 1994. Exhibition catalogue, illustrated with b/w photos.

Mast, Gerald. *A Short History of the Movies*. 5th ed. Revised by Bruce F. Kawin. New York: Macmillan Publishing Co., 1992. Includes information on stop-action and animated film in Europe and America.

Mégroz, R.L. *Profile Art through the Ages*. New York: Philosophical Library, 1949. Study of silhouette art in Western culture (including ancient Egypt) from cave paintings to shadow-puppet films.

Meschke, Michael, in collaboration with Margareta Sörenson. *In Search of Aesthetics for the Puppet Theatre*. Translated from Swedish by Susanna Stevens. New Delhi: Indira Gandhi National Centre for the Arts/Sterling Publishers, Private Limited, 1985. Exploration of puppet aesthetics plus a practicum by a major puppet artist.

Montanaro, Ann. "A Concise History of Pop-up and Movable Books." Essay for catalogue of virtual exhibition by Rutgers University Libraries. http://www.libraries.rutgers.edu/rul/libs/scua/montanar/p-intro.htm. Covers Europe and America.

Nelson, Victoria. *The Secret Life of Puppets*. Cambridge, MA: Harvard University Press, 2001. A range of material shaped to support theory that the suprascientific and sacred are fundamental to human experience. Purports to "out" would-be rationalists.

Plassard, Didier, editor. *Les Mains de lumière: Anthologie des écrits sur l'art de la marionnette*. Charleville-Mézières, France: Editions Institut International de la Marionnette, 1996. Anthology of writings about puppetry, from antiquity to the present, mainly from Europe but including some Middle Eastern and Asian material.

Philpott, A.R. *Dictionary of Puppetry*. Boston: Plays, Inc., 1969.

————, editor. *Puppets and Therapy*. Boston: Plays, Inc., 1977. (Originally published by Educational Puppetry Assocation, London.) Several dozen short reports from Europe and North America.

Ransome, Grace Greenleaf, editor. *Puppets and Shadows: A Selective Bibliography to 1930. Mellen Studies in Puppetry*, vol. I. Lewiston, New York: Edwin Mellen Press, 1997.

Rawlings, Keith. "Observations on the Historical Development of Puppetry." http://www.sagecraft.com/puppetry/definitions/historical. November 1999. Updated: April 2003.

Reusch, Rainer, editor. *Schattentheater/Shadow Theater, Vol. 2: Art and Technique*. Schwäbisch Gmünd, Germany: Einhorn-Verlag, 2001. Bilingual (German/English). Essays by 13 contemporary shadow puppeers from Europe, America, and Australia.

Ridgeway, William. *The Dramas and Dramatic Dances of non-European Races*. New York: Benjamin Blom, 1964. (Reissue of work published in 1915.) Covers ancient Greece, Egypt, and Asia, including puppets.

Robertson, Andrea. *Museum of Automata*. York, England: Museum of Automata, 1992. Covers automatons from ancient creations to contemporary robots, focusing on Europe and Japan.

Schönewolf, Herta. *Play with Light and Shadow: The Art and Techniques of Shadow Theater*. Translated from German by Alba Lorman. New York: Reinhold Book Corporation, 1968. Primarily a practicum.

Sherzer, Dina and Joel Sherzer, editors. *Humor and Comedy in Puppetry*. Bowling Green, OH: Bowling Green State University Popular Press, 1987. Essays on puppet comedy worldwide.

The Shrine to Music Museum: A Pictorial Souvenir. Photos by Simon R.H. Spicer. Vermillion, SD: Shrine to Music Museum, 1988. Includes anthropomorphic instruments.

Tillis, Steve. *Towards An Aesthetics of the Puppet*. Contributions in Drama and Theatre Studies, #47. Westport, CT: Greenwood Press, 1992. Just what the title says: an exploration of the aesthetics of puppetry.

Simmen, René. *The World of Puppets*. Photographs by Leonardo Bezzola. London: Phaidon Press. Includes many color and b/w photos, organized by puppetry technique.

Sorell, Walter. *The Other Face: The Mask in the Arts*. London: Thames and Hudson, Ltd., 1973. Ranges from ancient Greece to the 1960s avant-garde across several genres of art. Includes many color and b/w plates.

Stephenson, Ralph. *The Animated Film*. New York: A.S. Barnes and Co., 1973. History and detailed worldwide survey, with b/w photos.

UNIMA (Union Internationale de la Marionnette). *Figur und Spiel im Puppentheater der Welt*. Edited by Dezsõ Szilágyi. Introduction by Henryk Jurkowski. Berlin: Henschelverlag Kunst und Gesellschaft, 1977. Photo compendium of productions mainly from 1960s and 1970s.

UNIMA (Union Internationale de la Marionnette) under chairmanship of Margareta Niculescu. *The Puppet Theatre of the Modern World: An International Presentation in Word and Picture*. Boston: Plays, Inc. 1967. English reprint of German edition, published 1965. Picture book of contemporary theater from around the world.

von Boehn, Max. *Dolls and Puppets*. Translated by Josephine Nicoll with a note on puppets by George Bernard Shaw. Boston: Charles T. Barnford Company, 1956. A classic history of puppets and dolls from antiquity through the early 20th century, focusing on Europe, but also including a short section on Asia. Translated from German, originally published in English in 1932. Includes a good bibliography.

STUDIES OF ONE GEOGRAPHICAL AREA OR INDIVIDUAL TRADITIONS, ARTISTS, OR COMPANIES

AFRICA

Arnoldi, Mary Jo. *Playing with Time: Art and Performance in Central Mali*. Bloomington, IN: Indiana University Press, 1995. Fine, beautifully illustrated scholarly study of masquerades in Mali.

Beckwith, Carol, and Angela Fisher. *African Ceremonies*. New York: Harry N. Abrams, Inc., 1999. Lavish two-volume collection of Beckwith and Fisher's breathtaking photos with explanatory texts.

Bodson, Lucile, text. *Yaya Coulibaly: Marionnettiste*. Montreuil, France: Editions de l'Oeil, 2003. One of Editions de l'Oeil's series of small-format, 24-page, heavily illustrated books for young readers.

Christoph, Henning, and Hans Oberländer. *Voodoo: Secret Power in Africa*. New York: Taschen, 1996. Extraordinary photographs (by the authors) of Voodoo (or Vodun) rituals, many including inanimate objects endowed with life.

Dagan, E[sther]. A. *Emotions in Motion: Theatrical Puppets and Masks from Black Africa*. [La Magie de l'imaginaire: Marionnettes et masques théâtraux d'Afrique noire.] Montreal, Canada: Galerie Amrad African Arts, 1990. Overview of types of puppets in Africa, with more than 200 b/w images. Bilingual (English/French).

Darkowska-Nidzgorski, Olenka, and Denis Nidzgorski. *Marionnettes et masques au coeur du théâtre africain*. Saint-Maur, France: Sepia, 1998. The most significant broad study of sub-Saharan African puppets, organized by the functions of puppetry.

Darkowska-Nidzgorski, Olenka, in collaboration with Lucettte Albaret. *Tchitchili Tsitsawi: Marionnettes d'Afrique*. Photographs by Denis Nidzgorski. Paris: Cahiers de l'ADEIAO, 1996.

Friedman, Gary. "Puppets for Political Change." Unpublished article.

Gordon, Gill. *Puppets for Better Health: A Manual for Community Workers and Teachers*. Illustrations by Sue Gordon. London: Macmillan Education Ltd., 1986.

Huet, Michel, photographs. *Les Hommes de la danse*. Lausanne, Switzerland: Editions Clairefontaine, 1954. Lavish b/w photographs (with some text) of dance in sub-Saharan Africa, including many puppets.

Huet, Michel, photographs. *The Dances of Africa*. Text by Claude Savary. New York: Harry N. Abrams, Inc., 1995. B/w photos (from Huet's 1954 book) along with his color photos of the same subjects, including many puppets.

Lamp, Frederick. "The Art of the Baga: A Preliminary Study." *African Arts*: Vol. 19, no. 2, February 1986, 64–67.

————. "Dancing the Hare: Appropriation of the Imagery of Mande Power among the Baga," in *The Younger Brother in Mande: Kinship and Politics in West Africa*, 105–115. Edited by Jan Jansen and Clemens Zobel. Leiden, Netherlands: Research School CNWS, 1996.

L'Association Urbis. *Resonances: Arts traditionnels du Burkina Faso*. Amiens, France: Association Urbis, 1992. Illustrated (b/w and color) exhibition catalogue from Chapelle de la Visitation.

Lehuard, Raoul. "Trompes anthropomorphes du Bas-Congo." *Arts d'Afrique noire*, no. 6 (summer 1973), 4–15. Discussion of anthropomorphic trumpets in southern Congo.

L'Institut International de la Marionnette. *Marionnettes en territoire africain*. Text by Olenka Darkowska-Nidzgorski. Introduction by Margareta Niculescu. Charleville-Mézières, France: Editions Institut International de la Marionnette, 1991. Illustrated exhibition catalogue.

Magnin, André, with Jacques Soulillou. *Contemporary Art of Africa*. New York: Harry N. Abrams, Inc., 1995. Includes material on Johannes Segogela.

Musée de l'Homme. *Marionnettes et marottes de l'Afrique noire*. Introduction by Francine Ndiaye. Photographs by Béatrice Hatala. Paris: Editions du Muséum National d'Histoire Naturelle, 1992. Companion to an exhibition of puppetry.

Ndiaye, Francine. "Puppets of Black Africa," *Balafon* (published by Air Afrique), n.d.

"Three Cross River Puppets." *African Arts*, vol. 19, no. 2, February 1986, 68–69.

Tribal Arts Gallery Two. *Ekon Society Puppets: Sculptures for Social Criticism*. Text by Alfred L. Scheinberg. Photographs by Johan Elbers. New York: [Tribal Arts Gallery Two], 1977. Small exhibition catalogue, with b/w photographs.

Unima Informations. Special: *L'Afrique noire en marionnettes*. Edited by Olenka Darkowska-Nidzgorski. Translated into English by Prudence Borgniet. Illustrations and photographs by Denis Nidzgorski. Charleville-Mézières, France: 1988. Bilingual (French/English).

Widman, Ragnar. *The Niombo Cult among the Babwende*. Monograph Series, Publication No. 11. Stockholm: Ethnographical Museum of Sweden, 1967.

Witte, Hans. *Wereld in Beweging: Gelede-marionetten van de Anago-Yoruba*. *World in Motion: Gelede Puppets of the Anago Yoruba*. Photographs by Ferry Herrebrugh. Translated from Dutch by Kevin Cook. Berg en dal, Netherlands: Afrika Museum, 2001. Companion to an exhibition, lavishly illustrated, with detailed explanations.

THE AMERICAS

Berrin, Kathleen, and Esther Pasztory, editors. *Teotihuacan: Art from the City of the Gods.* New York: Thames and Hudson, Inc., 1993. Lavishly illustrated exhibition catalogue.

Blumenthal, Eileen. "Ants Invade BAM. Puppets in Cahoots." Sunday *New York Times,* October 16, 1988, Arts & Leisure, 3, 17. On Bunraku puppetry in Lee Breuer/Bob Telson *Warrior Ant.*

———. "The Fading British Empire as Performance Art." Sunday *New York Times,* May 20, 1990, Arts & Leisure, sec. 2. On *Half a World Away,* by Janie Geiser and A. Leroy.

———. "Serious Puppets." *American Theatre,* vol. 5, no. 10 (January 1989), 20–24. On Puppetry of the Americas Conference and Festival, 1988, Atlanta, GA.

———. "The Solo Performances of Winston Tong." *The Drama Review,* T81 (March 1979), 87–94.

Blumenthal, Eileen, and Julie Taymor. *Julie Taymor: Playing with Fire.* Revised edition. New York: Harry N. Abrams, Inc., 1999.

Bradley, David I., editor. *Festival of Puppet Theatre: The Thirty-First Annual Festival of the Puppeteers of America.* Nashville, TN: Williams Printing Co., 1971. Includes essays on North American puppetry, current and past.

Brecht, Stefan. *Peter Schumann's Bread and Puppet Theater.* 2 vols. New York: Routledge, 1988.

Brown, Forman. *Small Wonder: The Story of the Yale Puppeteers and Turnabout Theatre.* Forward by Ray Bradbury. Metuchen, NJ: the Scarecrow Press, 1980.

Broyles-Gonzalez, Yolanda. *El Teatro Campesino: Theater in the Chicano Movement.* Austin, TX: University of Texas Press, 1994. Mainly about El Teatro Campesino's live-actor and masked theater, but includes their puppetry.

Bunzel, Ruth L. *Zuñi Kachinas: A Paper from the Bureau of American Ethnology Annual Report 47, 1929–1930.* Glorieta, NM: the Rio Grande Press, Inc., 1973 (reprint of 1932 edition).

Carmichael, Elizabeth, and Chloë Sayer. *The Skeleton at the Feast: The Day of the Dead in Mexico.* Austin, TX: University of Texas Press, 191. History and interviews, with extensive b/w and color photos.

Cleveland Center for Contemporary Art. *Outside the Frame: Performance and the Object. A Survey History of Performance Art in the USA Since 1950.* Catalogue coordination by Gary Sangster. Cleveland, OH: Cleveland Center for Contemporary Art, 1994.

Cooper Union School of Art. *Ghostcatching.* New York: Cooper Union School of Art, 1999. Companion to performance by Bill T. Jones of virtual dance work, illustrated with b/w and color images.

Copeland, Roger. *Merce Cunningham: The Modernizing of Modern Dance.* New York: Routledge, 2004. Includes description of Cunningham's work with motion capture, as well as some work with constructed actors by Nam June Paik and others.

Davis, Nancy Yaw. *The Zuñi Enigma.* New York: W.W. Norton & Company, 2000. Some information on kachina dolls.

Dircks, Phyllis T., editor. *American Puppetry: Collections, History and Performance.* Jefferson, NC: McFarland, 2004.

Easby, Elizabeth Kennedy, and John F. Scott. *Before Cortés: Sculpture of Middle America.* New York: The Metropolitan Museum of Art, 1970. Lavishly illustrated exhibition catalogue.

Fewkes, Jesse Walter. *Hopi Snake Ceremonies: An Eyewitness Account by Jesse Walter Fewkes.* Selections from Bureau of American Ethnology annual reports nos. 16 and 19 for the years 1894–95 and 1897–98. Albuquerque, NM: Avanyu Publishing, 1986. Includes b/w sketches and photos.

Finch, Christopher. *Jim Henson: The Works.* New York: Random House, 1993.

Geertz, Armin W., and Michael Lomatuway'ma. *Children of Cottonwood: Piety and Ceremonialism in Hopi Indian Puppetry.* Lincoln, NE: University of Nebraska Press, 1987.

Gold, Donna Lauren. "Far from Sicily, The Manteos' Puppets Carry On," photographs by Martha Cooper, *Smithsonian,* vol. 14, no. 5, August 1983, 68–73.

Green, Susan. *Bread and Puppet: Stories of Struggle and Faith from Central America.* Introduction by Peter Schumann. Foreword by Grace Paley. Burlington, VT: Green Valley Film and Art, Inc., 1985.

Grooms, Red. *Ruckus Rodeo.* New York: Harry N. Abrams, Inc., 1988. Includes pop-up version of the original installation.

King, Elizabeth. *Attention's Loop: A Sculptor's Reverie on the Coexistence of Substance and Spirit.* Photos by Katherine Wetzel. New York: Harry N. Abrams, Inc., 1999.

Lamphier, Mary Jane. *Zany Characters of the Ad World: Collector's Identification and Value Guide.* Paducah, KY: Collector Books, 1995.

Leet, Richard. *Bil Baird . . . He Pulled Lots of Strings.* Mason City, IA: Charles H. MacNider Museum, 1988. Companion to *Bil Baird Memorial Exhibit.*

L'Institut International de la Marionnette. *Marionnettes en territoire brésilien.* Edited by Bruno Mikol. Charleville-Mézières, France: Editions Institut International de la Marionnette, 1994. Illustrated exhibition catalogue.

Lipman, Jean, editor, with Nancy Foote. *Calder's Circus.* New York: E.P. Dutton, in association with the Whitney Museum of American Art, 1972.

Los Angeles County Museum of Art. *Sculpture of Ancient West Mexico. Nayarit, Jaslico, Colima. The Proctor Stafford Collection.* Exhibition catalogue by Kan, Michael, Clement Meighan, and H.B. Nicholson. Los Angeles, CA: Los Angeles County Museum of Art, 1970.

Marlborough Gallery. *Red Grooms: New York Stories.* With interview by David Shapiro. New York: Marlborough Gallery, Inc. 1995. Illustrated exhibition catalogue, including "The Bus."

McPharlin, Paul. *The Puppet Theatre in America. A History 1524–1948.* With a supplement: "Puppets in America Since 1948" by Marjorie Bachelder McPharlin. Boston, MA: Plays, Inc., 1969. The first broad survey—and still the best—of American puppetry.

The Mantell Manikins Return Home to Everett. Everett, WA: Arts Council of Snohomish County, 1999. Catalogue with color photos for *The Art of Puppetry: An Exhibit of the Alan G. Cook Collection.*

"Mini Music Hall." *Time* magazine, Jan. 4, 1971, 53. About Jerome Robbins and the Little Players.

Musée de l'Homme. *La Vie et l'art des Inuit du nord québécois.* [No publication information given], 1988. Exhibition catalogue with extensive b/w photos.

Museum of Fine Arts, Houston, Texas. *Alexander Calder: Circus Drawings, Wire Sculpture, and Toys.* Houston, TX: Museum of Fine Arts, 1942. Museum catalogue with several b/w plates.

Pendleton, Ralph, editor. *The Theatre of Robert Edmond Jones.* Middletown, CT: Wesleyan University Press, 1958. Includes basic information about 1931 production of Stravinsky *Oedipus Rex.*

Ray, Dorothy Jean. *Eskimo Masks: Art and Ceremony.* Photographs by Alfred A. Blaker. Seattle, WA: University of Washington Press, 1967.

Ritzenthaler, Robert, and Lee A. Parsons, editors. *The Samuel A. Barrett Collection: Masks of the Northwest Coast.* Text by Marion Johnson Mochon. Milwaukee, WI: Milwaukee Public Museum, 1966.

Shank, Theodore. *American Alternative Theatre.* New York: St. Martin's Press, 1982. Study of the 1960s and 1970s avant-garde, including some puppet theater.

Tate, Carolyn, and Gordon Bendersky. "Olmec Sculptures of the Human Fetus." P.A.R.I. Online Publications: Newsletter #30, winter 1999.

Taymor, Julie, and Elliot Goldenthal. "Juan Darien: A Carnival Mass." Scenario and notes. *Theater,* vol. 20, no. 2 (summer 1989), 43–55.

Tick Tock Toys. "Food Character Premiums." http://www.ticktock.simplenet.com (no longer available). Virtual catalogue of food advertising premiums geared toward collectors.

TV Acres. "Puppets & Puppetry." http://www.tvacres.com. Virtual encyclopedia of television puppets in the U.S.

Vincent, Gilbert T., text. *Masterpieces of American Indian Art from the Eugene and Clare Thaw Collection.* Photographs by John Bigelow Taylor. New York: Harry N. Abrams, Inc., 1995. Some information on kachina dolls.

Whittaker, Wayne. "The $500,000 Puppet Show," *Popular Mechanics,* September 1952, 81–85. On a puppet opera theater in Chicago.

ASIA

Adachi, Barbara. *Backstage At Bunraku.* Photographs by Joel Sackett. New York: John Weatherhill, Inc., 1985.

Barbican Art Gallery. *Karakuri Ningyō.* Texts by Sue Henny, Kitō Hideaki, Nishitsuonoi Masahiro, Yamazaki Kōsei, and Wada Jun. London: Barbican Art Gallery, 1985. Lavishly illustrated exhibition catalogue.

Blackburn, Stuart. *Inside the Drama-House: Rama Stories and Shadow Puppets in South India*. Berkeley, CA: University of California Press, 1996.

Blumenthal, Eileen. "The Coarse and the Sacred Are Fused in Shadow Plays." Sunday *New York Times*, Feb. 21, 1988, Arts & Leisure, 7. On Indonesian Shadow Puppet Theater.

Bondan, Molly, Teguh S. Djamal, Haryono Guritno, and Pandam Guritno. *Lordly Shades: Wayang Purwa Indonesia*. Jakarta: privately published, 1984. Short texts providing an overview, plus 80 pages of exceptional color plates.

Brandon, James, editor. *On Thrones of Gold: Three Javanese Shadow Plays*. Honolulu: University of Hawaii Press, 1993 (reprint, first published by Harvard University Press in 1970).

Bridhyākorn, H.H. Prince Dhaninivat Kromamün Bidyalabh Bridhyākorn, *Shadow Play (The Nan)*. Bangkok: Fine Arts Department, 1973. (Reprint, first published in 1954.)

Broman, Sven. *Chinese Shadow Theatre Libretti*. Bangkok: White Orchard Books, n.d. (c. 1981). English translations of texts of ten Chinese shadow plays. Includes the original Chinese texts.

———. *Chinese Shadow Theatre*. Ethnographical Museum of Sweden, Monograph Series no. 15. Stockholm: The National Museum of Ethnography, 1981. Extensive catalogue of characters, costumes, props, and set pieces, with numerous b/w images and color plates.

Brunet, Jacques. *Nang Sbek: Théâtre d'ombres: danse du Cambodge*. Berlin: Internationalen Instituts für Vergleichende Musikstudien und Dokumentation, 1969.

Center For Puppetry Arts. *Puppetry of China*. Atlanta, GA: Center for Puppetry Arts, 1984. Small lavishly illustrated companion volume to exhibition.

Center For Puppetry Arts. *Puppetry of India*. Atlanta, GA: Center for Puppetry Arts, 1986. Small lavishly illustrated exhibition catalogue.

Chandavij, Natthapatra, and Promporn Pramualratana. *Thai Puppets and Khon Masks*. Bangkok: River Books, 1998. Lavishly illustrated volume covering three-dimensional Thai puppetry and masks of Thai dance-drama.

Clark, Sharri. "Embodying Indus Life." http://www.harappa.com/figurines. In *Harrapa: Glimpses of South Asia before 1947*. www.Harrapa.com

Contractor, Meher. *The Shadow Puppets of India*. Darpana Monograph Series, no. 2. Ahmedabad: Darpana Academy of the Performing Arts, 1984. A 20-page overview, including music, puppet construction, and staging.

Cuisinier, Jeanne. *Le Théâtre d'ombres à Kelantan*. Paris: Gallimard, 1957. Study of shadow puppetry on the Malaysian peninsula by pioneering scholar of southeast Asian dance and theater.

Dinh, Quang, et al. *Le Théâtre Vietnamien*. Hanoi: The Gioi Publishers, 1998.

Dubuffet Foundation. "Coucou Bazar, an animated painting." http://www.dubuffetfondation.com/coucoubazar_ang.htm.

Dunn, C.J. *The Early Japanese Puppet Drama*. London: Luzac and Company, Ltd., 1966.

Hemmet, Christine. *Nang Talung: The Shadow Theatre of South Thailand*. Amsterdam: KIT Press, Royal Tropical Institute, 1996. A 32-page overview, with b/w photos and sketches.

Herbert, Mimi, with Nur S. Rahardjo. *Voices of the Puppet Masters: The Wayang Golek Theater of Indonesia*. Jakarta: The Lontar Foundation, and Honolulu, HI: University of Hawai'i Press, 2002. Lavishly illustrated study of the work of ten master puppeteers.

Hironaga, Shuzaburo. *The Bunraku Handbook: A Comprehensive Guide to Japan's Unique Puppet Theatre with Synopses of All Popular Plays*. Tokyo: Maison Des Arts, Inc., 1976.

Hobart, Angela. *Dancing Shadows of Bali*. New York: KPI, Ltd., 1987. Includes study of the repertoire, symbolism, and role in society.

Indian Puppets. Edited by Mulk Raj Anand. Texts by Meher Contractor. Bombay: Marg Publications, n.d. [c. 1968] Survey of types of Indian puppetry and some major puppeteers. Includes b/w photos.

Irvine, David. *Leather Gods and Wooden Heroes: Java's Classical Wayang*. Singapore: Times Books, 1996.

Janin, Stéphane, text. *Sovanna Phum: Théâtre d'ombres*. Montreuil, France: Editions de l'Oeil, 2003. On shadow puppets of Cambodia. One of Editions de l'Oeil's series of small-format, 24-page, heavily illustrated books for young readers.

Jilin, Liu. *Chinese Shadow Puppet Plays*. Translation from Chinese, Fang Zhenya and Fang Guoping. Beijing: Morning Glory Publishers, 1988. Description of history, art, and technique, lavishly illustrated with color plates.

Keeler, Ward. *Javanese Shadow Plays, Javanese Selves*. Princeton, NJ: Princeton University Press, 1987.

Keene, Donald. *Bunraku: The Art of the Japanese Puppet Theatre*. Photographs by Kaneko Hiroshi. Introduction by Tanizaki Junichirō. Tokyo: Kodansha International Ltd., 1965. The classic English-language work on Bunraku. An oversize book, lavishly illustrated with b/w photos.

Keene, Donald. *Bunraku: The Art of the Japanese Puppet Theatre*. Photographs by Kaneko Hiroshi. Tokyo: Kodansha International, Ltd., 1973. A revised, paperback edition of Keene's classic work.

Laubu, Michel, text. *Ka Bong Lao: Théâtre d'objects*. Montreuil, France: Editions de l'Oeil, 2003. On Laotian puppetry. One of Editions de l'Oeil's series of small-format, 24-page, heavily illustrated books for young readers.

Law, Jane Marie. *Puppets of Nostalgia: The Life, Death, and Rebirth of the Japanese Awaji Ningyō Tradition*. Princeton, NJ: Princeton University Press, 1997.

Le Louvre des Antiquaires. *Marionnettes et ombres d'Asie*. Edited by Françoise Gründ. Paris: La Maison des Cultures du Monde, 1985. Illustrated exhibition catalogue on Asian puppet theater.

Le Roi singe et autres mythes: Marionnettes, ombres, et acteurs du théâtre chinois. Texts by Roger Darrobers, Jacques Pimpaneau, Michel Revelard, et al. Paris: Somogy Éditions d'Art, 2004. Lavishly illustrated companion to 2004 exhibition at Musée de l'Hôtel Dieu de Mantes-la-Jolie.

Masterpieces of Japanese Sculpture. Photographs by Irie, Yasukichi, Ken Domon, Shihachi Fujimoto, and Manshichi Sakamoto. Introduction, text, and commentaries by J. Edward Kidder Jr. Tokyo, Japan, and Rutland, VT: Bijutsu Shuppan-sha and Charles E. Tuttle Co., 1961.

Mellema, R.L. *Wayang Puppets: Carving, Colouring, Symbolism*. Amsterdam: Royal Tropical Institute, 1954. On Javanese shadow theater.

Miller, Terry E. and Jarernchai Chonpairot. "Shadow Puppet Theatre in Northeast Thailand." *Theater Journal*, vol. 31, no. 3, October 1979.

Musée de l'Hôtel-Dieu. *Aspects de l'Art populaire indien: Jean-Baptiste Faivre et les Peintres santals*. Compiled by Evelyne Le Roy-Kourouma. Mantes-La-Jolie, France: Musée de l'Hôtel-Dieu, 1997. Lavishly illustrated companion to exhibition.

Musée d'Ethnographie de Genève. *Théâtres d'Orient: Masques, marionnettes, ombres, costumes*. Texts by Laurent Aubert and Jérôme Ducor. Photographs by Jonathan Watts. Ivrea, Italy: Priuli & Verlucca, 1997. Overview, with 72 oversize color plates of objects in museum setting.

Nguyen, Huy Hong, and Tran Trung Chinh. *Vietnamese Traditional Water Puppetry*. Hanoi: The Gioi Publishers, 1996. Contains b/w sketches and photos as well as color photos.

Nguyen, Huy Hong. *Water Puppetry of Vietnam*. Hanoi: Foreign Languages Publishing House, 1986. An earlier book, with a few b/w sketches.

Nguyen, Vay Huy, editor-in-chief, and Frank Proschan, editor. *Lien hoan quoc te ve mua roi tai Ha Noi. Hanoi International Puppetry Festival, 6–15/10/2000*. Hanoi: Bao tang Dan toc hoc Viet Nam, 2000. Exhibition catalogue, including some photos, mainly of Vietnamese puppetry, with a section on Sicilian marionettes.

Obraztsov, Sergei. *The Chinese Puppet Theatre*. Translated from Russian by J. T. MacDermott. Boston: Plays, Inc., 1975. (Reprint of Faber and Faber edition, 1961. Originally published in Russian, 1957.)

Pani, Jiwan. *Living Dolls: The Story of Indian Puppets*. New Delhi: Ministry of Information and Broadcasting, 1986. Overview by type and region. Illustrated with sketches, some b/w and color photos.

Scott, A.C. *The Puppet Theatre of Japan*. Rutland, VT: Charles E. Tuttle Company, Inc., 1980. (Reprint of 1963 edition.) Small paperback with overview of Bunraku and summary of 10 plays. Some b/w photos.

Singer, Noel F. *Burmese Puppets*. New York: Oxford University Press, 1992. History plus descriptions of puppets and performances from the 15th century through the late 20th century.

Stalberg, Roberta Helmer. *China's Puppets*. San Francisco, CA: China Books, 1984. History and overview of types of puppetry in China, extensive b/w illustrations.

Sweeney, Amin. *Malay Shadow Puppets: The Wayang Siam of Kelantan*. London: The British Museum, 1972. Small 84-page paperback, giving an overview including plot summaries. Includes b/w sketches and color plates.

Thanegi, Ma. *The Illusion of Life: Burmese Marionettes*. Bangkok: White Orchid Books, 1994. Includes extensive color photos.

Tilakasiri, Jayadeva. *The Asian Shadow Play*. Sri Lanka: Vishva Lekha, 1999. Comprehensive study of Asian shadow theater up to the turn of the 21st century.

———. *Puppetry in Sri Lanka*. Sri Lanka: Department of Cultural Affairs, 1976 (reprint of 1961). Small paperback, with overview and 18 b/w and color plates.

———. *The Puppet Theatre of Asia*. Peradeniya, Sri Lanka: Department of Government Printing, Ceylon, 1968. A survey of two- and three-dimensional puppet forms in East, Southeast, and South Asia. Nearly forty years old, but still the best resource.

Ueno-Herr, Michiko. "Masters, disciples, and the art of the bunraku puppeteer's performance." Ph.D. dissertation, University of Hawaii, 1995.

Van Ness, Edward C., and Shita Prawirohardjo. *Javanese Wayang Kulit*. New York: Oxford University Press, 1953. A small paperback giving an overview plus descriptions of shows. Many plates, b/w and color, including some following the action of a play.

Venu, G. *Tolpava Koothu: Shadow Puppets of Kerala*. New Delhi: Sangeet Natak Akademi, 1990. Includes extensive b/w photos.

———. *Puppetry and Lesser Known Dance Traditions of Kerala*. Kerala, India: Natana Kairali, 1990.

Wickert, Utta, and Tizar Purbaya. *Wayang: Stories and Pictures*. Translated from German by Lilo Oldenberg. Jakarta: PT Intermasa, n.d. Bilingual (English/German).

Zurbuchen, Mary Sabina. *The Language of Balinese Shadow Theater*. Princeton, NJ: Princeton University Press, 1987.

EUROPE

And, Metin. *Karagöz Turkish Shadow Theatre*. Istanbul: A Dost Publication, 1979. (Revision of original 1975 edition.) The classic work on karagöz, with b/w and color illustrations.

Balzer, Richard. *Peepshows: A Visual History*. New York: Harry N. Abrams, Inc., 1998. Primarily illustrations, b/w and color, of European peepshows, with a very few non-European examples.

Bayer, Herbert, Walter Gropius, and Ise Gropius, editors. *Bauhaus 1919–1928*. New York: The Museum of Modern Art, 1990 (reprint of 1938 edition). Companion to exhibition.

Bell, John Thomas. "Mechanical Ballets: The Rediscovery of Performing Objects on European Stages from the 1890s to the 1930s." Ph.D. dissertation, Columbia University, 1993. Comprehensive study of performing objects including those in live-actor theater, dance, and the visual arts, during this very fertile period.

Blackham, Olive. *Puppets Into Actors*. London: Rockliff, 1948. Mainly a practicum by the director of Britain's Roel Puppet Theatre.

Blumenthal, Eileen. "Mass Requiem." *Village Voice*, Aug. 26–Sep. 1, 1981, 101. Interview with Tadeusz Kantor and review of *Wielopole Wielopole*, at the Caracas Theater Festival.

———. "Puppets in the Line of Fire." *American Theatre*, no. 2005 (May–June, 2003), 42. On Rezo Gabriadze *The Battle of Stalingrad*.

[Boer, Christien, and Hanny Alkema.] *Poppen-, Object- en Beeldend Theater in Nederland*. Amsterdam: Nederlands Poppenspel Institut, 1991. Comprehensive, illustrated (b/w) catalogue of puppet and object theater in the Netherlands as of 1991.

[Bollebakker, J.J., G,J,M, Sonnemans, and I. Vink.] *Theater uit handen: Nederlands poppen- en schimmentheater na 1900*. Rotterdam, Netherlands: Historisch Museum Rotterdam, 1992. A study of 20th-century Dutch puppet theater, lavishly illustrated.

Bührer, Michel. *Mummenschanz*. Translated from French by Mavis Guinard. Alstätten, Switzerland: Panorama Verlag AG, 1984. Extensive b/w, some color photos.

Bussell, Jan. *Fanfare for Puppets*. London: David & Charles, 1985. Puppeteer Bussell's overview of world puppetry, arranged by technique, drawing examples from around the world, illustrated with b/w and some color photos.

———. *Puppet's Progress*. London: Faber and Faber, 1953. One of several volumes of autobiographical narrative by director of the Hogarth Puppets.

———. *Through Wooden Eyes*. London: Faber and Faber, 1956. English puppeteer's memoir of puppets and puppeteers he encountered while traveling in Europe and South Africa.

Byrom, Michael. *The Puppet Theatre in Antiquity*. Bicester, England: DaSilva Puppet Books, 1996. A 40-page, illustrated (b/w) study of puppetry in ancient Greece and Rome.

———. *Punch in the Italian Puppet Theatre*. London: Centaur Press, 1983.

Castelo di Rivoli and Museo d'Arte Contemporanea. *Sipario/Staged Art: Balla De Chrico Savino Picasso Paolini Cucchi*. Texts by Maurizio dell'Arco et al translated from Italian by Marguerite Shore. Text by Alain Mousseigne translated from French by Charles Penwardin. Milan: Edizioni Charta, 1997. Lavishly illustrated exhibition catalogue.

Cate, Phillip Dennis, and Mary Shaw, editors. *The Spirit of Montmartre: Cabarets, Humor, and the Avant Garde, 1875–1905*. New Brunswick, NJ: Zimmerli Art Museum, 1996. Companion to exhibition, extensive b/w illustrations.

Chester, Lewis. *Tooth and Claw: The Inside Story of Spitting Image*. Boston, MA: Faber and Faber, 1986. History of this satiric team of British television puppets, based on interviews with company members.

Collodi, Carlo. *Pinocchio: The Adventures of a Puppet*. Translated from Italian by M. A. Murray. New York: A.L. Burt Company, n.d. [before 1924].

Cooper, Douglas. *Picasso Theatre*. Paris: Editions Cercle d'Art, 1987. Lavishly illustrated companion to exhibition.

Coult, Tony and Baz Kershaw, editors. *Engineers of the Imagination: The Welfare State Handbook*. London: Metheun, 1999.

Craig, Edward Gordon. *On the Art of the Theatre*. London: William Heinemann, 1911.

dell'Arco, Maurizio Fabiolo. *Balla: The Futurist*. Image editor, Paolo Sprovieri. Translated from Italian by Margaret Kunzle. New York: Rizzoli, 1987.

Der Figurenspiegel Richard Teschner. Edited and designed by Jarmila Weißesböck. Vienna: Böhlau Verlag, 1991. Illustrated exhibition catalogue, with several essays and b/w and color photos.

Early, Alice K. *English Dolls: Effigies and Puppets*. London: B.T. Barsford, Ltd., 1955. A study of English dolls from prehistoric times through the 19th century.

Eudel, Paul. *Les Ombres chinoises de mon père*. Paris: Rouveyre, 1885. Eudel's presentation of his father's puppets and puppet plays for "Chinese shadows" in 19th-century France.

Fields, Armond. *Henri Rivière*. Salt Lake City, UT: Gibbs M. Smith, Inc., 1983.

Fournel, Paul. *Guignol: Les Mourguet*. Paris: Editions du Seuil, 1995. Illustrated (b/w and color) history of the Guignol hand-puppet theater.

Friedman, Martin, et al. *Hockney Paints the Stage*. New York: Abbeville Press, 1980. Lavishly illustrated companion to exhibition at the Walker Arts Center, Minneapolis.

Galleria Daverio, Milan, and Galleria Sprovieri, Rome. *Futurism 1911–1918*. New York: Philippe Daverio Gallery, 1988. Lavishly illustrated companion (in English) to exhibition.

Garduño, Flor, and Guyette Lyr. *Mummenschanz 1972–1997*. Alstätten, Switzerland: Tobler Verlag AG, 1997. Trilingual (English/French/German). Extensive b/w photos.

Gordon, Michael R. "A Puppet Boris Gives Bill Advice He Doesn't Really Need." *New York Times*, Feb. 15, 1998. Includes an account of the Yeltsin/Clinton episode of *Kukly*.

Gudas, Rom. *The Bitter-Sweet Art: Karaghiozis, The Greek Shadow Theater*. Athens: Gnosis Publishing Co., 1986. Includes b/w sketches and color plates.

Haining, Peter. *Movable Books: An Illustrated History*. London: New English Library, 1979. Lavishly illustrated history of pop-ups and other "movable" books.

Halász, Lázló, Péter Molnár Gál, György Kroó, and Dezsö Sazilágyi. *Contemporary Hungarian Puppet Theater*. Edited by Dezsö Sazilágyi. Translated by Elisabeth Hoch. Photographs by Éva Kelati. Budapest: Corvina Press, 1978.

Hames, Peter, editor. *Dark Alchemy: The Films of Jan Švankmajer*. Wiltshire, England: Flick Books, 1995.

Hinot, Claude. *Le Fils à guignol*. Paris: Librairie Larousse, n.d. (c. 1895). Three plays, including texts and some music, illustrated with engravings.

Impe, Jean-Luc. *Opéra baroque et marionnette: Dix lustres de répertoire musical au siècle des lumières*. Charleville-Mézières, France: Editions Institut International de la Marionnette, 1994.

International Instutute of Puppet Arts in Prague and Alice Dubská. *Czech Puppet Theatre over the Centuries*. Translated from Czech by E. Fisher. Prague: International Institute of Puppet Arts, n.d.(after 1988).

Joannis, Claudette, and Bertrand Tillier. *Les Marionnettes de Maurice Sand*. Paris: Editions du Patrimoine, 1997. Exhibition catalogue with color photos.

Jurkowski, Henryk. *Ecrivains et marionnettes: Quatre siècles de littérature dramatique*. Translated from Polish by Max Blusztajn, adapted by Jean Allemand. Charleville-Mézières, France: Editions Institut International de la Marionnette, 1991. Survey of dramatic writing for puppets in Europe.

———. *A History of European Puppetry*. 2 vols. Collaborating editor, Penny Francis. Lewiston, NY: Edwin Mellen Press, 1996 & 1998. The landmark contemporary history of European puppetry, with attention to Eastern as well as Western Europe, illustrated with a few b/w pictures.

———. *Métamorphoses: La marionnette au xxe siècle*. Adapted by Bruno Mikol. Charleville-Mézières, France: Editions Institut International de la Marionnette, 2000. Comprehensive study of 20th-century European puppet art.

Kan, Michael, Clement W. Meighan, and H. B. Nicholson. *Sculpture of Ancient West Mexico: Nayarit, Jalisco, Colima*, second edition. Los Angeles and Albuquerque: Los Angeles County Museum of Art and University of New Mexico Press, 1989.

Kantor, Tadeusz. *A Journey through Other Spaces: Essays and Manifestos, 1944–1990*. Edited and translated by Michal Kobialka. Berkeley, CA: University of California Press, 1993.

Kelley, Catriona. *Petrushka: The Russian Carnival Puppet Theatre*. New York: Cambridge University Press, 1990.

Kirby, E. T. *Total Theatre: A Critical Anthology*. New York: E.P. Dutton & Co. Inc., 1969.

Kirby, Michael. *Futurist Performance*. New York: E. P. Dutton & Co, 1971.

Kennard, Joseph Spencer. *Masks and Marionettes*. Port Washington, NY: Kennikat Press, Inc., 1935. Reissued 1967. Study of commedia dell'arte and Italian puppet theater.

Kolland, Dorothea and Puppentheater-Museum Berlin. *Front Puppen Theater: Puppenspieler im Kriegsgeschehen*. Berlin: Elefanten Press, 1997. Twenty-one essays on puppets in wartime, published in conjunction with exhibition at the Puppentheater-Museum Berlin, 1997–98. Includes b/w images, some of them remarkable.

Kostelanetz, Richard, editor. *Moholy-Nagy*. New York: Allen Lane (Penguin Books), 1974.

Law, Roger, with Lewis Chester and Alex Evans. *A Nasty Piece of Work: The Art and Graft of Spitting Image*. London: Booth-Clibborn Editions, 1992. Lavishly illustrated history of *Spitting Image* by one of the founders.

Lawner, Lynne. *Harlequin on the Moon: Commedia dell'Arte and the Visual Arts*. New York: Harry N. Abrams, Inc., 1998.

Le Maréchal, A. *Les Santons de Provence*. Photos by P. Caudron and H. Chappe. Marseilles, France: Editions PEC, 1992.

Legrand, Pierre-Emile. *Un "regroleur" dit Gnafron. Un Canut nommé Guignol*. Lyon, France: Editions E.G.E., 1975.

Léger, Fernand. *Functions of Painting*. Translated from French by Alexandra Anderson. New York: Viking Press, 1973.

Lenoir, Michel. *La Préhistoire*. Paris: Editions Jean-Paul Gisserot, 1998. Extensively illustrated (color) 32-page booklet. Includes prehistoric "Venuses."

Lindsay, Frank Whiteman. *Dramatic Parody by Marionettes in Eighteenth-Century Paris*. New York: King's Crown Press, 1946.

Lorca, Federico García. *Four Puppet Plays, Divan Poems and other Poems, Prose Poems and Dramatic Pieces, Play without A Title*. Translated from Spanish by Edwin Honig. Riverdale-on-Hudson, NY: The Sheep Meadow Press, 1990.

Marshack, Alexander. *The Roots of Civilization: The Cognitive Beginnings of Man's First Art, Symbol, and Notation*. New York: McGraw-Hill Book Company, 1972. A study of Paleolithic art that includes the "Venuses."

Magnin, Charles. *Histoire des Marionnettes en Europe*. Paris: Michel Lévy Frères, 1862. Nearly 150 years old, a groundbreaking scholarly history of puppet art in Europe.

Malík, Jan, and Erik Kolàr. *The Puppet Theater in Czechoslovakia*. Translated from Czech by Jessie Kochanová. Prague: Orbis, 1970.

Martinovitch, Nicholas N. *The Turkish Theatre*. New York: Benjamin Blom, 1968.

McCormick, John. *The Victorian Marionette Theatre*. Iowa City, IA: University of Iowa Press, 2004.

McCormick, John, and Bennie Pratasik. *Popular Puppet Theatre in Europe, 1800–1914*. New York: Cambridge University Press, 1998. A major illustrated (b/w) study of the puppets, puppeteers, repertory, and audiences for popular puppetry during this period.

McDermott, Leroy. "Self-Representation in Upper Paleolithic Female Figurines." *Current Anthropology* 37, no. 2 (April 1966), 227–75. Study linking Paleolithic "Venuses" to pregnant women's view of their own bodies.

Mozart und die Marionetten von Salzburg. Salzburg, Austria: Salzburger Marionettentheater, 1969. Profusely illustrated souvenir program. Trilingual (German/English/French).

Musée du Vieil Aix. Edited by Marie-Christine Gloton, Marcel Bernos, and Nicole Martin-Vignes. Aix-en-Provence, France: L'Association du Vieil Aix, 1995. Beautifully illustrated 32-page museum guide, including several mechanical crèches.

Musée Historique de Lyon (Musée Gadagne). *Jiri Trnka: Cinéaste d'Animation*. Lyon, France: Musée Historique de Lyon (Musée Gadagne), 1992. Exhibition catalogue, including some b/w photos.

Museo Internazionale delle Marionette Antonio Pasqualino. *Historical Sicilian Marionettes*. Palermo, Italy: Museo Internazionale delle Marionette Antonio Pasqualino, [1997] Exhibition catalogue. A series of essays, lavishly illustrated.

Myrsiades, Kostas, translation [of plays]. Text by Linda S. Myrsiades. *The Karagiozis, Heroic Performance in Greek Shadow Theater*. Hanover, NH: University Press of New England, 1988.

Myrsiades, Linda S. and Kostas Myrsiades. *Karagiozis, Culture and Comedy in Greek Puppet Theater*. Lexington, KY: University of Kentucky Press, 1992.

Neirynck, Freek, and Hetty Paërl. *Marionnettes traditionnelles en Belgique*. Translated from original German edition. Ghent, Belgium: Vlaams Figurenteaterarchief, 1994. Companion to an exhibition of traditional Belgian puppets at the Institut International de la Marionnette in Charleville-Mézières, France. Contains only line drawings.

New York Public Library. *Artist of the Theatre: Alexandra Exter*. New York: The New York Public Library, 1974. Exhibition catalogue, including four essays plus some b/w photos and thumbnails.

Obraztsov, Sergei. *My Profession*. English translation of the revised Russian text (revised from 1981 Russian edition). Translated from Russian by Doris Bradbury. Moscow: Raduga Publishers, 1985. Obraztsov's account of his own career plus other thoughts about puppetry.

Onofrio, J[ean-Baptiste], editor. *Théâtre Lyonnais de Guignol*. Illustrations by Eugène Lefebvre. Preface (to reprint edition) by Jean-Guy Morguet. Lyon, France: Lafitte Reprints, [1998]. (Reprint of 1909 edition. Originally published in 2 volumes, 1865 and 1879.) Texts of 20 19th-century Guignol plays.

Paërl, Hetty. *Heerekrintjes: Over Jan Klaassen en Katrijn en hun Buitenlandse soortgenoten*. Amsterdam: Uniepers bv, 1987. Illustrated survey of European puppetry.

———. *Schattenspiel und das Spiel mit Silhouetten*. Munich: Heinrich Hugendubel Verlag, 1981.

Pfeiffer, John E. *The Creative Explosion: An Inquiry into the Origins of Art and Religion*. New York: Harper & Row, 1982. A study of Paleolithic art that includes the "Venuses."

Passuth, Krisztina. *Moholy-Nagy*. Translated from Hungarian by Éva Grusz, Judy Szöllösy, and László Baránszky Jób, from German by Mátyás Esterházy. Translation revised by Kenneth McRobbie and Ilona Jánosi. New York: Thames and Hudson, Inc., 1987.

Piron, Maurice, editor. *Les Marionnettes liégoises dans leur histoire*. Liège, Belgium: Service des Affaires Culturelles de la Province de Liège, 1979. Essays from colloquium in conjunction with exhibition.

Plassard, Didier. *L'acteur en Effigie: Figures de l'homme artificiel dans le théâtre des avant-gardes historiques—Allemagne, France, Italie*. Part of Théâtre Années Vingt series. Lausanne: Editions l'Age de l'Homme, 1992. Fine study of avant-garde puppetry in Western Europe during first two decades of the 20th century.

Purschke, Hans R. *The German Puppet Theatre Today*. Translated from German by Patricia Crampton. Bonn–Bad Godesberg, Germany: Inter Nationes, 1979. Published for 50th anniversary of UNIMA (Union Internationale de la Marionnette). Extensive b/w illustrations.

———. *Puppenspiel in Graphik und Malerei*. Frankfurt/Main, Germany: Perlicko-Perlacko, 1974–1976. Series of privately published booklets with b/w images documenting paintings and graphics depicting puppets in Europe.

Reiniger, Lotte. *Schattentheater, Schattenpuppen, Schattenfilm*. Tübingen: Schattenfilm Text Verlag, 1981.

Revelard, Michel, and Guergana Kostadinova. *Le Livre des masques: Masques et costumes dans les fêtes et carnavals traditionnels en Europe.* Tournai, Belgium: La Renaissance du Livre, 1998. Based on the collection of the International Museum of Carnival and Masks, Binche, Belgium.

Ribi, Hana. *Fred Schneckenburgers Puppet Cabaret.* Munich: Münchner Stadtmuseum, and Zürich: Museum Bellerive Zürich, 1991. Lavishly illustrated exhibition catalogue.

Rickard, Charles. *Les Automates.* Photographs by the author. Rennes, France: Ouest France, 1981. Lavishly illustrated 32-page booklet on famous automatons of 18th- and 19th-century Europe.

Rischbieter, Henning. *Art and the Stage in the 20th Century: Painters and Sculptors Work for the Theater.* Documented by Wolfgang Storch. Translated from German by Michael Bullock. Greenwich, CT: New York Graphic Society, Ltd., 1968. Excellent study of European artists' work in live-actor and puppet theater. Extensively illustrated, mainly in b/w.

Roser, Albrecht, et al. *Gustaf und sein Ensemble.* Gerlingen, Germany: Bleicher Verlag, 1992.

Salzburger Marionettentheater. Texts by Gottfried Kraus and Aretl Aicher. Salzburg, Austria: Salzburger Marionettentheater, 1993. Profusely illustrated souvenir program. Trilingual (German/English/French).

Schlemmer, Oskar, László Moholy-Nagy, and Farkas Molnár. *The Theater of the Bauhaus.* Edited and with an introduction by Walter Gropius. Translated by Arthur S. Wensinger. Middletown, CT: Wesleyan University Press, 1961.

Segal, Harold B. *Pinocchio's Progeny.* Baltimore, MD: Johns Hopkins University Press, 1995. Study of all manner of constructed actors in experimental theater, primarily in 20th-century Europe.

Shaw, [George] Bernard. "Shakes Versus Shaw," in *Buoyant Billions, Farfetched Fables, and Shakes Versus Shaw, 133–143.* London: Constable and Company Ltd., 1950. Shaw's puppet play written for the Malvern Marionette Theatre of Waldo Lanchester.

Söorenson, Margareta, editor. *. . . are but tugs on strings: The Marionette Theatre over 40 Years.* Photo editor, Arina Stoenescu. Stockholm: Stockholmia Förlag, 1988. Illustrated (mostly b/w) history of Michael Meschke's Marionetteatern.

Spatharis, Sotiris. *Behind the White Screen.* "Memoirs" translated by Mario Rinvolucri. "The History and Art of Karagiosis" translated by Leslie Finer. New York: Red Dust, 1976. Memoir of a karagiosis puppeteer, and his account of the history and art of karagiosis.

Speaight, George. *The Earliest English Puppet Play?* Bichester, England: DaSilva Puppet Books, 1997.

———. *The History of the English Puppet Theatre.* 2nd edition. Carbondale, IL: Southern Illinois University Press, 1990. The classic study of English puppet theater.

———. *Juvenile Drama: The History of the English Toy Theatre.* London: Macdonald & Co., Ltd., 1946. Includes b/w illustrations and a few color plates.

———. *Punch and Judy: A History.* Boston, MA: Plays, Inc., 1970. (Reprint of 1955 edition.)

Speranski E. *Biographia v Fotographia [Biography in photography].* Moscow: Vserossiskoe Theatralnoe Obshchectvo, 1973. Biography of Sergei Obraztsov in the form of captioned b/w photographs.

Spitting Image. The Appallingly Disrespectful Spitting Image *Book and the Inevitable* Spitting Image. London: Faber and Faber, n.d.

Spitting Image. Spitting Images. Text by Sean Kelly. New York: Harcourt Brace Jovanovich Publishers, 1987. Includes full-page, glossy color images of the company's over-the-top puppets.

Stead, Philip John. *Mr. Punch.* London: Evans Brothers Limited, 1952. History of Punch and some related puppets in Europe.

Steinlein, Jean-Marie, Martine Grinberg, et al. *Carnavals et fêtes d'hiver.* Paris: Centre Georges Pompidou, 1984. Exhibition catalogue of Steinlein's photographs of carnivals and winter ceremonies in Europe.

Teschner, Richard. "Richard Teschner's Figuren Theater." *The London Studio, 31–33.* January 1935.

Therén, Karen. *Marionetteatern.* Malmö, Sweden: LiberFörlag Malmö, 1983. History of the Stockholm Marionetteatern, directed by Michael Meschke.

The Tragical Comedy of Comical Tragedy of Punch and Judy. Illustrations by George Cruikshank. Boston: Routledge and Kegan Paul, 1980. (Reprint of 1860 edition.) The classic, with Cruikshank's famous images.

Tietze, Andreas. *The Turkish Shadow Theater and the Puppet Collection of the L.A. Mayer Memorial Foundation.* Volume IV of the L.A. Mayer Memorial Studies in Islamic Art and Civilization. Berlin: Gebr. Mann Verlag, 1977.

Till, Wolfgang. *Puppentheater: Bilder, Figuren, Dokumente.* Munich: Universitätsdruckerei und Verlag, 1986. Lavishly illustrated book based on puppet collection of the Munich Stadtmuseum.

Van der Elst, Elisabeth. *Puppets in Belgium.* Sprimont, Belgium: Mardaga, n.d. Trilingual edition (French, German, English). Less-than-reliable text, but good color and b/w illustrations.

Vibaek, Janne. *International Museum of Marionettes Antonio Pasqualino: Guide.* Translated from Italian by Simon Guadagnino. Sicily: Museo Internazionale delle Marionette Antonio Pasqualino, n.d.

von Schlosser, Julius. *Histoire du portrait en cire.* Translated from German to French by Valérie Le Vot. Paris: Macula, 1997. History of human images in wax from antiquity through modern times.

Young, Susan. *Shakespeare Manipulated: The Use of the Dramatic Works of Shakespeare in* teatro di figura *in Italy.* Madison, NJ: Fairleigh Dickinson University Press, 1996. Study of puppet performances of Shakespeare in Italy.

AUSTRALIA, NEW ZEALAND, PACIFIC ISLANDS

Luomala, Katherine. *Hula Ki'I: Hawaiian Puppetry.* [Laie], HI: Institute for Polynesian Studies, 1984.

Vella, Maeve, and Helen Rickards. *The Theatre of the Impossible: Puppet Theatre in Australia.* Roseville, NSW, Australia: Craftsman House, 1989.

[Hausberg, Norbert] *Strings Attached Puppet Theatre.* Wellington, New Zealand: Strings Attached Puppet Theatre, 1993.

Wardwell, Allen. *Island Ancestors.* Photographs by Dirk Bakker. [Seattle, WA]: University of Washington Press, 1994. Lavishly illustrated companion volume to exhibition of Oceanic art, including puppets, by the Detroit Institute of Arts.

MAJOR JOURNALS FOCUSING ON PUPPET AND OBJECT THEATER

(A few articles outside these journals that were drawn on for this study are integrated into other sections of this bibliography.)

Alternatives Théâtrales. Nos. 65–66: Le Théâtre dédoublé. No. 72: Voix d'auteurs et marionnettes. No. 80: Objects Danse. Coeditions with Editions Institut International de la Marionette. Covers a range of innovative puppet and object theater.

American Theatre. No. 2102 (February 2004). Issue devoted to puppetry.

E Pur Si Mouve: La Marionnette Aujourd'hui. Charleville-Mézières, France: Editions Institut International de la Marionette, 2002–. New semiannual journal covering contemporary puppetry, puppet history, and puppet events, including festivals worldwide. English, French, and Spanish editions.

Marionnettes. Bulletin of THEMAA (Théâtres de Marionnettes et Arts Associés, UNIMA-France). Articles on contemporary and historical puppet theaters.

Puck: La Marionnette et les autres arts. No. 1 (1988)–no. 13 (2004), ongoing. Charleville-Mézières, France: Editions Institut International de la Marionette, 1988–. Annual (mostly) journal with articles by puppeteers and scholars covering a wide range of innovative puppet and object theater as well as puppet history. Edited by Brunella Eruli. Extensive b/w illustrations.

Puppetry International: The puppet in contemporary theatre, film, and media. Vol. 1– (1994–) journal of UNIMA-USA (Union Internationale de la Marionette, North American Center). Articles on a range of contemporary (plus some historical) puppet and object theater.

Puppetry Journal. Vol. 1– (1949–). Continuation of *Puppetry Yearbook.* Quarterly journal published by Puppeteers of America. Articles and news about contemporary puppetry, aimed largely at puppeteers.

Puppetry Yearbook. Vol. 1–16 (1930–1948). Annual journal, after 1937 the official publication of Puppeteers of America. Articles on a wide range of American and non-American puppetry, mainly contemporary.

TDR. T163 fall 1999. *Puppets, Masks, and Performing Objects.* Guest editor: John Bell.

Picture Credits

Chapter 1

p. 1 © Studio Cyril Kobler; p. 2 Photo by Hendrik Planting, Courtesy Henk Boerwinkel (puppet artist); pp. 4–5 Photo by Eileen Blumenthal; p. 6 © Gary Gruby; p. 8 Courtesy Eileen Blumenthal; p. 10 © The National Museum of Ethnography, Stockholm, Sweden. Photo by Bo Gabrielsson; p. 11 Erich Lessing/Art Resource, NY; p. 12 (left) Photo by Laurence Fosse, Louvre Museum; p. 12 (right) Photo courtesy the Hermitage Museum, St. Petersburg; p. 13 (top) Courtesy New York Public Library; p. 13 (bottom) Bodleian Library, University of Oxford, MS. Bodl. 264, fol. 76; p. 14 (left) Courtesy Dr. Marek Waszkiel; p. 14 (right) © Robert Sargent Austin Estate; p. 15 (left) Inv.N427.32. Gravure de Giranne, *La Creche*, in the Collection of the Musée de Gadagne, Ville de Lyon. Photo by Studio Basset; p. 15 (right) Courtesy Munchner Stadtmuseum, Puppentheatermuseum; p. 16 Courtesy The International Museum of Marionettes Antonio Pasqualino, Palermo; p. 17 Photo by Gretl Aicher, courtesy Salzburger Marionettentheater; p. 18 (top) Photo AKG London; p. 18 (bottom) Courtesy New York Public Library; p. 19 Brigitte Pougeoise; p. 20 Photo by Susan Simpson © 1999, from the collection of Alan Cook; p. 21 Victoria and Albert Picture Library; p. 22 (top) Courtesy Musée d'Ethnographie de Geneve; p. 22 (bottom) Photo by Manshichi Sakamoto, courtesy Pacific Press Service; p. 23 (top) Private collection; p. 23 (bottom) Tsubouchi Memorial Theatre Museum, Waseda University, Serial #030-235; p. 24 (top) P. Jitendra and S. Olaniya; p. 24 (bottom) KITLV 3982, Royal Institute of Linguistics and Anthropology, Leiden, the Netherlands. First appeared in *Shadow Theatre in Java* by Alit Djajasoebrata; p. 25 Courtesy Musée d'Ethnographie de Geneve; p. 26 Le Centre des archives d'outre mer, Archives Nationales de France; p. 27 Photo © Denis Nidzgorski; p. 29 Archivos, Museo Nacional del Titere; p. 30 (top) Museum Bellerive, Zurich. Photo © Michael Wolgensinger, Zurich; p. 30 (bottom) Courtesy the Obraztsov Museum, Moscow; p. 31 (top) Theatremuseum de Universidat, Koln; p. 31 (bottom) Private collection. Licensed by Art Resource, New York; p. 32 (left) © Bettmann/CORBIS; p. 32 (right) For the League of Composers in association with Leopold Stokowski, from the book *The Theatre of Robert Edmond Jones*, edited by Ralph Pendleton; p. 33 Agnès Patrix; p. 34 © Disney; p. 35 (top) Courtesy Julie Taymor, photo by Kenneth van Sickle; p. 35 (bottom) Martha Swope/TIMEPIX

Chapter 2

p. 36 Angela Fisher/Carol Beckwith, courtesy Robert Estall Photo Agency; p. 37 Photo by Alfred A. Baker from the book *Eskimo Masks: Art & Ceremony* by Dorothy Jean Ray; p. 38 (top) Courtesy of the Obraztsov Museum, Moscow; p. 38 (bottom) Photo by Bernd Uhlig; p. 39 (top) From the book *The Eskimo about Bering Strait* (1899, Vol. 18, pt. 1, pl. C of Bureau of Ethnology) by Edward William Nelson; p. 39 (bottom) Von G. Heine illustrator, Chronik der zeit, 18865.185; p. 40 © Jean-Marie Steinlein; p. 41 (top) Photo by Felix Speiser, courtesy Museum der Kulturen, Basel; p. 41 (bottom) Private collection; p. 42 Carol Rosegg; p. 43 Michel Friang; p. 44 (top) Photo courtesy Musée International du Carnaval et du Masque; p. 44 (bottom) *Livres Danses D'Afrique,* photo by Michel Huet © HOA-QUI; p. 45 Phillipe Genty; p. 46 Courtesy of Hans Jürg Toblen, Mummenschantz Foundation; p. 47 (top) Courtesy of Hans Jürg Toblen, Mummenschantz Foundation; p. 47 (bottom) Richard Termine; p. 48 Photo by Mark Williams, courtesy River Books Ltd.; p. 50 Brigitte Pougeoise; p. 51 Richard Termine; p. 52 Photo by Linda MacMinn, courtesy Joseph Cashore, The Cashore Marionettes; p. 53 (top) Photo by Irene de Groot & Paul Romijn, Fotobureau/Tropenmuseum; p. 53 (bottom) Photo by Paulo Nuno Silva, courtesy Teatro Garcia de Resende; p. 54 Palermo, Museo Internazionale delle marionette Antonio Pasqualino; p. 55 Courtesy of Margareta Niculescu; p. 57 Carolina Salguero; p. 58 © Théâtre de l'Arc-en-Terre; p. 59 Photo by Eileen Blumenthal; pp. 60–61 Brigitte Pougeoise; p. 62 (bottom) Photo by Eileen Blumenthal; p. 63 Photo by Olaf Faustmann, © Prasanna Rao; p. 64 (left) Koninklijk Instituut voor de Tropen, Tropenmuseum; p. 64 (right) Mary Jo Arnoldi; p. 65 (left) Courtesy Sangeet Natak Akademi, New Delhi; p. 65 (right) From the book *The Puppet Theatre in America, A History 1524 to 1948* by Paul McPharlin; published by Plays, Inc., Boston, 1948; p. 66 (top) Brigitte Pougeoise; p. 66 (bottom) © CORBIS/Nik Wheeler; p. 67 (left) From *Arts d'Afrique Noire*, no. 6, p. 11, 1973. Photo by Raoul Lehuard; p. 67 (right) Courtesy Burke Museum of Natural History and Culture, Catalog #1-1653, photo by Eduardo Calderon; p. 68 Philippe Genty; p. 69 Photo by Manuela Seeber, courtesy The Henson Foundation

Chapter 3

p. 70 Brigitte Pougeoise; p. 71 Photo by Tom Sandler, courtesy Puppetmongers; pp. 72–73 © CORBIS/Jack Fields; p. 74 Chrystie Sherman ; p. 75 (top) Photo by Richard Termine, courtesy Sandglass Theatre, VT; p. 75 (bottom) Yves Joly; p. 76 Photo by René Wopereis, Deventer, courtesy TAM-TAM Objektentheater; p. 77 Courtesy Julie Taymor, photo by Kenneth van Sickle; p. 78 (left) Photo by Wolfgang Kraft, courtesy Teatro Hugo & Ines.; p. 78 (right) Culver Pictures; p. 79 (top) Culver Pictures; p. 79 (bottom) The Center for Puppetry Arts; p. 80 (left) © 2001 Sylvia Plachy; p. 80 (right) Photo by Marijke Mooy, courtesy Impresariaat Wim Visser; p. 81 (left) © Henk Boerwinkel, photo © Hendrik Planting; p. 81 (right) Photo by C. C. Somerville; p. 82 Brigitte Pougeoise; p. 83 (left) Brigitte Pougeoise; p. 83 (right) M. Wanjnrych, courtesy Martine Godat, Companie Nicole Mossoux & Patrick Bonte; p. 84 Van Bucher; p. 85 Richard Termine

Chapter 4

p. 86 © Keizo Kanoko, courtesy Kodansha International Ltd.; p. 87 Photo by Patrick Argirakis; p. 88 (top) Courtesy Torokko Puppetry Library; p. 88 (bottom) Cyril Kobler; p. 89 Brigitte Pougeoise; p. 90 The Ballard Institute and Museum of Puppetry, University of Connecticut, The Rufus Rose Marionettes. Photo by Fran Funk/ The Chronicle; p. 91 Photo by Harry Burnett, courtesy Caltech Archives; p. 92 (top) Richard Termine; p. 92 (bottom) Richard Termine; p. 93 (left) Collection Theater Instituut Nederland; p. 93 (right) Private collection; p. 94 (left) © Robert Frerck/ Odyssey/Chicago; p. 94 (right top) Courtesy Munchner Stadtmuseum, Puppentheatermuseum; p. 94 (right bottom) Courtesy Munchner Stadtmuseum, Puppentheatermuseum; p. 95 Courtesy Richard Bradshaw; p. 96 (left) Courtesy of the Marionettmuseet, Stockholm; p. 96 (right) Courtesy of the Marionettmuseet, Stockholm; p. 97 (top and bottom) Transparency Nos: 1993(2) and 2004(2), photo by Arthur Singer, courtesy Department of Library Services, American Museum of Natural History; p. 98 (left) Photo by Hendrik Planting, courtesy Henk Boerwinkel (puppet artist); p. 98 (right) Photo by Ruphin Coudyzer, courtesy The Henson Foundation; p. 99 Photo by Arie de Zanger; p. 100 (top left) Photo by Wolfgang Ramsbott; p. 100 (top right) Photo by Cyril Kobler © 2005 Artists Rights Society (ARS), New York/VG Bild-Kunst, Bonn; p. 100 (bottom) Courtesy Jane Phillips; p. 101 (left) Photo by Nat Messik, courtesy of Peter Baird; p. 101 (right) Courtesy Musée de l'Homme; p. 102 Photo by Donna Gray; p. 103 *El Periferico de Objectos*, from Cámara Gesell, photo by Magdalena Viggiani

Chapter 5

p. 104 Courtesy Theatre Tandarica; p. 105 Photo by Kolin Smith, courtesy Jonathan Edward Cross, CLOCKWORKS; p. 106 Richard Termine; p. 107 (left) Courtesy Puppetsweat Theater; p. 107 (right) Courtesy Puppetsweat Theater; p. 108 (left) Brigitte Pougeoise; p. 108 (right) Courtesy Institut International des Marionnettes; p. 109 HERE Arts Center; p. 110 (top left) Photo by Raymond Irons, courtesy Little Angel Theatre; p. 110 (top right) Stephano Rossi; p. 110 (bottom) Carolina Salguero; p. 111 (top) Private collection; p. 111 (bottom) Photo by Ann Mundy; p. 112 (top) Schenkung LK, Klee-Museum, Bern, Ref No.s 2341, 3092, 3680; © 2005 Artists Rights Society (ARS), New York/VG Bild-Kunst, Bern; p. 112 (bottom) Courtesy Osterreichisches Theatermuseum; p. 113 (top) Setting for the ballet, *Mercure*, first produced Paris, June 15, 1924. Scenery and costumes by Pablo Picasso. Courtesy The Museum of Modern Art, New York, © 2005 Estate of Pablo Picasso/Artists Rights Society (ARS), New York; p. 113 (bottom) Statkewicz as the American Manager in the first performance of the ballet, *Parade,* Theatre du Chatelet, Paris, May 18, 1917. Curtain, scenery, and costumes by Pablo Picasso. Courtesy the Museum of Modern Art, New York, © 2005 Estate of Pablo Picasso/Artists Rights Society (ARS), New York; p. 114 (top) Museo di Arte moderna di Trento e Rovereto; p. 114 (bottom) © 2001 The Oskar Schlemmer Theatre Estate, I-28824 Oggebbio, Italy; Photo Archive C. Raman Schlemmer, 1-28824 Oggebbio, Italy; p. 115 Carolina Salguero; p. 116 Chrystie Sherman; p. 117 (top) Chrystie Sherman; p. 117 (bottom) Chrystie Sherman; p. 118 (top) Courtesy Meredith Monk, photo by Johan Elbers; p. 118 (bottom) © Puppetsoup Theater of Objects, photo by David Emery Photography; p. 119 Richard Landry; pp. 120–121 (spread, top) Courtesy Puppetsweat; p. 121 (middle) Richard Termine; p. 121 (bottom) Richard Termine; p. 122 Private collection; p. 123 (top) The Museum of Modern Art/Film Stills Archive; p. 123 (bottom) © The Henson Foundation

Chapter 6

p. 124 Photo by Nat Messik, courtesy Peter Baird; p. 125 Photo by Hillel Burger, courtesy Peabody Museum, Harvard University; p. 126 From the book *Marionettes et Masques, au Couer du Theatre Africain* by Olenka Darkowska-Nidzgorski and Denis Nidzgorski; published by Sepia, 1998, photo by Henri Labouret; p. 127 Photo © Denis Nidzgorski; p. 128 CORBIS/© Werner Forman; p. 129 Brigitte Pougeoise; p. 130 (top) Richard Termine; p. 130 (bottom left) Phillipe Genty; p. 130 (bottom right) Phillipe Genty; p. 131 Photo by Rene Sauloup, courtesy Compagnie Philippe Genty; p. 132 (left sequence of 4 images) Photos courtesy of the Obraztsov Museum, Moscow; p. 132 (right) Courtesy Krzysztof Rau, Teatr 3/4 Zusno; p. 133 (left) Black Belly Dancer String-Puppet © Albrecht Roser, Stuttgart, Germany, Donation to Takeda International Museum, Jida, Japan, Photo © Ingrid Höfer; p. 133 (right) Richard Termine; p. 134 Private collection; p. 135 © 2001 Sylvia Plachy; p. 136 Brigitte Pougeoise; p. 137 (top) © 2001 Sylvia Plachy; p. 137 (bottom) Photo by Gail S. Goodman; p. 138 Courtesy Grupo Contadores de Estorias—Teatro Espaco; p. 139 © Disney, photo by Richard Termine; p. 140 J. Daniel Vancas, Vanguard Gallery International; p. 141 (left) Photo by Jorg P. Anders, Berlin, Staatliche Museen zu Berlin, Preußischer Kulturbesitz Nationalgalerie, © 2005 Artists Rights Society (ARS), New York/Pro Litteris, Zurich; p. 141 (right) From the book *The Bitter-Sweet Art: Karaghiozis, The Greek Shadow Theatre* by Rom Gudas, published by Gnosis, 1986

Chapter 7

p. 142 Giraudon/Art Resource; p. 144 Carlos da Fonte; p. 145 *Bima clubs an enemy with a severed head,* photo by Larry Reed; p. 146 (sequence of 4 images) Photos courtesy of the Obraztsov Museum, Moscow; p. 147 Palermo, Museo Internazionale della Marionette Antonio Pasqualino; p. 148 Collection Theater Instituut Nederland; p. 149 (top) © Robert Frerck/Odyssey/Chicago; p. 149 (bottom) Photo courtesy of the Obraztsov Museum, Moscow; p. 150 (left) Courtesy Theatre Tandarica; p. 150 (right) and p. 151 (spread) Photo by Kata Kádár, courtesy Kolibri Szinhaz; p. 152 Photo by Arie de Zanger; p. 153 Courtesy Munchner Stadtmuseum, Puppentheatermuseum; p. 154 Courtesy Vit Horejš; p. 155 © Disney; p. 156 (top) Richard Termine; p. 156 (bottom) © 1981 Theodore Shank, all rights of reproduction reserved; p. 157 Photo by Frank Ward; p. 158 (top) © 2005 Artists Rights Society (ARS), New York/ADAGP, Paris; p. 159 Photo by Beata Bergstrom, courtesy Marionetteatern/Marionettemuseet, Stockholm; p. 160 (top) Courtesy Fundacio Joan Miro, Barcelona © 2005 Artists Rights Society (ARS) New York/ADAGP, Paris; p. 160 (bottom) Photo © F. Catala-Roca, Barcelona; p. 161 Brigitte Pougeoise

Chapter 8

p. 162 © Spitting Image, photo © John Lawrence Jones; p. 163 Photo © Denis Nidzgorski; p. 164 (left) Martha Zamora © Banco de México; p. 164 (right) Courtesy Munchen Stadtmuseum, Puppentheatermuseum; p. 165 (left) Arko Datta/AFP Photos; p. 165 (right) Courtesy NYC Labor Union 78; p. 166 © Hulton-Deutsch Collection/CORBIS; p. 167 (left) Photo by Marco de Nood, collection of Historisch Museum Rotterdam/Stichting Poppenspelcollecties Dordrecht; p. 167 (right) Photo © Michael Wolgensinger, Zurich; p. 169 Brigitte Pougeoise; p. 170 Richard Termine; p. 171 Brigitte Pougeoise; p. 172 (top) Jiri Trnka Studio; p. 172 (bottom) CORBIS/Hulton-Deutsch Collection; p. 173 Photo by Cylla von Tiedemann; p. 174 (left) Courtesy Carole Sidlow; p. 174 (right) Courtesy of Mr. Melviut Ozham, UNIMA, Turkey; p. 175 (left) Photo by Sebastien Boffredo © Théâtre de l'Arc-en-Terre; p. 175 (right) Photo by Fausto Fleury, courtesy Magda Modesto; p. 176 Courtesy Munchner Stadtmuseum, Puppentheater-museum; p. 177 (left) Federal Theatre Project Collection, Special Collections & Archives, George Mason University Libraries; p. 177 (right) Stiftung Archiv der Akademie der Künste, Berlin, nr. 308, "The Conservative Man" (and John Heartfield), John Heartfield © 2005 Artists Rights Society (ARS), New York/VG Bild-Kunst, Bonn; p. 178 Photo by Ron Levine, first appeared on the cover of *Bread and Puppet: Stories of Struggle and Faith from Central America,* published by Green Valley Media, Burlington, VT, 1985; p. 179 (right) Carolina Salguero; p. 180 Photo by James R. Moore; p. 181 Photo by Valerie Osterwalder, courtesy Theodora Skipitares; p. 182 Richard Termine; p. 183 Brigitte Pougeoise; p. 184 Photo by Igor Mukhin, courtesy Konstantin Leifer, Russia; p. 185 Photo by Igor Mukhin, courtesy Konstantin Leifer, Russia

Chapter 9

p. 186 Courtesy Peter Baird; p. 187 Private collection; pp. 188–189 © The British Museum; p. 189 (bottom) Richard Termine; p. 190 (top) © 1976 George Ballis/Take Stock; p. 190 (bottom) Richard Termine; p. 190 Irene de Groot, Fotobureau/Tropenmuseum; p. 191 Brigitte Pougeoise; p. 192 Irene de Groot, Fotobureau/Tropenmuseum; p. 193 (left) Private collection; p. 193 (right) Private collection; p. 194 © Lauren Piperno/Kingston; p. 195 Courtesy Department of Library Services, American Museum of Natural History, neg. no. 22840, photo by R. C. Andrews; p. 196 CORBIS/Hulton-Deutsch Collection; p. 197 (top) Courtesy Munchner Stadtmuseum, Puppentheatermuseum; p. 198 (left) Photo by Jean-Loup Charmet, collection of La Bibliotheque des Arts Decoratifs, Paris; p. 198 (right) Sherif Sonbol; p. 199 (top left) Courtesy Musée de l'homme; p. 199 (top right) Courtesy Musée de l'homme; p. 199 (bottom) Gerd Kaminski, Ludwig Boltzmann Institute for Research on China, Austria; pp. 200–201 Gregg Butensky; p. 202 Tropenmuseum/E. L. den Otter; p. 203 Photo by Teguh S. Djamal, courtesy Haryono Guritno and Marc Hoffman; pp. 204–205 Brigitte Pougeoise; p. 206 Jane Voorhees Zimmerli Art Museum, Rutgers, the State University of New Jersey, photo by Jack Abraham; p. 207 (top) Baird Collection; p. 207 (bottom) Archives Départementales des Vosges, 48 J Construction, Imagerie d'Epinal S.A., A.M. 1989 (cliché J. Laurençon)

Chapter 10

p. 208 Photo by Susan Simpson © 1999, from the collection of Alan Cook; p. 210 (top) Photo by Michele Laurent, courtesy Gamma Liaison, Paris; p. 210 (bottom) Photo by Petr Nykl, Courtesy Artworks, Prague; p. 211 Guy Charrie; p. 212 (top) Photo by Erich Malter; p. 212 (bottom) Brigitte Pougeoise; p. 213 Courtesy Artificio Milano; p. 214 (left) Photo by B. Lawson, Fotobureau/Tropenmuseum; p. 214 (right) Photo by B. Lawson, Fotobureau/Tropenmuseum; p. 215 From *Arts d'Afrique Noire,* no. 2, 25, 1973; p. 216 Angela Fisher/Carol Beckwith, courtesy Robert Estall Photo Library; p. 217 (left) © Charles & Josette Lenars/CORBIS; p. 217 (right) Marionette éphémère (Compagnie Coatimundi), photo by Jean-Claude Leportier; p. 218 Photo by Eileen Blumenthal; p. 219 Photo by H. M. Nooy-Palm, Fotobureau/Tropenmuseum; p. 220 (left) Courtesy Museo Nacional de Antropología; p. 220 (right) Alaska State Library/Case and Draper/PCA 39–65; p. 221 Photo © Denis Nidzgorski; p. 222 Angela Fisher/Carol Beckwith, courtesy Robert Estall Photo Library; p. 223 Michel Friang; p. 224 (left) Courtesy The Eugene and Clare Thaw Collection, New York State Historical Association, photo by John Bigelow Taylor; p. 224 (right) Catalog No. 2000-6853, Department of Anthropology, Smithsonian Institute; p. 225 Collection of L. Bateson, Duke Art Museum; pp. 226–227 Photos by Teguh S. Djamal, courtesy Haryono Guritno and Marc Hoffman

Chapter 11

p. 228 "Pierrot Ecrivain" ("Writing Clown") automate par G. Vichy a Paris, fin XIXème siècle, Musée National de Monaco (collection de Galea), photo by Andre Soriano; p. 229 Photo by Araldo De Luca; p. 230 © C.A.A.C., The Pigozzi Collection, Geneva, photo by Michael Hall; p. 231 Photo by Jerry L. Thompson, © 2000 Whitney Museum of American Art, New York © 2005 Estate of Alexander Calder/Artists Rights Society (ARS), New York; p. 232 Photo by Joe Viesti, The Viesti Collection Inc.; pp. 232–233 © Jean Bernard, courtesy Musée du Vieil Aix; p. 234 From the book *Automata and Mechanical Toys* by Mary Hillier, Bloomsbury Books, London, 1976; p. 235 Photo courtesy Lord & Taylor; p. 236 (left) Jean-Baptiste Faivre, from Collection Musée de l'Homme; p. 236 (right) Courtesy Munich Stadtmuseum, Puppentheater; p. 237 Sophea Sek; p. 238 (left) Photo by Jean-Marie Steinlein; p. 238 (right) The Center for Puppetry Arts, photo by Richard Termine; p. 239 (top) Photo by Michel Frison, courtesy Amoros & Augustin; p. 239 (bottom) Photo by Michel Frison, courtesy Amoros & Augustin; p. 240 courtesy Tony Oursler and Metro Pictures; p. 241 (left) Photo © Michael Wilson, 2000; p. 241 (right) Photo © Michael Wilson, 2000; p. 242 Jacob Gole, courtesy Deutsches Volkslierarchiv; p. 243 Josef Ptácek; p. 244 Photo by Dan Dennehy, courtesy The Walker Art Center, Minneapolis, MN; p. 245 Charlotte Victoria, courtesy Meredith Monk; p. 246 Federico Pedrotti; p. 247 © 1999 Paul Kaiser and Shelley Eshkar; pp. 248–249 Brigitte Pougeoise

Chapter 12

p. 250 © KIT, Amsterdam, inv.nr.792-9 (wayang wong) no. 46, Gusti Pangeran Ario Hadikusumo (uncle of the Sultan of Yogjarkarta) as Arjuno, photo by Tassilo Adam, c. 1921; p. 251 Photo by Eileen Blumenthal; pp. 252–253 Photo by Michele Laurent, courtesy Gamma Liaison, Paris; p. 255 Courtesy Fondation Dubuffet. © 2005 Artists Rights Society (ARS), New York/ADAGP, Paris; p. 272: Courtesy Munchner Stadtmuseum, Puppentheatermuseum; Endpapers: Puppentheater-sammlung Stadtmuseum Munchen, photo by Claus Hansmann

Picture research by Carousel Research, Inc.

Index

Fourteenth-century Egyptian shadow puppet,
detail. See page 15.

EDITOR: Andrea Danese
DESIGNERS: Ellen Nygaard Ford, Shawn Dahl
PRODUCTION MANAGERS: Justine Keefe, Jane Searle
PICTURE RESEARCH: Carousel Research, Inc. (Fay Torres-yap,
  Mary Teresa Giancoli, Laurie Platt Winfrey)

LIBRARY OF CONGRESS CATALOGING-IN-PUBLICATION DATA
Blumenthal, Eileen, 1948–
  Puppetry : a world history / by Eileen Blumenthal.
    p. cm.
  Includes bibliographical references and index.
  ISBN 0–8109–5587–3
  1. Puppet theater—History. I. Title.

  PN1972.B57 2005
  791.5'3—dc22

          2004029349

Printed and bound in China
10 9 8 7 6 5 4 3 2 1

Harry N. Abrams, Inc.
100 Fifth Avenue
New York, N.Y. 10011
www.abramsbooks.com

Abrams is a subsidiary of
LA MARTINIÈRE
GROUPE